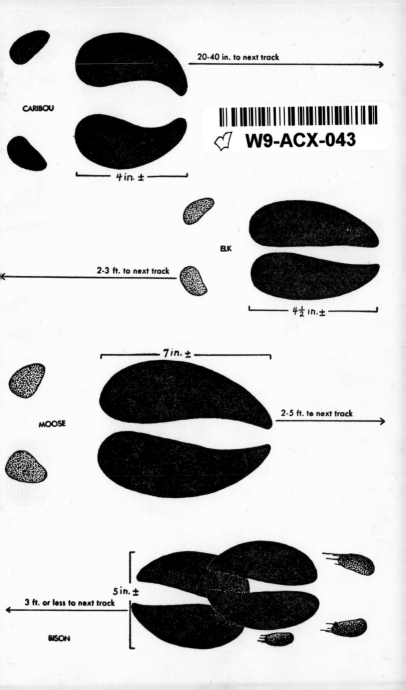

CARIBOU

20-40 in. to next track

4 in. ±

W9-ACX-043

ELK

2-3 ft. to next track

4½ in. ±

MOOSE

7 in. ±

2-5 ft. to next track

BISON

5 in. ±

3 ft. or less to next track

A Field Guide
to the Mammals

THE PETERSON FIELD GUIDE SERIES
EDITED BY ROGER TORY PETERSON

THE PETERSON FIELD GUIDE SERIES

A Field Guide
to the Mammals

Field marks of all species
found north of the Mexican boundary

Text and Maps by
WILLIAM HENRY BURT

Illustrations by
RICHARD PHILIP GROSSENHEIDER

Second Edition
Revised and Enlarged

Sponsored by the National Audubon Society
and National Wildlife Federation

HOUGHTON MIFFLIN COMPANY BOSTON

SEVENTH PRINTING   W

LIBRARY OF CONGRESS CATALOG CARD NUMBER: 63–8125

ISBN : 0–395–07471–1

PRINTED IN THE U.S.A.

Editor's Note

OUR views of mammals are often so brief that it is even more important than it is with birds to know exactly what to look for — to know their "field marks." A large percentage of mammals are nocturnal; we find their tracks in the mud by the riverbank, and in the snow, but except for the squirrels and a few others, we get scarcely more than an occasional glimpse of these shy creatures.

With this new edition the *Field Guide to the Mammals* has come of age. Having undergone the scrutiny of tens of thousands of students, the maps have been perfected to reflect our current knowledge of mammal distribution on the North American continent. The species accounts have also been strengthened and expanded with sections on habitat, habits, reproduction, and economic status. Although these inclusions have added many pages to the book it still fits the pocket easily and will be far more satisfying to many readers who may wish to know a bit more about each species than just its recognition marks.

William H. Burt and Richard P. Grossenheider combined their talents to produce this *Field Guide*, one which Ernest Thompson Seton would have enthusiastically endorsed, because it was he who pointed out that each animal has its particular badge, or identification tag, by which it may be known at a glance. This idea was first developed fully in *A Field Guide to the Birds*, in which all eastern birds were reduced to simple patterns. An added innovation was the use of arrows pointing to distinctive field marks. The success of the book and its companion volume, *A Field Guide to Western Birds*, was immediate, far exceeding the expectations of the author and the publisher. It was inevitable that students would urge us to extend the system to other fields of natural history; thus the Field Guide Series was launched.

A Field Guide to the Mammals is the second book on which Mr. Burt and Mr. Grossenheider have collaborated. Their earlier work was the well-known volume *The Mammals of Michigan*. Dr. Burt, through years of teaching at the University of Michigan, his custodianship of the mammal collection at the Museum of Zoology in Ann Arbor, and through a term as editor of the *Journal of Mammalogy*, is ideally equipped to inform us in the clearest, most direct terms about North American mammals. Familiar with mammals both in the wild and in the hand, he knows where to draw the line between field marks and taxonomic characters. A few small mammals, it will be seen, simply cannot be identified with certainty except in the hand, by means of dentition and skull characters. Dr. Burt has avoided the problem of subspecies, since that too is more properly within the realm of the specialist and the specimen tray. Moreover, had he treated them at this stage in our taxonomic knowledge the book would probably become obsolete in a short time.

Richard Grossenheider's drawings are so sensitive in handling that one must study them carefully to appreciate fully their artistry. He loves the small mammals in particular, and no one has ever portrayed them with greater understanding. The exquisite textural quality of his drawings reminds one of an earlier master, Albrecht Dürer.

George Sutton, the distinguished wildlife artist, in eulogizing Grossenheider's work writes: "Those who study these drawings will, I am confident, concur that they possess that rarest of qualities — the life-spark. This subtle quality in a picture invariably puzzles me. I have studied living birds and mammals for years, and believe I know *why* they look alive. But the aliveness of a picture is amazing and wondrous nonetheless. There must be something of the small mammal in Dick Grossenheider himself — something very sensitive to sounds, something keenly aware of passing shadows, something ever on the alert for signs and warnings — else how could his drawings have the *autobiographical* authenticity they possess?"

When you start out on a camping trip take this book with you. Do not leave it on your library shelf; it is a field guide intended to be used.

ROGER TORY PETERSON

CONSERVATION NOTE

Mammals and all wildlife are part of our American heritage. They contribute to our happiness and standard of living.

Help support the cause of wildlife conservation by taking an active part in the work of the National Wildlife Federation, National Audubon Society, World Wildlife Fund, and other conservation organizations. They deserve your support.

Should your interest in mammals be scientific, even in an amateur way, you shall want to subscribe to the *Journal of Mammalogy* or the *Journal of Wildlife Management*.

Preface

WHEN *A Field Guide to the Mammals* was published in 1952, it included distribution maps for 313 species of North American land mammals (all of those north of Mexico except a few that were restricted to islands). This innovation in the Peterson Field Guide Series was also a first in North American mammalogy. Although distribution maps for many of the species had been published, they had not been assembled in one book. Since then much additional information on the geographic distribution of North American mammals has appeared in journals and other publications. I have incorporated all additional information known to me in this second edition, and consequently most of the maps have been modified to fit our present concepts. These undoubtedly will be modified further in the future, owing to subsequent information and expansion or contraction of geographic ranges of some of the species.

The 291 maps of the present edition show distribution for as many species of land mammal. As in the first edition, range maps are not included for species restricted to islands, for those mainland species known from a single locality, or for those restricted to an area such as a single mountaintop. Instead, a statement is made in the text under the heading *Range*.

Another, and more important, change in the present book is the addition of sections on *Habitat, Habits, Young,* and *Economic status*. These are condensed accounts; they include what I consider essential information that the reader might wish to have at his fingertips.

The treatment of subspecies again has been omitted purposely. It is my opinion that the ordinary person will be satisfied to know which species he is seeing. If he is concerned about the subspecies, he should turn to the more technical literature, some of which is listed under "References," and to the specialist in mammalogy.

For those who wish to keep a record of the kinds of mammals they have seen and identified, there is a Checklist (p. xix) of all species treated in the text.

I wish to thank my many colleagues, especially the graduate students, for help and constructive advice. To single out any one would be unfair to the others — they all contributed in a substantial way. Also, many readers of the first edition have given me valuable information on the occurrence of mammals in parts of the country unfamiliar to me. To those individuals, my most sincere thanks.

The photographs for the plates on skulls (Plates 25–32) were made by Luis de la Torre when he was a student at the University of Michigan.

To those on the staff of Houghton Mifflin Company whose expertise and patience make for a most cordial publisher-author relationship, my sincere gratitude. The continued interest of Paul Brooks, the book production skills of Morton Baker and Katharine Bernard, and, above all, the unsurpassed editorial competence of Helen Phillips, all go to make an author's dream materialize. As always, the counsel of Roger Tory Peterson is invaluable.

WILLIAM HENRY BURT

Contents

Illustrations

How to Use This Book

MOST mammals, unlike birds, are nocturnal and secretive in their habits. They are therefore much more difficult to see and identify in the field. An exception is the squirrel family. Tree squirrels, ground squirrels, chipmunks, Woodchucks, and prairie dogs are active by day and present themselves in favorable situations for the field naturalist. Also in this category are many of the big game mammals, deer, Elk, Moose, caribou, sheep, goats, Bison, Pronghorns, and Muskox, as well as the marine mammals, whales, dolphins, seals, and sea lions. Cats, foxes, Coyotes, rabbits, and hares, too, although most active at night, are often seen by day. Most of the small mammals — bats, moles, shrews, mice, and rats — sleep during the day and come out only as darkness falls. Although one occasionally sees these small mammals in daytime, particularly in early morning or just before darkness, they are difficult to identify except at very close range. Even then, some are puzzling and cannot be determined by external characters alone. If characterizations sometimes seem vague it is because those species being discussed do not possess outstanding field marks. I consider it better to treat obscure species in this way than to give characters nobody can see.

Recognition: To use this *Field Guide* effectively for identifying mammals, the following procedure is suggested. First, by thumbing through the plates of illustrations, determine the kind or large group to which the mammal in question belongs. Arrows point to the outstanding recognition marks mentioned on the legend page opposite the drawing. In many instances these and the indication of general area where the mammal is found which is given on the legend pages (see p. xvi for explanation) will suffice for proper identification. If not, then turn to the maps showing the ranges of the species in this group. A rapid perusal of the maps will show you which kinds are to be found in your area. You need be concerned *only* with these. If but one species occurs there you need look no further. If you have two or more kinds to select from, turn to the text where one of the species is treated. Read the characters given and also those given under *Similar species. Be concerned only with those found in your area;* this should give you the answer in most instances. If it is one of the similar species, turn to the account of that one and see if the characters fit.

Here is an example — follow this through and you will know how to use the book. You are in northern Wisconsin. You see a small mammal in the woods; it is brightly colored, brownish, and has stripes on its sides and face. While looking through the illustrations you come to a plate (p. 116) showing squirrel-like mammals, all having stripes on them. The animal you saw fits those labeled "chipmunk." You now turn to the maps (pp. 115–22) where the ranges of chipmunks are shown. You discover that in northern Wisconsin there are two species, the Eastern and Least Chipmunks. You need not be concerned about the other 14 species. Since both chipmunks are illustrated on Plate 11, you should determine the kind from the drawings alone. If you are not certain of the identification, turn to the Eastern Chipmunk (p. 113) and read the account under *Recognition*. If this does not fit, under *Similar species* look for the Least Chipmunk. Here you will find that the body stripes reach to the base of the tail, and the rump is not reddish. If the animal you saw has these marks, it is a Least Chipmunk. To double-check, turn to the account under Least Chipmunk. This should not be necessary, but it is always good to have an extra check on any identification.

Mammal skulls are often picked up in the field or taken from owl pellets. Many of these can be identified, at least to the large group to which they belong, by comparing them with the pictures (Plates 25–32, pp. 244–61). In many instances they may be identified to the species by just counting the teeth and referring to the list of "Dental Formulae."

The measurement "head and body" is of the outstretched animal from tip of nose to base of tail. The tail measurement does not include the hairs at the tip — it is of the tail vertebrae. Measurements are given in feet and inches, weight in pounds and ounces. In the short list of characters under *Recognition* the most important ones are in *italics*.

Similar species: Under this subheading the most similar species is given first, the least similar is listed last. Only those species occurring in the same area are listed. Cross-reference pages are given for those similar species occurring under another section grouping or for those in the same section which are separated by several pages of text.

Habitat: The place where a mammal is seen is sometimes an important clue to its identification, particularly with those kinds confined to limited sets of conditions. Tree squirrels are restricted to wooded areas and prairie dogs to open grasslands. The information on *Habitat* has been added to indicate the types of places where each species is most likely to be found.

Habits: In this new part the time, day or night, when a particular kind of mammal is most active is indicated. Also, when known, information is given on food, nests, populations, longevity, breeding season, and other habits considered to be of interest.

Young: When known, the number of young in a litter and the number of litters a year, as well as the gestation period and other details, are given here.

Economic status: Sometimes this is given under the intro-
ductory family or general description, if it applies to all within
that group. In other instances it is under the last subheading to
the species entry.

Range: Distributions of marine mammals, mammals confined to
islands, and some mainland species with restricted ranges or known
from a single locality are not shown on maps. Instead, a statement
under the subheading *Range* will indicate where they occur.

Distribution maps: Except for the bats and marine species,
migrations of mammals are slight or nonexistent. Most mammals
stay put. This is an aid to identification by elimination. The
maps are arranged throughout the text so that each is near its
respective species account. The shaded parts of the maps represent the approximate areas within which the different species may
be expected. This does not mean that the species will be found
over the entire area, but possibly wherever suitable conditions
exist within the area. The outer boundaries represent approximate
limits of distribution. Present, not past, distributions are indicated. Many game species have been introduced into areas beyond
their original ranges. Occasionally they become established, many
disappear. Some of these are shown on the maps, others are
indicated in the text, if known to the author.

Number of species: There are 378 species accounts in the text.
This is probably a minimum; several doubtful species are included
under *Recognition*. In some cases, two or more so-called species
have been grouped under a single entry heading because it is
difficult or impossible to give distinctive characters that the non-
specialist would be able to use. Further study may show some of
these to be subspecies, not species.

Common names: There is no official list of common names for
mammals. Usage has determined most of the names, and many
of these do not indicate relationships. The Mountain Beaver
(*Aplodontia rufa*) is not even closely related to the Beaver (*Castor
canadensis*); yet in certain areas the name persists instead of the
proper one, Aplodontia. Common names also change from one
locality to another; this is especially true for wide-ranging species.
The name Mountain Lion for *Felis concolor* is appropriate for the
western mountain country, but in Florida, where there are no
mountains, the name is quite inappropriate. In this instance, as
in several others, alternate names are provided in parentheses.

The spelling of some of the common names used herein needs
some explanation. A system worked out by the American Fisheries
Society for uniform spelling of common names for fishes seemed to
me to be a good one. It was used in part in the first edition and is
followed in part in this one. The rule to which I have adhered is
that if an unpaired structure is involved in the name (tail, nose,
etc.), compounded words are written as one word without a hyphen
(longtail, longnose, etc.), but if paired structures are involved they

are hyphenated (white-footed, big-eared, etc.). This is a deviation from the rule followed by the American Fisheries Society. This society hyphenates only where orthographically essential, where a special meaning is involved, or where it is necessary to avoid misunderstanding. I have attempted, not always with success, to use euphonious names.

Area designations on legend pages: The general section of the North American continent where the species occurs is indicated by N and S for north and south of the 40th parallel, E and W for east and west of the 100th meridian. Some species overlap these arbitrary boundaries, but the major part of the range will be found in the sector indicated. In a few instances where the range is confined to the central plains the term Central has been used, sometimes with N, S, E, or W modifications; also, Arctic and Subarctic are used for a few species confined to the Far North. See map below for the area breakdowns.

Classification: The primary purpose of any classification is to

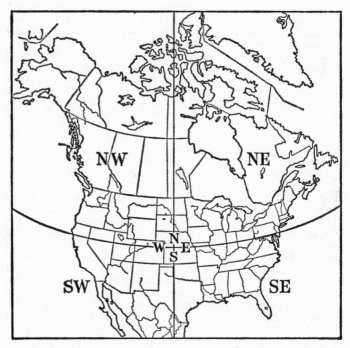

Key to area designations given on legend pages of Plates 1–24.

arrange things in an orderly manner. In the classification of mammals we also try to arrange them in a way that will indicate relationships and at the same time tell us something of their evolutionary history. This, of course, is impossible with our present knowledge. But we think we can approach the solution in a few groups where there have been adequate studies in comparative anatomy, paleontology, and, in a very few kinds, physiology and genetics.

In this revised edition the arrangement of the Orders and Families is nearly the same as it was in the first edition. The shrews (Soricidae) and moles (Talpidae) have been reversed in their order of appearance. The Walrus (Odobenidae) has been placed before the hair seals (Phocidae) and the Aplodontia, or Mountain Beaver (Aplodontiidae), has been transferred to the beginning of the rodents (Rodentia). In theory, the most primitive (or oldest) group (marsupials) is listed first and the least primitive (youngest) group last. But some groups are equally primitive or equally advanced in comparison with others, so their place in the classification becomes somewhat arbitrary. If we did know the true relationships, it would be physically impossible to arrange them in linear fashion to show those relationships — we would need a third dimension to do it properly. I have retained, in general, the order used in the first edition. I believe it is quite as satisfactory as some of the rearrangements by recent authors.

Checklist

KEEP your "life list" up to date by checking the mammals you have seen.

..../..OPOSSUM
....MASKED SHREW
....MOUNT LYELL SHREW
....MALHEUR SHREW
....SMOKY SHREW
....ARCTIC SHREW
....UNALASKA SHREW
....PRIBILOF SHREW
....MERRIAM SHREW
....SOUTHEASTERN SHREW
....LONGTAIL SHREW
....GASPÉ SHREW
....TROWBRIDGE SHREW
....VAGRANT SHREW
....DUSKY SHREW
....PACIFIC SHREW
....ORNATE SHREW
....ASHLAND SHREW
....SANTA CATALINA SHREW
....SUISUN SHREW
....INYO SHREW
....DWARF SHREW
....NORTHERN WATER SHREW
....PACIFIC WATER SHREW
....PYGMY SHREW
....GRAY SHREW
....LEAST SHREW
....SHORTTAIL SHREW
....SHREW-MOLE
....STARNOSE MOLE
....EASTERN MOLE
....HAIRYTAIL MOLE
....TOWNSEND MOLE
....PACIFIC MOLE

....CALIFORNIA MOLE
....LEAFCHIN BAT
....LEAFNOSE BAT
....HOGNOSE BAT
....LONGNOSE BAT
....LITTLE BROWN MYOTIS
....YUMA MYOTIS
....MISSISSIPPI MYOTIS
....GRAY MYOTIS
....CAVE MYOTIS
....ARIZONA MYOTIS
....KEEN MYOTIS
....LONG-EARED MYOTIS
....FRINGED MYOTIS
....INDIANA MYOTIS
....LONG-LEGGED MYOTIS
....CALIFORNIA MYOTIS
....SMALL-FOOTED MYOTIS
....SILVER-HAIRED BAT
....WESTERN PIPISTREL
....EASTERN PIPISTREL
....BIG BROWN BAT
....RED BAT
....SEMINOLE BAT
....HOARY BAT
....EASTERN YELLOW BAT
....WESTERN YELLOW BAT
....EVENING BAT
....SPOTTED BAT
....WESTERN BIG-EARED BAT
....EASTERN BIG-EARED BAT
....MEXICAN BIG-EARED BAT
....PALLID BAT
....MEXICAN FREETAIL BAT

....POCKETED FREETAIL BAT

....BIG FREETAIL BAT

....WESTERN MASTIFF BAT

....UNDERWOOD MASTIFF BAT

....EASTERN MASTIFF BAT

..✓.BLACK BEAR

..✓.GRIZZLY BEAR

....BIG BROWN BEAR

..✓.POLAR BEAR

..✓.RACCOON

....COATI

....RINGTAIL

....MARTEN

....FISHER

....SHORTTAIL WEASEL

....LEAST WEASEL

.✓..LONGTAIL WEASEL

....BLACK-FOOTED FERRET

.✓..MINK

.✓..RIVER OTTER

....SEA OTTER

....WOLVERINE

....BADGER

....SPOTTED SKUNK

....STRIPED SKUNK

....HOODED SKUNK

....HOGNOSE SKUNK

....COYOTE

....GRAY WOLF

....RED WOLF

.✓..RED FOX

....SWIFT FOX

....KIT FOX

....ARCTIC FOX

.✓..GRAY FOX

....JAGUAR

....MOUNTAIN LION

....OCELOT

....MARGAY CAT

....JAGUARUNDI CAT

....LYNX

.✓..BOBCAT

....NORTHERN SEA LION

....CALIFORNIA SEA LION

....GUADALUPE FUR SEAL

....ALASKA FUR SEAL

....WALRUS

....HARBOR SEAL

....RINGED SEAL

....RIBBON SEAL

....HARP SEAL

....GRAY SEAL

....BEARDED SEAL

....CARIBBEAN MONK SEAL

....HOODED SEAL

....ELEPHANT SEAL

....APLODONTIA

....WOODCHUCK

....YELLOWBELLY MARMOT

....HOARY MARMOT

....OLYMPIC MARMOT

....VANCOUVER MARMOT

....BLACKTAIL PRAIRIE DOG

....WHITETAIL PRAIRIE DOG

....CALIFORNIA GR. SQUIRREL

....ROCK SQUIRREL

....TOWNSEND GROUND SQUIRREL

....WASHINGTON GR. SQUIRREL

....IDAHO GROUND SQUIRREL

....RICHARDSON GR. SQUIRREL

....UINTA GROUND SQUIRREL

....BELDING GROUND SQUIRREL

....COLUMBIAN GROUND SQUIRREL

....ARCTIC GROUND SQUIRREL

....THIRTEEN-LINED GR. SQUIRREL

....MEXICAN GROUND SQUIRREL

....SPOTTED GROUND SQUIRREL

....MOHAVE GROUND SQUIRREL

....ROUNDTAIL GROUND SQUIRREL

....FRANKLIN GROUND SQUIRREL

....GOLDEN-MANTLED SQUIRREL

....YUMA ANTELOPE SQUIRREL

....WHITETAIL ANTELOPE SQ.

....SAN JOAQUIN ANTELOPE SQ.

....EASTERN CHIPMUNK

....ALPINE CHIPMUNK

....LEAST CHIPMUNK
....TOWNSEND CHIPMUNK
....CLIFF CHIPMUNK
....SONOMA CHIPMUNK
....YELLOW PINE CHIPMUNK
....MERRIAM CHIPMUNK
....GRAYNECK CHIPMUNK
....LONG-EARED CHIPMUNK
....REDTAIL CHIPMUNK
....COLORADO CHIPMUNK
....UINTA CHIPMUNK
....PANAMINT CHIPMUNK
....LODGEPOLE CHIPMUNK
....CHARLESTON MT. CHIPMUNK
....WESTERN GRAY SQUIRREL
....TASSEL-EARED SQUIRREL
✓..EASTERN GRAY SQUIRREL
....ARIZONA GRAY SQUIRREL
✓..EASTERN FOX SQUIRREL
....APACHE FOX SQUIRREL
....RED SQUIRREL
....CHICKAREE
✓..SOUTHERN FLYING SQUIRREL
....NORTHERN FLYING SQUIRREL
....VALLEY POCKET GOPHER
....BAILEY POCKET GOPHER
....PYGMY POCKET GOPHER
....NORTHERN POCKET GOPHER
....SIERRA POCKET GOPHER
....MAZAMA POCKET GOPHER
....TOWNSEND POCKET GOPHER
....GIANT POCKET GOPHER
....PLAINS POCKET GOPHER
....SO. TEXAS POCKET GOPHER
....SOUTHEASTERN POCKET GO.
....MEXICAN POCKET GOPHER
....MEXICAN POCKET MOUSE
....WYOMING POCKET MOUSE
....PLAINS POCKET MOUSE
....MERRIAM POCKET MOUSE
....SILKY POCKET MOUSE
....APACHE POCKET MOUSE
....LITTLE POCKET MOUSE

....ARIZONA POCKET MOUSE
....SAN JOAQUIN POCKET MOUSE
....GREAT BASIN POCKET MOUSE
....WHITE-EARED POCKET MOUSE
....WALKER PASS POCKET MOUSE
....DESERT POCKET MOUSE
....ROCK POCKET MOUSE
....NELSON POCKET MOUSE
....SAN DIEGO POCKET MOUSE
....CALIFORNIA POCKET MOUSE
....SPINY POCKET MOUSE
....LONGTAIL POCKET MOUSE
....BAILEY POCKET MOUSE
....HISPID POCKET MOUSE
....DARK KANGAROO MOUSE
....PALE KANGAROO MOUSE
....BANNERTAIL KANGAROO RAT
....HEERMANN KANGAROO RAT
....PANAMINT KANGAROO RAT
....STEPHENS KANGAROO RAT
....GIANT KANGAROO RAT
....ORD KANGAROO RAT
....PACIFIC KANGAROO RAT
....SANTA CRUZ KANGAROO RAT
....BIG-EARED KANGAROO RAT
....GREAT BASIN KANGAROO RAT
....DESERT KANGAROO RAT
....TEXAS KANGAROO RAT
....MERRIAM KANGAROO RAT
....FRESNO KANGAROO RAT
....BEAVER
....EASTERN HARVEST MOUSE
....PLAINS HARVEST MOUSE
....WESTERN HARVEST MOUSE
....SALT MARSH HARVEST MOUSE
....FULVOUS HARVEST MOUSE
....CACTUS MOUSE
....MERRIAM MOUSE
....CALIFORNIA MOUSE
....CANYON MOUSE
....DEER MOUSE
....SITKA MOUSE
....OLDFIELD MOUSE

....WHITE-FOOTED MOUSE

....COTTON MOUSE

....BRUSH MOUSE

....WHITE-ANKLED MOUSE

....PIÑON MOUSE

....ROCK MOUSE

....FLORIDA MOUSE

....GOLDEN MOUSE

....PYGMY MOUSE

....NO. GRASSHOPPER MOUSE

....SO. GRASSHOPPER MOUSE

....EASTERN WOODRAT

....SOUTHERN PLAINS WOODRAT

....WHITETHROAT WOODRAT

....DESERT WOODRAT

....STEPHENS WOODRAT

....MEXICAN WOODRAT

....DUSKY-FOOTED WOODRAT

....BUSHYTAIL WOODRAT

....RICE RAT

....HISPID COTTON RAT

....LEAST COTTON RAT

....YELLOWNOSE COTTON RAT

....HUDSON BAY COLL. LEMMING

....GREENLAND COLL. LEMMING

....SOUTHERN BOG LEMMING

....NORTHERN BOG LEMMING

....BROWN LEMMING

....MOUNTAIN PHENACOMYS

....PACIFIC PHENACOMYS

....TREE PHENACOMYS

....TUNDRA REDBACK VOLE

....BOREAL REDBACK VOLE

....CALIFORNIA REDBACK VOLE

....MEADOW VOLE

....MOUNTAIN VOLE

....CALIFORNIA VOLE

....TOWNSEND VOLE

....TUNDRA VOLE

....LONGTAIL VOLE

....CORONATION ISLAND VOLE

....MEXICAN VOLE

....YELLOW-CHEEKED VOLE

....YELLOWNOSE VOLE

....RICHARDSON VOLE

....OREGON VOLE

....ALASKA VOLE

....INSULAR VOLE

....PRAIRIE VOLE

....PINE VOLE

....SAGEBRUSH VOLE

....FLORIDA WATER RAT

..✓.MUSKRAT

....NORWAY RAT

....BLACK RAT

....HOUSE MOUSE

....MEADOW JUMPING MOUSE

....WESTERN JUMPING MOUSE

....PACIFIC JUMPING MOUSE

....WOODLAND JUMPING MOUSE

....PORCUPINE

....NUTRIA

....PIKA

....COLLARED PIKA

....ARCTIC HARE

....TUNDRA HARE

....WHITETAIL JACKRABBIT

....SNOWSHOE HARE

....EUROPEAN HARE

....ANTELOPE JACKRABBIT

....BLACKTAIL JACKRABBIT

.✓.EASTERN COTTONTAIL

....MOUNTAIN COTTONTAIL

....NEW ENGLAND COTTONTAIL

....DESERT COTTONTAIL

....BRUSH RABBIT

...✓.MARSH RABBIT

.✓..SWAMP RABBIT

....PYGMY RABBIT

.✓.PECCARY

....WILD BOAR

....ELK

....MULE DEER

.✓..WHITETAIL DEER

....MOOSE

....WOODLAND CARIBOU

....BARREN GROUND CARIBOU
....GREENLAND CARIBOU
....PRONGHORN
....BISON
....MOUNTAIN GOAT
....MUSKOX
....BIGHORN SHEEP
....WHITE SHEEP
....ARMADILLO
....MANATEE
....BAIRD BEAKED WHALE
....SOWERBY BEAKED WHALE
....ATLANTIC BEAKED WHALE
....GERVAIS BEAKED WHALE
....TRUE BEAKED WHALE
....PACIFIC BEAKED WHALE
....GOOSEBEAK WHALE
....BOTTLENOSE WHALE
....SPERM WHALE
....PYGMY SPERM WHALE
....WHITE WHALE
....NARWHAL
....CUVIER DOLPHIN
....SPOTTED DOLPHIN
....LONGSNOUT DOLPHIN
....LONGBEAK DOLPHIN

....COMMON DOLPHIN
....ATLANTIC BOTTLENOSE DOLPH.
....PACIFIC BOTTLENOSE DOLPHIN
....RIGHT WHALE DOLPHIN
....ATLANTIC WHITE-SIDED DOLPH.
....PACIFIC WHITE-SIDED DOLPHIN
....WHITEBEAK DOLPHIN
....ATLANTIC KILLER WHALE
....PACIFIC KILLER WHALE
....GRAMPUS
....FALSE KILLER
....COMMON BLACKFISH
....SHORT-FINNED BLACKFISH
....PACIFIC BLACKFISH
....ATLANTIC HARBOR PORPOISE
....PACIFIC HARBOR PORPOISE
....DALL PORPOISE
....GRAY WHALE
....FINBACK WHALE
....RORQUAL
....PIKED WHALE
....BLUE WHALE
....HUMPBACK WHALE
....ATLANTIC RIGHT WHALE
....PACIFIC RIGHT WHALE
....BOWHEAD WHALE

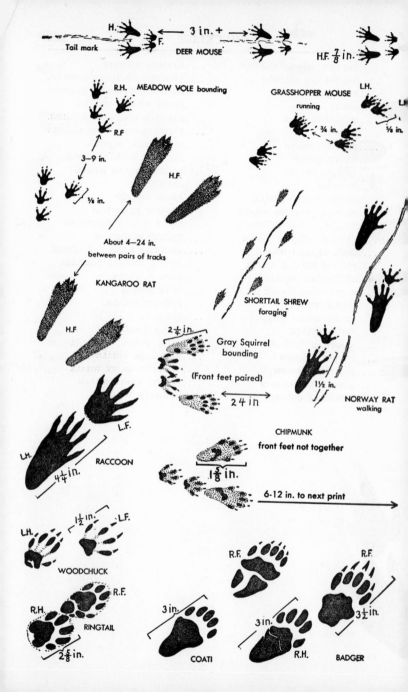

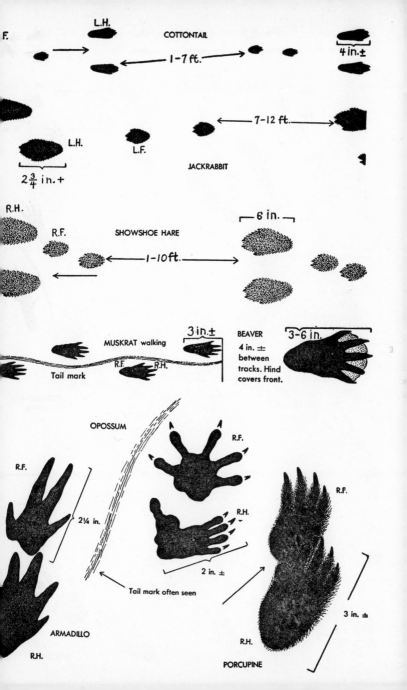

L.H.

COTTONTAIL

F.

1-7 ft.

4 in. ±

L.H.

L.F.

7-12 ft.

JACKRABBIT

2¾ in. +

R.H.

R.F.

SHOWSHOE HARE

6 in.

1-10 ft.

MUSKRAT walking

3 in. ±

BEAVER

3-6 in.

4 in. ± between tracks. Hind covers front.

Tail mark

R.F.

R.H.

OPOSSUM

R.F.

R.F.

R.H.

R.F.

2¼ in.

2 in. ±

3 in. ±

Tail mark often seen

ARMADILLO

R.H.

R.H.

PORCUPINE

A Field Guide
to the Mammals

Pouched Mammals: Marsupialia

YOUNG are born premature and complete their development in fur-lined pouch on belly of female, in most kinds.

Opossums: Didelphiidae

THE only marsupials in N. America. Five toes on each foot; inside toe on hind foot opposable (an aid in climbing) and without claw; prehensile tail scaly and similar to a rat's. Among the most primitive of living mammals. As fossils, date back to Upper Cretaceous time.

OPOSSUM *Didelphis marsupialis* p. 196
Recognition: Head and body 15–20 in.; tail 9–20 in.; wt. 9–13 lb. Often seen in beam of auto headlights or dead along highways. About the size of a House Cat, but body heavier, legs shorter, nose pointed, *face white*, paper-thin *ears black*, often tipped with whitish; *tail* ratlike, round, prehensile, and black for basal ⅛ to ½, white on end. Ears and tail may be partially missing in North, owing to freezing. Usually whitish gray in North, gray to nearly black in South. Eyeshine dull orange. Skull (p. 260) has 50 teeth. Up to 17 mammae in pouch.
  Formerly known as Virginia Opossum; now considered same species as the one in Mexico.
Similar species: Nutria (p. 210) has sparsely haired tail same color throughout, webs between toes of hind foot, and blunt (not pointed) face suggestive of large Muskrat.
Habitat: Farming areas preferred, also found in woodlands and along streams.
Habits: Usually active only at night. Eats fruits, vegetables, nuts, meat, eggs, insects, carrion. Seeks shelter in old dens, beneath outbuildings, in hollow trees or logs, culverts, brushpiles. May feign death, "play possum," when cornered. Usual home range 15–40 acres, but may wander widely, especially in fall. Has extended its range northward and become more numerous in recent years. May live 7 years or more.
Young: Up to 14 per litter; gestation period about 13 days; 1 or 2 litters per year. Tiny at birth, weigh $\frac{1}{15}$ oz. each; entire litter may be put in a teaspoon. Remain in pouch about 2 months; later may travel on mother's back with tails grasping hers.

Economic status: Sometimes hunted for sport, especially in the South. Edible, but meat oily. Occasionally raids poultry yards, but also destroys many mice and insects. Fur salable, but of small value.   Map below

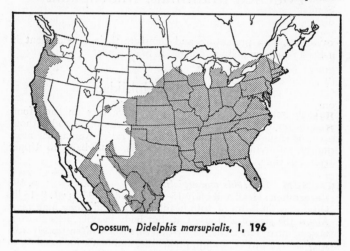

Opossum, *Didelphis marsupialis*, I, **196**

Insect-eaters: Insectivora

NORTH AMERICAN representatives of this group, nearly worldwide in distribution, are relatively small (largest, length about 9 in.), with long pointed noses and tiny beadlike eyes; 5 toes on each foot.

Shrews: Soricidae

THESE bundles of energy are *mouse size; beadlike eyes not* covered with skin; ears concealed or nearly concealed by soft fur; always *5 toes* on each foot (most mice have 4 toes on front foot); teeth usually pigmented in part with chestnut. Many shrews are difficult to identify; if identification questionable, they should be sent to a museum. Found over most of N. America. Usually prefer moist situations, but some are found in sagebrush regions of arid West. Date back to Lower Oligocene as fossils.

Economic status: Either neutral or beneficial; eat many insects and do no harm.

MASKED SHREW *Sorex cinereus*   p. 20
   Recognition: Head and body 2–2½ in.; tail 1¼–2 in.; wt. ⅒–

⅛ oz. Body grayish brown, tail bicolored; underparts paler than upperparts. In the North and along Rocky and Appalachian Mts., particularly in *moist habitat*, usually the commonest shrew. Skull (p. 244) has 32 teeth. There are 6 mammae.

Similar species: (1) Pygmy Shrew — slightly smaller; can be distinguished for certain only by the unicuspids (single-cusped teeth in upper jaw), 3 instead of 5 on each side. (2) Smoky Shrew — larger; dark underparts. (3) Merriam Shrew — pale grayish; whitish underparts. (4) Arctic, (5) Longtail, (6) Vagrant, (7) Dusky, and (8) Trowbridge Shrews — all larger. (9) Gaspé and (10) Dwarf Shrews — tail not distinctly bicolored. (11) Southeastern Shrew — about same size, but ranges overlap only slightly. (12) Least Shrew — shorter tail.

Habitat: Moist situations — forests, open country, brushland.

Habits: Active day or night; when not sleeping, searching for food. Eats more than own weight each day; a captive ate more than 3 times own weight; food mostly insects, but includes many other small animals. Nest of dry leaves or grasses, in stumps or under logs or piles of brush. Concentrations of these shrews have been observed several times. Recorded heartbeats, more than 1200 per min.; respirations equally high. Breeding season probably March–Oct.; some females may reach sexual maturity at ages 4–5 months.

Young: 2–10; probably more than 1 litter a year. Embryos reported for Jan., April, May, and Sept.   Map p. 4

MOUNT LYELL SHREW *Sorex lyelli*
Recognition: Head and body 2¼ in.; tail 1½ in. Found only in a small section of the high Sierra Nevada, *6900-ft. altitude and above*. Skull has 32 teeth.   Map p. 7

MALHEUR SHREW *Sorex preblei*
Recognition: Head and body 2–2¼ in.; tail 1½ in. One of the *smallest* western shrews. Skull has 32 teeth.
Similar species: (1) Merriam and (2) Vagrant Shrews — larger.
Habitat: As far as known, marshes and near streams.   Map p. 7

SMOKY SHREW *Sorex fumeus*
Recognition: Head and body 2½–3 in.; tail 1¾–2 in.; wt. ⅕–⅓ oz. A *dull brown* shrew; *uniformly colored* except for *bicolored tail* (yellowish below, brown above) and *pale feet*. A common shrew within its range. Skull has 32 teeth. There are 6 mammae.
Similar species: (1) Longtail Shrew — longer tail. (2) Masked Shrew — smaller, underparts paler than upperparts. (3) Pygmy and (4) Gaspé Shrews — smaller. (5) Arctic Shrew — shorter tail, body not uniform color. (6) Southeastern Shrew — smaller.
Habitat: Birch and hemlock forests with deep layer of leaf mold on ground preferred.

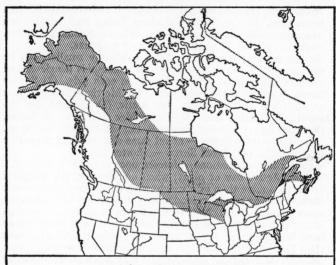

Arctic Shrew, *Sorex arcticus*, 5, **20**

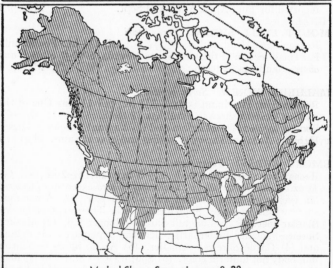

Masked Shrew, *Sorex cinereus*, 2, **20**

Habits: Makes own burrows or uses those of other small mammals through damp leaf mold. Food, insects and other small animals. Nest of dry vegetation in stumps, logs, and among rocks. May be abundant locally at times, suggests colonial habits; suspected that few live more than a year in the wild.

Young: Born April–June; possibly 2nd litter in July, Aug., or occasionally as late as Oct.; 2–7; gestation period probably 3 weeks or less (not known). Naked, blind.   Map p. 7

ARCTIC SHREW *Sorex arcticus*   p. 20

Recognition: Head and body 2¾–3 in.; tail 1¼–1⅔ in.; wt. ¼–⅓ oz. The most *brilliantly* colored and most attractive of the shrews — back, sides, and belly all contrast. In winter, *tricolored*, with back nearly black; in summer *dull brown.* Skull has 32 teeth There are 6 mammae.

On St. Lawrence I. known as *S. jacksoni.*

Similar species: (1) Smoky Shrew — longer tail, uniform body color. (2) Dusky and (3) Gaspé Shrews — not tricolored, but light brown. (4) Masked and (5) Pygmy Shrews — smaller, grayish brown.

Habitat: Tamarack and spruce swamps.

Habits: Food, chiefly insects and other invertebrates; not well known.

Young: Record of 1 female with 6 embryos.   Map opposite

UNALASKA SHREW *Sorex hydrodromus*

Range: Confined to *Unalaska I.* in Aleutians.

PRIBILOF SHREW *Sorex pribilofensis*

Range: Confined to *St. Paul I.*, Pribilofs.

MERRIAM SHREW *Sorex merriami*   p. 20

Recognition: Head and body 2¼–2½ in.; tail 1½ in. Upperparts *pale gray; underparts and feet whitish;* tail bicolored. Skull has 32 teeth.

Similar species: (1) Dwarf Shrew — tail indistinctly bicolored. (2) Malheur Shrew — smaller. (3) Gray Shrew — paler; shorter tail. (4) Masked Shrew — slightly larger, grayish brown. (5) Dusky Shrew — larger, brownish. (6) Vagrant Shrew — larger; dark feet. (7) Inyo Shrew — darker; high mts.

Habitat: Arid areas, sagebrush or bunchgrass.   Map p. 7

SOUTHEASTERN SHREW *Sorex longirostris*

Recognition: Head and body 2–2½ in.; tail 1–1½ in.; wt. ⅛–⅕ oz. This *dark brown* shrew with *paler underparts* is the only long-tailed shrew found over most of its range in the Atlantic Plain and Piedmont region. Skull has 32 teeth. There are 6 mammae.

Similar species: (1) Masked Shrew — about same; ranges overlap only slightly. (2) Other shrews — longer tail.
Habitat: Open fields and woodlots; moist areas preferred. This shrew not confined to one kind of habitat.
Habits: Probably eats insects, worms, and other small animals. Nest of dry grass or leaves in shallow depression.
Young: Born April; usually 4; probably 1 litter a year.
Map opposite

LONGTAIL SHREW *Sorex dispar*
Recognition: Head and body 2¾ in.; tail 2⅕–2½ in.; wt. ⅕± oz. In summer, *dark grayish* with slightly paler underparts and almost *uniformly colored tail;* in winter, slate color throughout; restricted range. Skull has 32 teeth. There are 6 mammae.
Similar species: (1) Masked and (2) Pygmy Shrews — smaller. (3) Smoky and (4) Southeastern Shrews — shorter tail.
Habitat: Cool, moist, rocky situations in deciduous or mixed deciduous-coniferous forests.
Habits: Food includes centipedes, spiders, insects, and possibly other small invertebrates. Sometimes found in concentrations.
Young: Born May; 5 reported; probably 1 litter a year.
Map opposite

GASPÉ SHREW *Sorex gaspensis*
Recognition: Head and body 2–2⅕ in.; tail 2 in. Similar to Longtail Shrew, but slightly smaller. Skull has 32 teeth. There are 6 mammae.
Similar species: (1) Masked, (2) Pygmy, and (3) Smoky Shrews — bicolored tail. (4) Arctic Shrew — tricolored body.
Habitat: Along streams in coniferous forests.
Range: Confined to Gaspé Pen.

TROWBRIDGE SHREW *Sorex trowbridgei*
Recognition: Head and body 2½–2⅘ in.; tail 2–2½ in.; wt. ⅕–⅓ oz. A fairly large shrew with nearly uniform dark *mouse-gray to brownish* body and a distinctly *bicolored tail, nearly white below.* Skull has 32 teeth. There are 6 mammae.
Similar species: (1) Pacific Shrew — larger; tail not bicolored. (2) Vagrant Shrew — shorter tail. (3) Ornate and (4) Masked Shrews — smaller. (5) Dusky Shrew — dull brown; underparts whitish. (6) Shrew-Mole (p. 16) — larger; front feet broad.
Habitat: Coniferous forests and other wooded areas.
Habits: Food consists of insects, isopods, probably other small invertebrates, and Douglas fir seeds. Few live as long as 18 months.
Young: Born March–May, occasionally July; 3–6; number of litters a year not known, probably 1. Brown until first molt in Sept.
Map p. 11

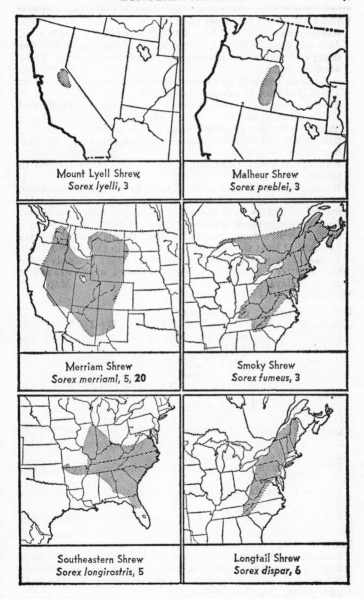

Mount Lyell Shrew
Sorex lyelli, 3

Malheur Shrew
Sorex preblei, 3

Merriam Shrew
Sorex merriami, 5, **20**

Smoky Shrew
Sorex fumeus, 3

Southeastern Shrew
Sorex longirostris, 5

Longtail Shrew
Sorex dispar, 6

8

LONGTAIL SHREWS

VAGRANT SHREW *Sorex vagrans*

Recognition: Head and body 2⅓–2⅖ in.; tail 1½–1⅖ in.; wt. ¼ ± oz. *Reddish brown* in summer, nearly *black* in winter; feet dark; common in our western mts. Skull has 32 teeth. There are 6 mammae.

Some authors consider the following two species, *S. obscurus* and *S. pacificus*, as subspecies of *vagrans*.

Similar species: (1) Dusky Shrew — dull brown. (2) Pacific and (3) Trowbridge Shrews — larger. (4) Masked and (5) Pygmy Shrews — smaller, grayish brown. (6) Dwarf Shrew — smaller, pale brown. (7) Merriam Shrew — smaller, pale gray. (8) Malheur Shrew — smaller.

Habitat: Marshes, bogs, wet meadows; also along streams in forests.

Habits: Active day and night. Known to eat insects, sow bugs, centipedes, spiders, earthworms, slugs, and some vegetable matter. Captives have eaten 1⅓ times own weight each day. Nest of dry grass or leaves in stumps or logs. Molts twice a year. Few live more than 16 months. Breeds as early as late Jan. and at least through May, then again in Oct. or Nov.

Young: 2–9; gestation period about 20 days; probably more than 1 litter a year. Eyes open in about 1 week; weaned at about 20 days.   Map p. 11

DUSKY SHREW *Sorex obscurus*

Recognition: Head and body 2½–3 in.; tail 1⅜–2½ in. Upperparts *dull brown*, underparts *whitish;* tail *bicolored*. Skull has 32 teeth. There are 6 mammae.

This shrew is difficult to distinguish from some others occurring in the same areas. In case of doubt, specimens should be sent to a museum. Some authors consider this and *S. vagrans* as same species.

Similar species: (1) Vagrant Shrew — reddish brown or blackish. (2) Arctic Shrew — tricolored. (3) Trowbridge Shrew — dark underparts. (4) Pacific Shrew — larger. (5) Masked, (6) Dwarf, and (7) Pygmy Shrews — smaller. (8) Merriam Shrew — smaller; pale gray; found on desert.

Habitat: Marshes, coniferous forests, heather, dry hillsides, rain-forest thickets.

Habits: Active day and night. Nests in stumps, logs, beneath debris.

Young: Recorded for July; 4–7.   Map opposite

PACIFIC SHREW *Sorex pacificus*

Recognition: Head and body 3⅛ in.; tail 2–2¾ in. This *large brown* western shrew is exceeded in size only by the Pacific Water Shrew. It is generally medium brown, including tail, feet, and underparts. Skull has 32 teeth.

Some authors consider this a subspecies of *S. vagrans*.
Similar species: (1) Vagrant, (2) Dusky, and (3) Trowbridge Shrews — smaller; bicolored tail. (4) Pacific Water Shrew — larger, blackish; stiff hairs on sides of hind feet.
Habitat: Redwood and spruce forests, marshes, swamps.

Map p. 11

ORNATE SHREW *Sorex ornatus*
Recognition: Head and body 2⅓–2½ in.; tail 1½–1⅘ in. This small *grayish brown* shrew, *pale beneath*, is the only shrew found over much of its range. Skull has 32 teeth.

It may be the same as the Ashland Shrew.
Similar species: (1) Trowbridge Shrew — larger; dark underparts. (2) Gray Shrew — pale ash-gray, found on desert.
Habitat: Near streams and in wet meadows.
Habits: Active both day and night.

Map p. 11

ASHLAND SHREW *Sorex trigonirostris*
Recognition: Head and body 2½ in.; tail 1⅓ in. A small *grayish-brown* shrew.

Dusky Shrew, *Sorex obscurus*, 8

May be the same as the Ornate Shrew (above).
Range: Known only from Ashland, Oregon.

SANTA CATALINA SHREW *Sorex willetti*
Recognition: Head and body 2⅗ in.; tail 1½ in.
Range: Known only from *Santa Catalina I.*, California. No other shrew is known from the island.

SUISUN SHREW *Sorex sinuosus*
Recognition: Head and body 2⅕–2½ in.; tail 1½ in. *Nearly* black.
Range: Known only from *Grizzly I.*, near Suisun, Solano Co., California.

INYO SHREW *Sorex tenellus*
Recognition: Head and body 2⅖ in.; tail 1⅗ in. *Grayish brown;* known only from a few *high mt. peaks* in California and Nevada. Skull has 32 teeth.
Similar species: Merriam Shrew — nearly white underparts; low deserts.
Habitat: Near water; rock ledges and old logs in bottom of canyons.
Habits: Active day and night. Map opposite

DWARF SHREW *Sorex nanus*
Recognition: Head and body 2½ in.; tail 1¾ in. A *small* shrew. Body *pale grayish brown,* tail indistinctly bicolored. Known from a few scattered locations within its general range. Skull has 32 teeth.
Similar species: (1) Merriam and (2) Masked Shrews — tail distinctly bicolored. (3) Dusky and (4) Vagrant Shrews — larger. Map opposite

NORTHERN WATER SHREW *Sorex palustris* p. 20
Recognition: Head and body 3⅓ in.; tail 2½–3 in.; wt. ⅓–½+ oz. A *large blackish-gray* shrew; in some areas underparts are silver, in others slightly paler than back. *Stiff hairs along sides of hind feet* will distinguish it from all but the Pacific Water Shrew. Skull has 32 teeth. There are 6 mammae.

The population from Pt. Gustavus, Glacier Bay, Alaska, is considered a distinct species (*S. alaskanus*) by some authors.
Similar species: (1) Pacific Water Shrew — larger, brownish. (2) Shrew-Mole (p. 16) — nose naked; front feet broad.
Habitat: Along cold, small streams with cover on banks, and in bogs; confined to mts. in South.
Habits: Adapted for swimming, readily takes to water, where it feeds on small aquatic organisms; sometimes caught in fish traps. Nest of dried sticks and leaves, diam. about 4 in., found in beaver lodge in New Hampshire.

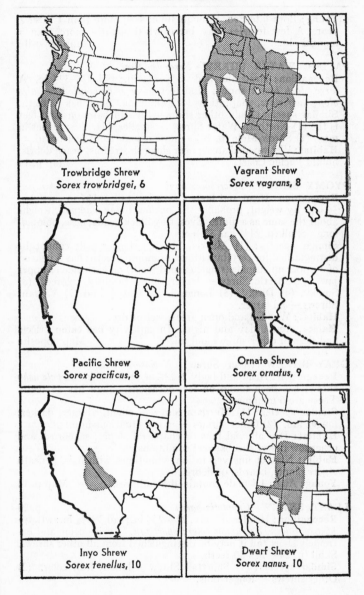

Trowbridge Shrew
Sorex trowbridgei, 6

Vagrant Shrew
Sorex vagrans, 8

Pacific Shrew
Sorex pacificus, 8

Ornate Shrew
Sorex ornatus, 9

Inyo Shrew
Sorex tenellus, 10

Dwarf Shrew
Sorex nanus, 10

Young: Born late Feb. through June; 4–8; more than 1 litter a year. A few females may breed when slightly more than 3 months old. Map opposite

PACIFIC WATER SHREW *Sorex bendirei*

Recognition: Head and body 3½–3⅘ in.; tail 2½–3⅕ in. A *large, dark brown* shrew; hind feet have *stiff, bristle-like hairs along their sides,* adaptations for swimming. Skull has 32 teeth.
Similar species: Only other shrew with stiff hairs on hind feet is the (1) Northern Water Shrew — smaller, blackish; higher in mts. (2) Shrew-Mole (p. 16) — nose naked; front feet broad.
Habitat: Wet wooded areas; near sluggish streams, beach debris; humid Pacific Coast. Map p. 14

PYGMY SHREW *Microsorex hoyi*

Recognition: Head and body 2–2½ in.; tail 1–1⅗ in.; wt. ⅑-⅐ oz. By weight, probably the *smallest living mammal;* weighs about the same as a dime. Eyes, tiny black beads; nose, pointed, long. Skull (p. 244) has 32 teeth.
Similar species: (1) Masked Shrew — longer tail; cannot be distinguished for certain without examining teeth; has 5 instead of 3 upper unicuspids (single cusped teeth) on each side of upper jaw. (2) Arctic Shrew — larger, more brightly colored. (3) Smoky, (4) Dusky, (5) Longtail, (6) Gaspé, and (7) Vagrant Shrews — all larger.
Habitat: Wooded and open areas, wet or dry.
Habits: Active day and night. In captivity has eaten insects and flesh of other shrews and mice. Map opposite

GRAY SHREW (Desert Shrew) *Notiosorex crawfordi*

Recognition: Head and body 2–2⅗ in.; tail 1+ in. A *pale ashy* shrew; has been found on few occasions. Skull has 28 teeth. There are 6 mammae.
Similar species: (1) Merriam Shrew — slightly larger, darker; longer tail. (2) Other shrews — moist situations in mts.
Habitat: Dry alluvial fans or chaparral slopes; sagebrush and other low desert shrubs; arid conditions.
Habits: Nest of fine vegetation, sometimes with hair, beneath *Agave* plants, boards, or debris.
Young: Aug.; 1 female contained 5 embryos. Map p. 14

LEAST SHREW *Cryptotis parva* p. 20

Recognition: Head and body, 2⅕–2½ in.; tail ½–¾ in.; wt. ⅐–¼ oz. Small, *cinnamon color; short tail.* By its color and extremely short tail it may be distinguished from all other shrews. Skull (p. 244) has 30 teeth.
Similar species: (1) Shorttail Shrew — larger, lead color. (2) Other shrews — longer tails.

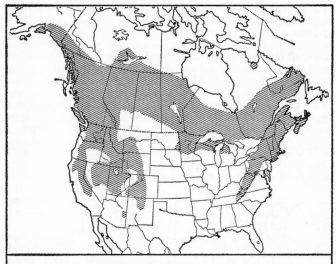

Northern Water Shrew, *Sorex palustris*, 10, **20**

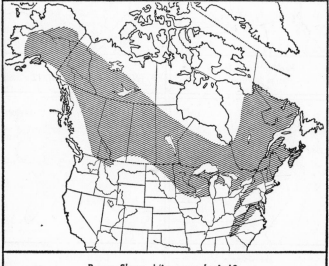

Pygmy Shrew, *Microsorex hoyi*, 12

Habitat: Open grass-covered areas, which may have scattered brush; also marshes.

Habits: Active day and night. Often uses same runways as voles. Eats insects and other small animals, may eat more than own weight in food each day. Nests under debris, if available, or beneath surface of ground, sometimes in beehives; as many as 31 have been found in 1 nest in winter. Breeds March–Nov. in North, also Feb. in South.

Young: 3–6; gestation period 21–23 days; more than 1 litter a year. Naked; eyes and ears closed; weaned at about 21 days; appearance of adults at 1 month.   Map below

SHORTTAIL SHREW   *Blarina brevicauda*   p. 20
    Recognition: Head and body 3–4 in.; tail ¾–1⅛ in.: wt. ⅖–⅘ oz. *Lead color*, short tail, *no external ears;* eyes so small they

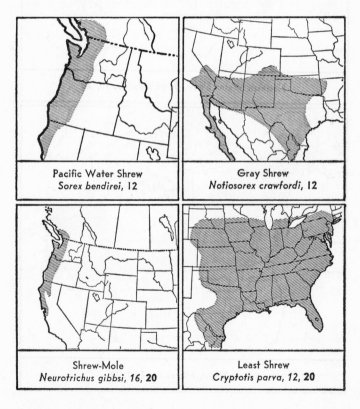

Pacific Water Shrew
Sorex bendirei, 12

Gray Shrew
Notiosorex crawfordi, 12

Shrew-Mole
Neurotrichus gibbsi, 16, **20**

Least Shrew
Cryptotis parva, 12, **20**

are *barely apparent*. Skull (p. 244) has 32 teeth. There are
6 mammae.

Those from the Dismal Swamp, Virginia, considered distinct
species (*B. telmalestes*) by some authors.
Similar species: (1) Least Shrew — smaller, cinnamon color.
(2) Other shrews — longer tails.
Habitat: Forests, grasslands, marshes, brushy areas; not restricted.
Habits: Active day and night throughout year. Makes own
tunnels in ground or snow; also uses those of other animals.
Feeds on insects, worms, snails, other invertebrates, and possibly
young mice; saliva poisonous. Nest of dry leaves, grass, hair
(diam. 6–8 in.), beneath logs, stumps, rocks, or debris. Home
range ½–1 acre. Populations as high as 25 per acre, usually
fewer. Longevity 1–2 years. Breeds March–May and Aug.–Sept.
Young: 5–8; gestation period 21+ days; 2–3 litters a year.
Naked, pink, about size of honeybee when born; eyes and ears
closed.   Map below

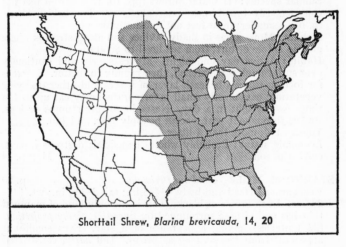

Shorttail Shrew, *Blarina brevicauda*, 14, **20**

Moles: Talpidae

MOLES live most of their lives *beneath* the surface of the ground.
Their presence may be detected by the *low ridges* pushed up as
they move just under the surface; also by the *mounds*, each con-
sisting of from ½ to 2 gallons of earth, which they push up from
below. No indication of entrance to burrow as in a pocket gopher

mound. Front feet *broad*, palms usually face outward. Eyes of *pinhead size* or smaller; some covered with a thin skin; *no external ears;* fur soft and thick. Do not occur in Rocky Mt. or Great Basin area. Length, from tip of nose to tip of tail, 4–9 in. As fossils, date back to Upper Eocene.

Local control of moles, when needed, is best achieved by use of special traps obtainable at most hardware stores and mail order houses. To locate an active subsurface runway, press down ridges of earth in several places and next day observe which ones have been raised. For control on large areas, poisoned raw peanuts or poisoned earthworms placed in active tunnels are most effective. These *should not* be used by the inexperienced person, however.

SHREW-MOLE   *Neurotrichus gibbsi*   p. 20
  Recognition: Head and body 2½–3 in.; tail 1–1½ in.; wt. ⅖ oz. Body and tail black. Front feet *longer than broad;* nose naked; nostrils open *to the sides;* eyes *small but apparent;* tail *haired.* Smallest of N. American moles. Skull (p. 244) has 36 teeth.
  Similar species: (1) Water Shrews (pp. 10, 12) — front feet not conspicuously broad; nose not naked. (2) Trowbridge Shrew (p. 6) — smaller; front feet not unusually broad.
  Habitat: Moist areas in shady ravines and along streams where ground is free of turf; from sea level to 8000 ft.
  Habits: Active day and night. Moves slowly and cautiously over surface unless frightened, then rapidly to shelter. Searches for food in tunnels beneath layer of leaves and other decaying vegetation; eats mostly small invertebrates; may eat up to 1½ times own weight in a day. Nests in rotting stumps or logs. Breeds throughout year, except possibly Dec. and Jan.
  Young: 1–4; more than 1 litter a year.
  Economic status: Probably wholly beneficial; destroys insects, cultivates soil.   Map p. 14

STARNOSE MOLE   *Condylura cristata*   p. 20
  Recognition: Head and body 4½–5 in.; tail 3–3½ in.; wt. 1⅕–2⅖ oz. Dark brown or black. This is the only kind of mammal that has end of nose surrounded by *fingerlike, fleshy projections* (22 tentacles), giving appearance of a star. Eyes small but apparent; front feet as long as broad. Tail *hairy,* constricted near body. Skull (p. 244) has 44 teeth. There are 8 mammae.
  Similar species: (1) Eastern and (2) Hairytail Moles — both have naked noses without fingerlike projections.
  Habitat: Low, wet ground near lakes or streams preferred.
  Habits: Active day and night. Pushes up mounds of black dirt 12 in. or more in diam. Often appears aboveground or in water; good swimmer. Tunnels not usually visible as ridges on surface of ground; may use same tunnels as Eastern Mole. Eats worms and insects, many aquatic. Detects food with sensitive tentacles on snout, but sense of smell poor. Underground spherical nest

of grass and leaves. Often gregarious; populations of 10 or more to an acre are common.

Young: Born April–June; 3–7; 1 litter a year. Independent at 3 weeks; mature at 10 months.

Economic status: Neutral. Occasionally does damage to greens on lawns or golf courses; destroys many insects; aerates soil. Fur of some value.   Map below

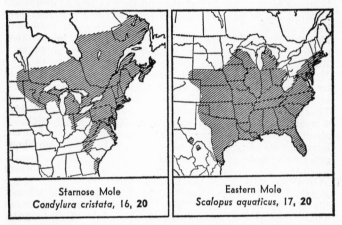

Starnose Mole
Condylura cristata, 16, **20**

Eastern Mole
Scalopus aquaticus, 17, **20**

EASTERN MOLE   *Scalopus aquaticus*   p. 20

Recognition: Head and body 4½–6½ in.; tail 1–1½ in.; wt. 2⅖–5 oz. Front *feet broader than long,* palms turn outward; snout pointed, end *naked,* nostrils open *upward; tail naked;* no external ears; tiny eyes covered with thin skin. Fur with a silvery sheen; slate color in North, brown to golden in South and West. Skull (p. 244) has 36 teeth. There are 6 mammae.

Similar species: (1) Hairytail Mole — tail haired, not naked. (2) Starnose Mole — end of nose surrounded with 22 fingerlike projections.

Habitat: This mole prefers moist sandy loam; lawns, golf courses, gardens, fields, meadows; avoids extremely dry soil.

Habits: Active day and night in burrows, all seasons. Feeds on worms, insects, and some vegetable matter, chiefly in ridge-covered burrows just below the surface which it makes by pushing through the soil with its piglike snout and spadelike forefeet. Grass-lined nest in burrow 18 to 24 in. below surface.

Young: Born March in South, May in North; 4–5; gestation period probably about 6 weeks; 1 litter a year. Naked at birth; independent at 1 month; do not breed until 1 year old.

Economic status: Damages lawns and gardens, but destroys many insects and aerates soil where not cultivated.

Map above

HAIRYTAIL MOLE   *Parascalops breweri*   p. 20
  Recognition: Head and body 4½–5½ in.; tail 1–1½ in.; wt.
  1½–2⅓ oz. Fur slate color, with sheen. Smallest of eastern
  moles. Front feet as broad as long; nose pointed; eyes not
  apparent; *tail* distinctly *haired*. Skull (p. 244) has 44 teeth.
  There are 8 mammae.
  Similar species: (1) Eastern Mole — larger; naked tail. (2)
  Starnose Mole — has 22 fingerlike projections around nose.
  Habitat: Sandy loam with good vegetative cover preferred, not
  heavy wet soils.
  Habits: Active day and night. Feeds chiefly on insects and
  earthworms; may consume 3 times own weight in 24 hrs.
  Burrows near surface as well as deep down (about 18 in.).
  Nests in deep tunnels; tunnels may be used for 8 years or more
  by successive generations. Home range about ⅓ acre; populations to 11 per acre, usually fewer. Longevity 4–5 years.
  Young: Born early May; usually 4; gestation period probably
  4 weeks; 1, possibly 2 litters a year. Naked; remain in nest
  about 1 month; sexually mature at 10 months.
  Economic status: Beneficial except when in lawns, gardens, and
  golf greens; destroys many insects.   Map opposite

TOWNSEND MOLE   *Scapanus townsendi*   p. 20
  Recognition: Head and body 6–7 in.; tail 2± in.; wt. 4–6 oz.
  Blackish brown to black. Front feet *broader than long;* nose
  naked; nostrils open *upward;* tail slightly haired. Skull (p. 244)
  has 44 teeth. There are 8 mammae.
  Similar species: Pacific Mole — smaller, paler.
  Habitat: Moist areas (meadows and floodplains) where soil is
  easily worked — fields, gardens, and coniferous forests.
  Habits: Not well known; more active at night than during day.
  Eats earthworms, sow bugs, insects, tubers, and some root crops.
  Has surface as well as deep tunnels. Males are in breeding
  condition in Feb.
  Young: Born March–April; 2–6; 1 litter a year. By May nearly
  as large as adults.
  Economic status: Does damage to some root crops and tubers.
  In wild areas, beneficial.   Map opposite

PACIFIC MOLE   *Scapanus orarius*
  Recognition: Head and body 5–5¼ in.; tail 1⅛ in.; wt. 2± oz.
  Front feet *broader than long*, nose naked; nostrils open above;
  tail slightly haired; color, blackish brown to black. Skull has
  44 teeth. There are 8 mammae.
  Similar species: (1) California Mole — difficult to distinguish
  in the flesh; where the two occur together, specimens should be
  sent to a museum for identification. (2) Townsend Mole —
  larger, darker.
  Habitat: Well-drained soils, meadows, deciduous forests.

Habits: Active day and night; rarely comes above surface. Eats insects and other small invertebrates. Males are in breeding condition in late Jan.
Young: Born March–April; usually 4; 1 litter a year.
Economic status: Mostly beneficial; does some harm to gardens and other cultivated areas.   Map below

CALIFORNIA MOLE *Scapanus latimanus*
Recognition: Head and body 5–6 in.; tail 1½ in.; wt. 2± oz. Front feet *broader than long;* nose naked; nostrils open upward; blackish brown to black; tail slightly haired. Skull has 44 teeth. There are 8 mammae.
Similar species: Pacific Mole — difficult to distinguish; where the two occur together, specimens should be sent to a museum for positive identification.
Habitat: Porous soils in valleys, meadows in mts.

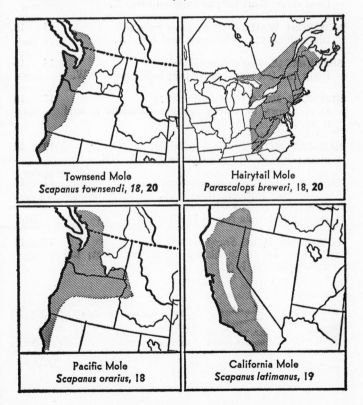

Townsend Mole
Scapanus townsendi, 18, **20**

Hairytail Mole
Parascalops breweri, 18, **20**

Pacific Mole
Scapanus orarius, 18

California Mole
Scapanus latimanus, 19

SHREWS AND MOLES

	Map	Text
MASKED SHREW, *Sorex cinereus*	4	2

Grayish brown; long tail; pointed nose. N.

MERRIAM SHREW, *Sorex merriami*   7   5

Pale gray; underparts whitish; small size. W.

LEAST SHREW, *Cryptotis parva*   14   12

Cinnamon color; short tail. SE.

ARCTIC SHREW, *Sorex arcticus*   4   5

Tricolored pattern in winter; darkest on back. N.

SHORTTAIL SHREW, *Blarina brevicauda*   15   14

Lead color; short tail; no external ears. E.

NORTHERN WATER SHREW, *Sorex palustris*   13   10

Blackish gray; stiff hairs on hind feet. N.

SHREW-MOLE, *Neurotrichus gibbsi*   14   16

Body and tail black; hairy tail; naked nose. NW.

STARNOSE MOLE, *Condylura cristata*   17   16

Dark brown or black; fleshy projections around
nose. NE.

HAIRYTAIL MOLE, *Parascalops breweri*   19   18

Slate color; broad front feet; hairy tail. NE.

EASTERN MOLE, *Scalopus aquaticus*   17   17

Broad front feet; naked tail. SE.
Pale phase: Light golden color.
Dark phase: Slate color.

TOWNSEND MOLE, *Scapanus townsendi*   19   18

Blackish brown to black; broad front feet; tail
slightly haired. NW.

Shrew-Mole snout
top view

H.F., Water Shrew,
fringe of stiff hairs

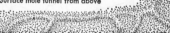
Surface mole tunnel from above

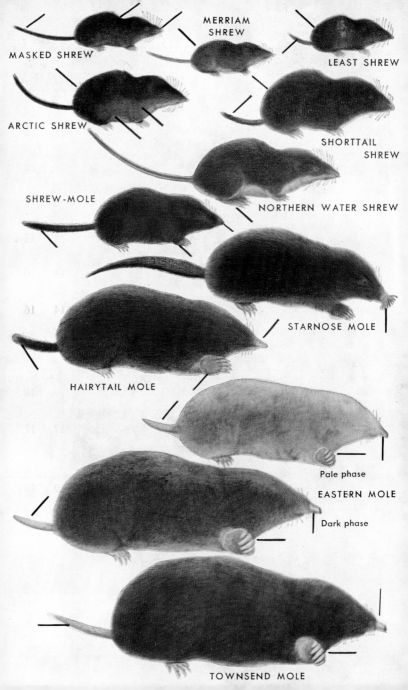

MASKED SHREW

MERRIAM SHREW

LEAST SHREW

ARCTIC SHREW

SHORTTAIL SHREW

SHREW-MOLE

NORTHERN WATER SHREW

STARNOSE MOLE

HAIRYTAIL MOLE

Pale phase

EASTERN MOLE

Dark phase

TOWNSEND MOLE

**LITTLE BROWN
MYOTIS**

LONG-EARED MYOTIS

**EASTERN
BIG-EARED BAT**

EASTERN PIPISTREL

**CALIFORNIA
MYOTIS**

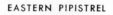

**SMALL-FOOTED
MYOTIS**

WESTERN PIPISTREL

PALLID BAT

BIG BROWN BAT

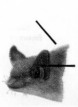

Plate 2   21

BATS

	Map	Text
LITTLE BROWN MYOTIS, *Myotis lucifugus*	26	25

Brown, with glossy sheen; medium-sized ears; small size. N, S, E, W.

| **LONG-EARED MYOTIS,** *Myotis evotis* | 30 | 30 |

Pale brown; large black ears. W.

| **EASTERN BIG-EARED BAT,** *Plecotus rafinesquei* | 44 | 43 |

Lumps on nose; large ears joined in middle. SE.

| **CALIFORNIA MYOTIS,** *Myotis californicus* | 31 | 32 |

Bases of hairs dark; small size. W.

| **SMALL-FOOTED MYOTIS,** *Myotis subulatus* | 34 | 33 |

Yellowish fur; black mask; small size. W, Central, NE.

| **EASTERN PIPISTREL,** *Pipistrellus subflavus* | 35 | 35 |

Yellowish brown to drab brown; blunt tragus. E.

| **WESTERN PIPISTREL,** *Pipistrellus hesperus* | 35 | 34 |

Pale ashy or yellowish gray; blunt tragus; small size. W.

| **PALLID BAT,** *Antrozous pallidus* | 46 | 44 |

Pale yellowish gray; large ears not joined; simple muzzle. W.

| **BIG BROWN BAT,** *Eptesicus fuscus* | 38 | 39 |

Pale brown to dark brown; blunt tragus; large size. N, S, E, W.

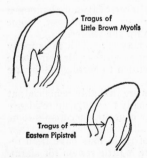

Tragus of Little Brown Myotis

Tragus of Eastern Pipistrel

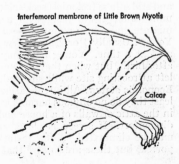

Interfemoral membrane of Little Brown Myotis

Calcar

Habits: Rarely comes aboveground. Feeds on insects, earthworms, and other small invertebrates; in captivity will eat 63–107 per cent of own weight in earthworms each day; also requires water.

Young: Born March–April; 2–5; 1 litter a year.

Economic status: In much of area, beneficial; may do damage to lawns or gardens.   Map p. 19

Bats: Chiroptera

THESE are the only *truly flying* mammals. The hand is formed into a wing with a double membrane of skin covering (and stretching between) the hand and finger bones, and extending to the forearm, side of body, and hind leg. Thumb is free and terminates in a claw. Most bats also have a membrane connecting the legs (including the tail) — the *interfemoral membrane.* The only measurement given in the following descriptions is that of forearm (from elbow to wrist). This indicates relative size of the animal fairly accurately. The *calcar,* a cartilaginous support for the free edge of the interfemoral membrane, is anchored to the inside of foot and extends out along edge of the membrane. If keeled, there will be a definite extension of the free edge of membrane beyond the calcar. If calcar lies along free edge, it is not keeled. The *tragus* is a leaflike structure in the ear.

Habits: All bats within area covered are nocturnal; nearly all eat insects, which they usually capture on the wing. Their small beady eyes are probably of little use in their night flights. To substitute for poor vision, they have evolved a sonar system for locating solid objects. As they fly they emit a series of supersonic sounds that bounce back from other objects and are picked up by the bats. This is called *echolocation;* it enables them to fly in absolute darkness. Some bats (solitary) pass the day hanging among the foliage of trees, others hang in hollow trees or attics of buildings, and still others (colonial) seek shelter in natural caves or abandoned mine tunnels. All hang with heads down when at rest. Some migrate and others go into hibernation for the winter.

Young: Usually 1 or 2, but a few bats may give birth to as many as 4 at a time. Young bats may cling to mother for some time after birth, but when they become a burden to her flight they are left at roosting site while she feeds.

Economic status: All insect-eating bats are probably beneficial; at least they do no obvious harm. Occasionally they take up residence in the attic or walls of a house and may cause the occupants some discomfort. If screen is placed over all possible entrances they may be eliminated. A few instances of rabid bats have been reported, but these are so rare that there is little reason for alarm.

However, it is not advisable to handle them with bare hands because of the slim chance of encountering a rabid individual. The guano deposits in some caves have been mined for fertilizer; many tons were taken from the Carlsbad Caverns, New Mexico.

Leafnose Bats: Phyllostomidae

MEMBERS of this family, except those of the genus *Mormoops*, have a *leaflike, triangular flap* of thick skin *projecting upward from tip of the nose.* They are the only ones considered here that possess these structures. Not known as fossils.

LEAFCHIN BAT *Mormoops megalophylla*
   Recognition: Forearm 2–2⅛ in. A brownish bat with prominent *leaflike folds of skin across chin*, reaching from ear to ear, the central one, in front of lower lip, covered with small *wartlike prominences;* end of tail appears on *upper side of interfemoral membrane;* face short; forehead high. We have no other bat with the above characters. Skull (p. 244) has 34 teeth.
   Habitat: Usually tunnels or caves; it may roost in buildings.
   Habits: Colonial; probably feeds on insects.
   Young: Born June or July in this area; 1.   Map p. 24

LEAFNOSE BAT *Macrotus californicus*   p. 36
   Recognition: Forearm 2 in. This *large-eared, grayish* bat has a distinct *leaflike flap* of thick skin *projecting upward from tip of nose;* tail extends to edge of complete interfemoral membrane. Skull (p. 244) has 34 teeth.
   Similar species: (1) Hognose Bat — long, slender rostrum; small ears; dark brown; interfemoral membrane about ½ in. wide in middle. (2) Longnose Bat — long rostrum; no tail.
   Habitat: Usually caves or old mine tunnels during day, sometimes buildings during night.
   Habits: Flies late; returns to roost when stomach is full; sexes usually separate except during mating season. When alighting they give a half roll and attach directly with the feet.
   Young: Born May–July; 1.   Map p. 24

HOGNOSE BAT *Choeronycteris mexicana*   p. 36
   Recognition: Forearm 1¾ in.; wt. ¾ oz. This bat has a *long, slender nose* with triangular *flap* of skin projecting upward from tip; ears small, barely projecting above head; color light brown; tail extends *less than halfway to edge of interfemoral membrane,* which is reduced. Skull (p. 244) has 30 teeth.
   Similar species: (1) Longnose Bat — no tail. (2) Leafnose Bat — ears large; tail extends to edge of interfemoral membrane.
   Habitat: By day, natural caves, old mine tunnels, and buildings.

Habits: During the day prefers area of deep shadow or twilight, not extreme darkness of tunnels. This bat is wary and takes flight when approached. Feeds, in part at least, on pollen and nectar.

Young: Born June or July in this area; 1.   Map below

LONGNOSE BAT *Leptonycteris nivalis*

Recognition: Forearm 2⅛ in.; wt. ¾ oz. This rather large, brownish bat has an extremely *long slender nose* with a *leaflike projection* of thick skin on its end. Ears extend well above top of head. Interfemoral membrane narrow; there is *no tail*. Skull (p. 244) has 30 teeth.

Similar species: (1) Hognose and (2) Leafnose Bats — tail present.

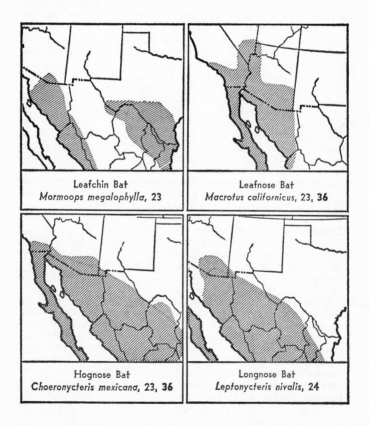

Leafchin Bat
Mormoops megalophylla, 23

Leafnose Bat
Macrotus californicus, 23, **36**

Hognose Bat
Choeronycteris mexicana, 23, **36**

Longnose Bat
Leptonycteris nivalis, 24

Habitat: This bat hangs in caves, old mine tunnels, and buildings by day.
Habits: Feeds chiefly on pollen and nectar; also some insects. Females may congregate in nurseries where young and adults intermingle during midsummer.
Young: Born April, May, or June in this area; 1–2.

Map opposite

Plainnose Bats: Vespertilionidae

MEMBERS of this family have *simple, unmodified muzzles*. They all have *complete* interfemoral membranes, and in all the *tail reaches to the back edge of the membrane but not noticeably beyond*. As fossils, date back to Lower Oligocene.

Myotis Group of Bats

THIS is the largest and most widely distributed group of bats. They are all relatively *small*, some shade of *brown*, have simple snouts. The *tragus* (a leaflike projection arising from the base of the inside of the external ear) is long and pointed. The membranes are always complete, and the tail reaches to the edge of the interfemoral membrane. This membrane is sometimes scantily haired, especially at the base, but *never thickly covered with hair*. Skull has 38 teeth. There are 2 pectoral mammae.

Many of the species are difficult to identify, even in a museum. When reading the following descriptions this should be borne in mind. In case of doubt, specimens should be sent to an authority for identification.
Similar species: (1) Big Brown Bat (p. 39) — larger; tragus blunt. (2) Evening Bat (p. 41) and (3) Pipistrels (pp. 34–35) — tragus blunt.

LITTLE BROWN MYOTIS *Myotis lucifugus*   p. 21
Recognition: Forearm 1½ in.; wt. ¼–⅓ oz. The ear is moderate in size; when laid forward it reaches to the nostril. Hairs on back have *long glossy tips;* this glossy sheen is fairly characteristic. Skull (p. 244) has 38 teeth.
Similar species: (1) Indiana Myotis — definite keel on calcar. (2) Mississippi Myotis — larger; duller color. (3) Gray and (4) Cave Myotis — larger. (5) Keen and (6) Long-eared Myotis — ears large (when laid forward, reach beyond nose). (7) Long-legged Myotis — larger; fur not glossy. (8) Yuma Myotis — smaller. (9) Fringed Myotis — conspicuous fringe of hairs along edge of interfemoral membrane. (10) California and (11) Small-footed Myotis — smaller.
Habitat: Caves, mine tunnels, hollow trees, or buildings serve as roosting places.

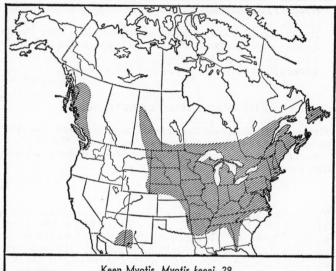

Keen Myotis, *Myotis keeni*, 29

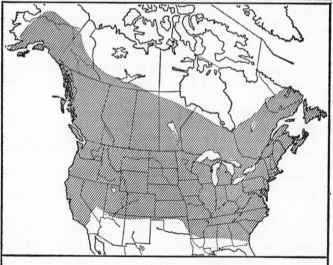

Little Brown Myotis, *Myotis lucifugus*, 25, **21**

Habits: Leaves daytime retreat at dusk, returns to roosting site just before dawn. Colonial. Feeds on insects on the wing near water or forests; flight erratic. In the North, most of them migrate South in the fall and go into hibernation in a cave or other suitable retreat. Although they become torpid, they do not go into a deep sleep. Have been known to return home in 3 weeks after being released at distance of 270 mi. One banded bat known to have lived more than 20 years. They may breed during late fall and winter, but embryonic development does not begin until Feb. in the North.

Young: Born May–July; usually 1, occasionally 2; gestation period about 80 days. Naked; eyes open in 2 or 3 days. May or may not be carried by mother; normally left hanging in roost. When about a month old, take to wing and become self-supporting.   Map opposite

YUMA MYOTIS   *Myotis yumanensis*

Recognition: Forearm 1⅓–1½ in.; wt. ⅛–¼ oz. Color *dull brownish* with hairs dark at bases; interfemoral membrane *haired nearly to knees.* One of the commonest of the western myotis.
Similar species: (1) Cave Myotis — larger. (2) Arizona Myotis — ochraceous, glossy fur. (3) Little Brown and (4) Long-legged Myotis — larger; hair glossy. (5) Keen and (6) Long-eared Myotis — ears large (when laid forward extend beyond nose). (7) Fringed Myotis — conspicuous fringe of hairs along edge of tail membrane. (8) California and (9) Small-footed Myotis — smaller.
Habitat: Caves, tunnels, or buildings; arid areas.
Habits: Late fliers, usually fly close to ground. Colonial. Hang in closely grouped clumps.
Young: Born May or June; 1. Clings to mother for a few days.
                    Map p. 32

MISSISSIPPI MYOTIS   *Myotis austroriparius*

Recognition: Forearm 1½–1⅗ in. Hair woolly, *dull yellowish brown*, dark at base.
Similar species: (1) Little Brown Myotis — smaller; glossy fur. (2) Indiana Myotis — smaller. (3) Gray Myotis — larger; hairs not dark at bases. (4) Keen Myotis — ears large.
Habitat: Mostly caves, but also mine tunnels, hollow trees, buildings, culverts, and beneath bridges.
Habits: Appears from roosting site when nearly dark; flies low over water and fields to feed. Colonial. Hangs in large clusters; density of cluster about 150 bats for each sq. ft.; up to 90,000 in a cave. Hibernates in caves in North, intermittently active all winter in Florida. Requires body of water and expanse of ceiling at least 6 ft. above. Has returned 45 mi. to home cave.

Females and some males enter maternity caves in South in mid-March.
Young: Born May in South, June in North; normally 2, occasionally 1. Able to fly and feed themselves at 5 or 6 weeks; sexually mature at 1 year. Females do not carry young when feeding. *Map below*

GRAY MYOTIS *Myotis grisescens*
Recognition: Forearm 1⅜–1⅘ in.; wt. ¼–⅓ oz. A *dull grayish-brown* bat with the hairs about the same color to the bases.
Similar species: (1) Mississippi, (2) Small-footed, and (3) Indiana Myotis — smaller. (4) Little Brown Myotis — smaller; fur glossy and dark at bases.
Habitat: Caves for roosting and bearing young.
Habits: Colonial. Hangs in compact clusters from ceilings of

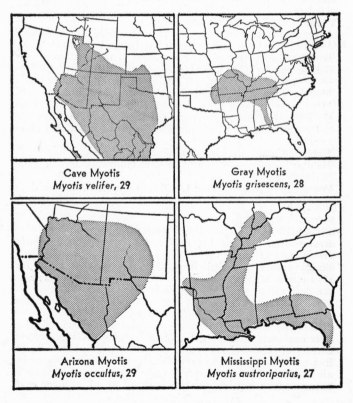

Cave Myotis
Myotis velifer, 29

Gray Myotis
Myotis grisescens, 28

Arizona Myotis
Myotis occultus, 29

Mississippi Myotis
Myotis austroriparius, 27

caves. May migrate from one cave to another. Sexes segregate when young are born.
Young: Born May in South, June in North; 1. Naked; clings to mother for less than a week, then remains in cave.
Map opposite

CAVE MYOTIS *Myotis velifer*
Recognition: Forearm $1\frac{3}{5}$–$1\frac{4}{5}$ in. Color *dull brown;* ears moderate in size; wing membrane arises *from base of toes.* Common in *caves* of Southwest.
Similar species: (1) Little Brown, (2) Arizona, (3) Yuma, (4) Long-legged, (5) California, and (6) Small-footed Myotis — smaller. (7) Long-eared Myotis — smaller; ears larger. (8) Fringed Myotis — fringe of hairs along edge of tail membrane.
Habitat: Typically, caves and mine tunnels; also buildings.
Habits: Colonial. Seeks crevices or vertical walls; moves from place to place.
Young: Born June or July; 1. Map opposite

ARIZONA MYOTIS *Myotis occultus*
Recognition: Forearm $1\frac{2}{5}$–$1\frac{3}{5}$ in. This is a relatively rare bat with a limited distribution in the Southwest. Color strongly *ochraceous;* hairs of back with burnished tips and a *glossy sheen.*
Similar species: (1) Long-legged Myotis — underside of wing furred to elbow. (2) Yuma Myotis — brownish. (3) Cave Myotis — larger. (4) Long-eared Myotis — ears large. (5) Fringed Myotis — fringe of hairs at edge of tail membrane. (6) California and (7) Small-footed Myotis — smaller.
Habitat: Buildings, mine tunnels, beneath bridges.
Habits: Colonial. Migratory. Feeds among trees. Sexes may segregate when young are born.
Young: Born late May or early June; 1. Map opposite

KEEN MYOTIS *Myotis keeni*
Recognition: Forearm $1\frac{2}{5}$–$1\frac{3}{5}$ in.; wt. $\frac{1}{4}$–$\frac{1}{3}$ oz. This northern member of the myotis group may be distinguished from all other myotis within its range, except the Long-eared Myotis, by the size of its ears. When laid forward, ears *extend about* $\frac{1}{16}$ in. *beyond the nose.* Long-eared Myotis has even larger ears. Keen Myotis is *dark brown.*
Similar species: (1) Long-eared Myotis — ears larger (extend $\frac{1}{5}$ in. beyond nose when laid forward). (2) Fringed Myotis — fringe of hairs on edge of tail membrane. (3) All other myotis — ears smaller.
Habitat: Mine tunnels, caves, buildings, hollow trees, storm sewers, forested areas.
Habits: Probably occurs in small, scattered colonies; may spend winter in hibernation in North; known to live $18\frac{1}{2}$ years in wild.
Young: Born late June or July; 1. Map p. 26

LONG-EARED MYOTIS *Myotis evotis* p. 21

Recognition: Forearm 1⅖–1⅗ in. May be distinguished from all other species of myotis by its *large black ears* (when laid forward they extend about ⅕ in. beyond the nose). General coloration is a *pale brown.*

Similar species: (1) Keen Myotis — slightly smaller ears; dark brown. (2) Little Brown, (3) Arizona, and (4) Yuma Myotis — smaller ears. (5) Cave Myotis — larger; smaller ears. (6) Long-legged, (7) California, and (8) Small-footed Myotis — smaller. (9) Fringed Myotis — distinct fringe of hairs on edge of interfemoral membrane; smaller ears.

Habitat: Thinly forested areas, around buildings or trees; occasionally caves.

Habits: Usually flies late, but at high altitudes may fly in early evening before temperature drops. Not known to occur in large colonies.

Young: Born late June or July; 1. Map below

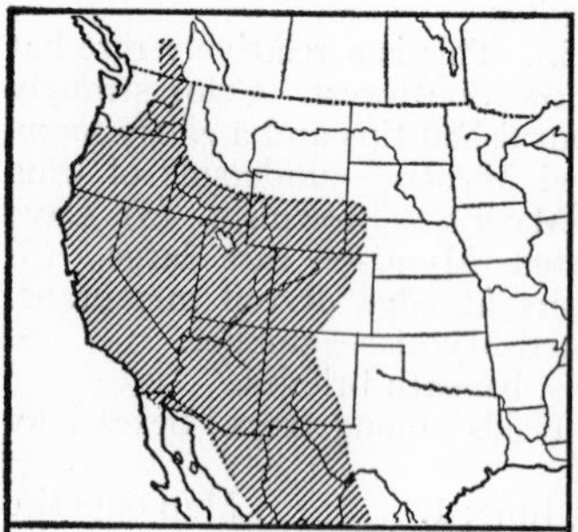

Fringed Myotis
Myotis thysanodes, 30

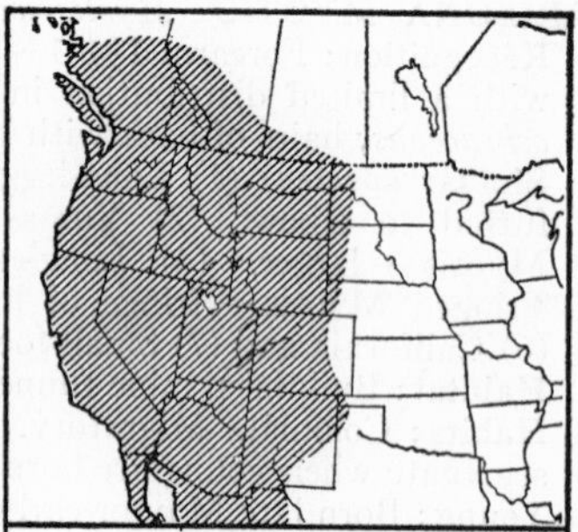

Long-eared Myotis
Myotis evotis, 30, **21**

FRINGED MYOTIS *Myotis thysanodes*

Recognition: Forearm 1⅗–1⅘ in. Buffy brown in color; this bat may be distinguished from all other myotis by presence of a *conspicuous fringe of stiff hairs along free edge of the interfemoral (tail) membrane.* It also has relatively large ears.

Similar species: The following species of myotis may be found within the range of the Fringed Myotis; all but the Cave Myotis are smaller, and none has the distinct fringe on edge of tail membrane: (1) Little Brown, (2) Yuma, (3) Cave, (4) Arizona, (5) Keen, (6) Long-eared, (7) Long-legged, (8) California, and (9) Small-footed Myotis.

Habitat: Caves, attics of old buildings.

Habits: Colonial. When in caves, hangs in clumps in deep
twilight zone; sexes separate during summer.
Young: Born June or July; 1.   Map opposite

INDIANA MYOTIS   *Myotis sodalis*
Recognition: Forearm 1⅖–1⅗ in.; wt. ¼–⅓ oz. Calcar with
definite *keel*. Very difficult to distinguish from the Little Brown
Myotis, especially in the field.
Similar species: (1) Little Brown Myotis — no definite keel on
calcar. (2) Mississippi Myotis — larger. (3) Gray Myotis —
larger; hairs not dark at bases. (4) Keen Myotis — larger ears.
(5) Small-footed Myotis — smaller.
Habitat: Caves in winter, man-made structures and possibly
hollow trees in summer.
Habits: Colonial in winter, may scatter in summer. Hangs in
compact clusters; sexes segregate for part of year.
Young: Born probably in June; immature bats taken in July.
                                                Map below

LONG-LEGGED MYOTIS   *Myotis volans*
Recognition: Forearm 1½–1⅗ in. Distinguished from other
species of myotis by the *short rounded ears, small foot,* well-
developed *keel on calcar,* and fur on the underside of the membranes as far out as the elbow and knee.

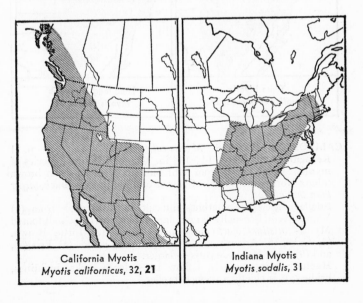

California Myotis
Myotis californicus, 32, **21**

Indiana Myotis
Myotis sodalis, 31

Similar species: (1) Cave Myotis — larger. (2) Little Brown, (3) Small-footed, (4) California, and (5) Yuma Myotis — smaller. (6) Arizona Myotis — underside of wing not furred to elbow. (7) Keen and (8) Long-eared Myotis — larger ears. (9) Fringed Myotis — larger; fringe on edge of tail membrane.
Habitat: Buildings, small pockets and crevices in rock ledges.
Habits: Colonial. Flight less erratic than with most myotis.
Young: Born June; 1.   Map below

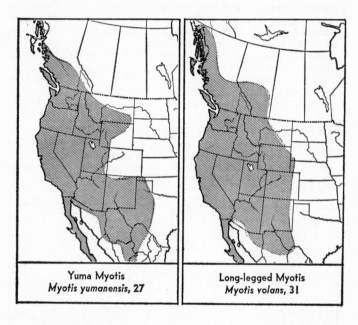

Yuma Myotis
Myotis yumanensis, 27

Long-legged Myotis
Myotis volans, 31

CALIFORNIA MYOTIS *Myotis californicus*   p. 21
Recognition: Forearm 1⅕–1⅖ in. One of the small species of myotis. Color varies from light buff (in desert) to rich brown (along Northwest Coast). Color of bases of hairs is *much darker than that of tips.*
Similar species: Sometimes difficult to distinguish from (1) Yuma Myotis (usually larger, larger foot) or (2) Small-footed Myotis (*distinct black mask across face*). (3) Little Brown, (4) Cave, (5) Arizona, (6) Keen, (7) Long-eared, (8) Fringed, and (9) Long-legged Myotis — larger.
Habitat: Mine tunnels, hollow trees, loose rocks, buildings, bridges; it is chiefly a crevice dweller.

Habits: Leaves roost shortly after sunset to forage near trees, rarely more than 15 ft. above ground; hangs up several times during night. Occurs in small colonies or singly. Moves from place to place, except females in nursery colonies. Hibernating temperature near that of surroundings. Sexes separate for most of year.

Young: Born May or June; 1. Naked. Map p. 31

SMALL-FOOTED MYOTIS *Myotis subulatus* p. 21

Recognition: Forearm 1⅕–1⅜ in.; wt. ⅕–⅛ oz. This is the *smallest* myotis in the eastern area and, except for the California Myotis, the western area also. *Long silky fur* is *yellowish;* it has a distinct *black mask* across face. Ears are black.

Similar species: (1) California Myotis — brown mask; ears dark brown (sometimes difficult to distinguish). (2) Yuma Myotis — larger, no black mask. (3) Little Brown, (4) Cave, (5) Arizona, (6) Keen, (7) Long-eared, (8) Fringed, (9) Indiana, (10) Gray, and (11) Long-legged Myotis — all larger.

Habitat: Caves, mine tunnels, crevices in rocks, buildings; in or near forested areas.

Habits: Appears fairly early in evening. Colonial or solitary. Hangs with wings partially spread; may move to different cave in winter. Feeds low among trees or over brush.

Young: Born May–July; 1. Map p. 34

Other Plainnose Bats

INCLUDED here are all of the genera in the Family Vespertilionidae except *Myotis*. A rather diverse group; all have simple unmodified noses, and complete interfemoral membranes; tail reaches to, but not beyond, edge of membrane.

SILVER-HAIRED BAT *Lasionycteris noctivagans* p. 36

Recognition: Forearm 1⅔ in.; wt. ⅓–⅔ oz. A *blackish-brown* bat with hairs on middle of back *tipped with white;* tail membrane furred above on basal half. Distinguished from all other bats by color. Skull (p. 244) has 36 teeth. There are 2 mammae.

Similar species: (1) Hoary Bat — larger; throat buffy. (2) Red Bat — brick or rusty red. (3) Seminole Bat — mahogany.

Habitat: Forested areas; buildings may be occupied or, occasionally, caves.

Habits: Solitary. Flies high and fairly straight. Feeds among trees. Probably migrates south in winter.

Young: Born June or July; usually 2, sometimes 1. Naked, blind. May cling to mother in flight for several days.

Map p. 34

WESTERN PIPISTREL   *Pipistrellus hesperus*   p. 21
Recognition: Forearm 1–1⅕ in.; wt. ⅙–⅕ oz. Tragus *blunt*, with tip bent forward; color *ashy gray or yellowish gray. Smallest* of the bats here considered. Small size and pale coloration distinguish it from other bats. Skull has 34 teeth. There are 2 mammae.

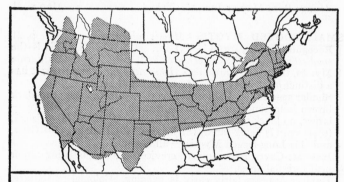

Small-footed Myotis, *Myotis subulatus*, 33, **21**

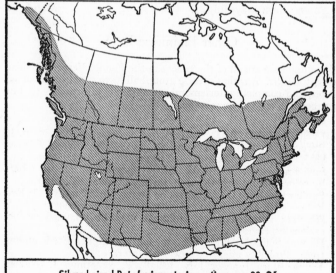

Silver-haired Bat, *Lasionycteris noctivagans*, 33, **36**

Similar species: (1) All Myotis (p. 25) — larger; pointed tragus.
(2) Other bats — larger.
Habitat: Caves, under loose rocks, crevices in cliffs, buildings;
arid conditions, but near watercourses.
Habits: Flies early in evening, sometimes before sundown; flight
erratic; feeds on insects.
Young: Born June or July; usually 2, occasionally 1. Cling to
mother for several days.   Map below

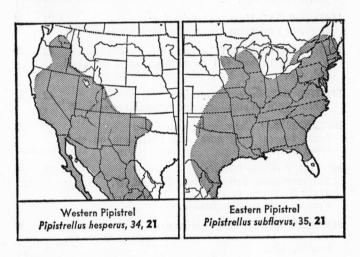

Western Pipistrel
Pipistrellus hesperus, 34, 21

Eastern Pipistrel
Pipistrellus subflavus, 35, 21

EASTERN PIPISTREL *Pipistrellus subflavus*   p. 21
Recognition: Forearm 1⅛± in.; wt. ⅙–⅕ oz. Tragus *blunt* and
straight; color *yellowish brown* to *drab brown*. One of the *smallest*
eastern bats. Small size and blunt tragus distinguish this from
other bats. Skull (p. 244) has 34 teeth. There are 2 mammae.
Similar species: (1) All Myotis (p. 25) — pointed tragus.
(2) Other bats — larger.
Habitat: Caves, mine tunnels, crevices in rocks, buildings,
wooded areas; near water.
Habits: Appears in early evening. Flight slow and erratic.
Hangs singly or in small clusters. Feeds on small insects;
probably rests several times during night. Some hibernate in
North; some may migrate and return to same roost following
year. Has returned 80 mi. to original roost. Known to live
7 years in wild.
Young: Born May in South, June or July in North; normally 2,
occasionally 1. Carried by mother on feeding flights for about
1 week, then left hanging at roost; fly at 4 weeks.   Map above

OTHER BATS

	Map	Text

SILVER-HAIRED BAT, *Lasionycteris noctivagans*   34 33
  Blackish brown, with white-tipped hairs. N, S, E, W.

MEXICAN FREETAIL BAT, *Tadarida brasiliensis*   46 45
  Chocolate-brown; tail beyond membrane; ears not
  joined; small size. S.

LEAFNOSE BAT, *Macrotus californicus*   24 23
  Grayish; projection on tip of nose; large ears. SW.

EASTERN YELLOW BAT, *Lasiurus intermedius*   42 40
  Yellowish brown; tail membrane furred on basal
  3rd. SE.

SPOTTED BAT, *Euderma maculata*   42 41
  White spots on shoulders and rump; large ears. W.

HOGNOSE BAT, *Choeronycteris mexicana*   24 23
  Light brown; long nose with projection on end;
  small ears. SW.

RED BAT, *Lasiurus borealis*   38 39
  Tail membrane furred above. N, S, E, W.
  Male: Brick-red, frosted.
  Female: Pale reddish, frosted.

SEMINOLE BAT, *Lasiurus seminolus*   42 39
  Tail membrane furred above; mahogany-brown,
  frosted. SE.

HOARY BAT, *Lasiurus cinereus*   40 39
  Tail membrane furred above; buffy throat; frosted
  body. N, S, E, W.

WESTERN MASTIFF BAT, *Eumops perotis*   44 47
  Chocolate-brown; tail beyond membrane; large
  size. SW.

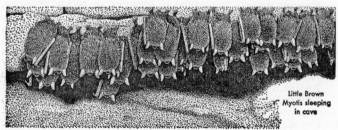

Little Brown
Myotis sleeping
in cave

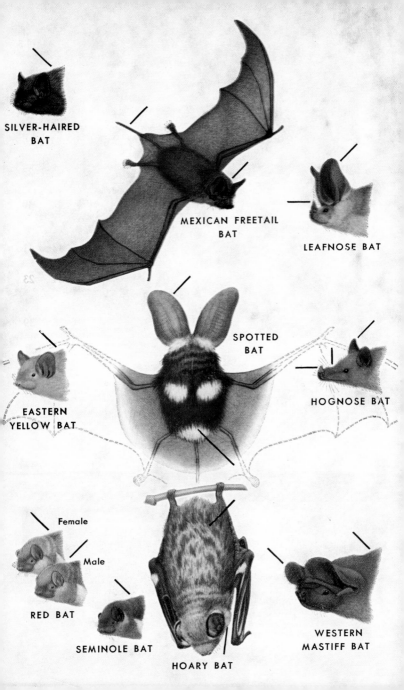

SILVER-HAIRED BAT

MEXICAN FREETAIL BAT

LEAFNOSE BAT

SPOTTED BAT

EASTERN YELLOW BAT

HOGNOSE BAT

Female

Male

RED BAT

SEMINOLE BAT

HOARY BAT

WESTERN MASTIFF BAT

Plate 4

BIG BROWN BEAR

GRIZZLY BEAR

POLAR BEAR

Blue phase   Cinnamon phase   Black phase

BLACK BEAR

Plate 4   37

BEARS

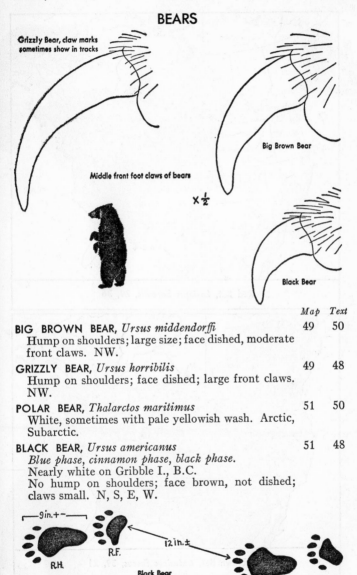

Grizzly Bear, claw marks
sometimes show in tracks

Big Brown Bear

Middle front foot claws of bears

X ½

Black Bear

	Map	Text
BIG BROWN BEAR, *Ursus middendorffi*	49	50
Hump on shoulders; large size; face dished, moderate front claws. NW.		
GRIZZLY BEAR, *Ursus horribilis*	49	48
Hump on shoulders; face dished; large front claws. NW.		
POLAR BEAR, *Thalarctos maritimus*	51	50
White, sometimes with pale yellowish wash. Arctic, Subarctic.		
BLACK BEAR, *Ursus americanus*	51	48
Blue phase, cinnamon phase, black phase. Nearly white on Gribble I., B.C. No hump on shoulders; face brown, not dished; claws small. N, S, E, W.		

┌─9in.+─┐

R.F.
12 in. ±

R.H.

Black Bear

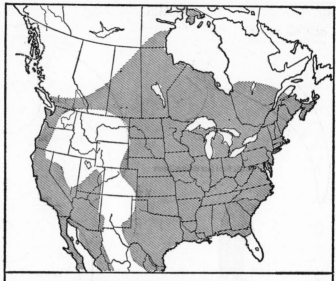

Red Bat, *Lasiurus borealis*, 39, **36**

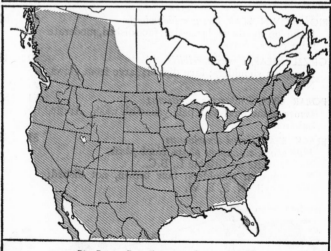

Big Brown Bat, *Eptesicus fuscus*, 39, **21**

BIG BROWN BAT   *Eptesicus fuscus*   p. 21
  Recognition: Forearm 1⅘–2 in.; wt. ⅖–⅗ oz. Pale brown (on
  desert) to dark brown; membranes black; *tragus blunt.* One of
  the commonest and most widely distributed of our bats. Large
  size and color distinguish this from all others. Skull (p. 244) has
  32 teeth. There are 2 mammae.
  Similar species: (1) Evening Bat — smaller. (2) All Myotis
  (p. 25) — smaller; pointed tragus.
  Habitat: Caves, tunnels, crevices, hollow trees, buildings,
  wooded areas.
  Habits: Roosts singly or in small clusters. Feeds on insects,
  chiefly beetles. Some migrate, others winter over in North.
  Common in buildings in winter.
  Young: Born May or June; usually 2, occasionally 1.
Map opposite

RED BAT   *Lasiurus borealis*   p. 36
  Recognition: Forearm 1½–1⅔ in.; wt. ⅓–½ oz. This is a
  brick-red to *rusty-red* bat with hairs *tipped with white;* tail
  membrane fully furred above. Females distinctly paler than
  males. Skull (p. 244) has 32 teeth. There are 4 mammae.
  Similar species: (1) Seminole Bat — mahogany-brown. (2) Yellow Bats — tail membrane not heavily furred to edge. (3) Hoary
  Bat — larger. (4) Silver-haired Bat — blackish brown.
  Habitat: Wooded areas; it normally roosts in trees, occasionally
  enters caves.
  Habits: Leaves roost at deep dusk. Solitary. Flight rather
  steady and rapid. Has regular feeding areas; they usually feed
  in pairs, working same route of about 100 yds. over and over.
  Migrates south in autumn; has been seen far out to sea.
  Young: Born June; 2–4. Cling to mother until too heavy to
  support in flight.   Map opposite

SEMINOLE BAT   *Lasiurus seminolus*   p. 36
  Recognition: Forearm 1½–2⅔ in.; wt. ⅓–½ oz. Rich *ma-
  hogany-brown* with hairs *tipped with white;* similar, in other
  respects, to Red Bat.
  Similar species: (1) Red Bat — brick-red or rusty red. (2)
  Eastern Yellow Bat — tail membrane heavily furred for only
  basal 3rd; yellowish brown. (3) Hoary Bat — larger. (4) Silver-
  haired Bat — blackish brown.
  Habitat: Wooded areas; trees for roost.
  Habits: Solitary. Similar to those of Red Bat.
  Young: Born June; 2–4. Cling to mother for several days.
Map p. 42

HOARY BAT   *Lasiurus cinereus*   p. 36
  Recognition: Forearm 2+ in.; wt. 1± oz. Yellowish brown to
  mahogany-brown, the hairs tipped with white over most of body;

throat buffy; tail membrane heavily furred on top to edges; ears rounded. Size and color distinguish it. Skull (p. 244) has 32 teeth. There are 4 mammae.

Similar species: (1) Silver-haired, (2) Red, and (3) Seminole Bats — all smaller. (4) Yellow Bats — hairs not frosted.

Habitat: Wooded areas.

Habits: Flies late, high. Solitary. Hangs in trees. Occasionally caves. Migrates south in autumn.

Young: Born June; 2. Carried by mother on feeding excursions for several days; able to fly at 4 weeks. Map below

EASTERN YELLOW BAT *Lasiurus intermedius* p. 36
Recognition: Forearm 2–2⅕ in. A large, pale, *yellowish-brown* bat with tail membrane heavily *furred only on basal 3rd.* Skull (p. 244) has 30 teeth. There are 4 mammae.
Formerly known as *Dasypterus.*
Similar species: (1) Hoary, (2) Red, and (3) Seminole Bats — all have tail membrane heavily furred to edge.
Habitat: Wooded areas.

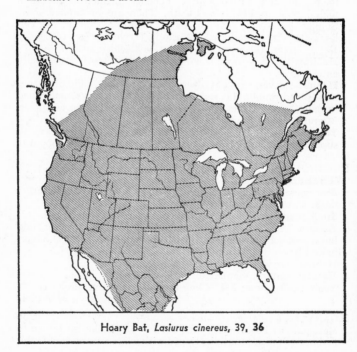

Hoary Bat, *Lasiurus cinereus*, 39, **36**

Habits: Probably solitary for most part; may occur in small colonies. Map p. 42

WESTERN YELLOW BAT *Lasiurus ega*

Recognition: Forearm 1⅘ in. This pale, *yellowish-brown* bat barely enters s. California. Tail membrane heavily *furred only on its basal 3rd.* Skull has 30 teeth.

Similar species: (1) Hoary and (2) Red Bats — tail membrane completely furred.

Habitat: Wooded areas.

Habits: Probably similar to those of Eastern Yellow Bat (above). Map p. 42

EVENING BAT *Nycticeius humeralis*

Recognition: Forearm 1⅖–1½ in.; wt. ¼–⅓ oz. Dark brown; black membranes; *blunt tragus.* Combination of size, color, and blunt tragus distinguishes this from all other species in its range. Skull (p. 244) has 30 teeth. There are 2 mammae.

Similar species: (1) Big Brown Bat — larger. (2) All Myotis (p. 25) — pointed tragus.

Habitat: Buildings and hollow trees.

Habits: Usually colonial, sometimes solitary. Flight fairly steady and straight. Sexes segregate when young are born. Common in South, rare in North.

Young: Born May or June; usually 2, occasionally 1. Map p. 42

SPOTTED BAT *Euderma maculata* p. 36

Recognition: Forearm 2 in. This rare and spectacular bat has *huge ears*, is *dark sepia*, with a *white spot* on *rump* and another on *each shoulder.* Only bat with such contrasting colors. Skull has 34 teeth.

Habitat: Arid country. It occasionally enters buildings and caves. Map p. 42

WESTERN BIG-EARED BAT *Plecotus townsendi*

Recognition: Forearm 1⅗–1⅘ in.; wt. ⅓–⅖ oz. Extremely *large ears* (over 1 in. high) *joined across forehead.* On nose, in front of eyes, are 2 prominent lumps. General color clove-brown; bases of ventral hairs gray or brown, tips brown or buffy; tail membrane naked. Skull (p. 244) has 36 teeth. There are 2 mammae.

Formerly known as *Corynorhinus rafinesquei.*

Similar species: (1) Eastern Big-eared Bat — bases of ventral hairs black, tips white. (2) Mexican Big-eared Bat — small lobe at inner base of ear. (3) Pallid Bat — ears separate; no prominent lumps on nose.

Habitat: Caves, mine tunnels, and buildings for roosts.

Habits: Colonial in nurseries and hibernation; may be solitary

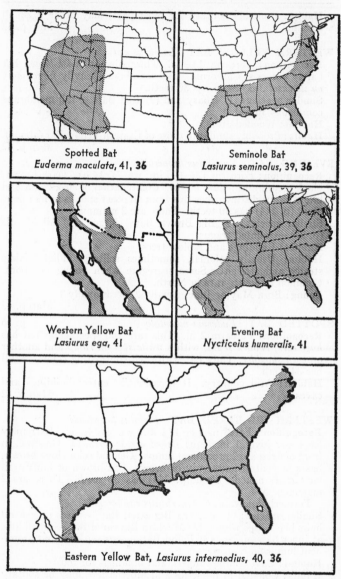

Spotted Bat
Euderma maculata, 41, **36**

Seminole Bat
Lasiurus seminolus, 39, **36**

Western Yellow Bat
Lasiurus ega, 41

Evening Bat
Nycticeius humeralis, 41

Eastern Yellow Bat, *Lasiurus intermedius*, 40, **36**

part of the year. Hangs in tight clusters. Moves from cave to cave, even in winter; when removed, has returned 28 mi. to roost in 2 days. When resting, ears folded back over neck or coiled like ram's horn. Body temperature approaches that of surroundings. Mates Oct.–Feb.; ovulation Feb.–April. Sexes segregate in summer.

Young: Born April–July; normally 1; gestation period 56–100 days. Naked; eyes open at 8–10 days; flies at 3 weeks; not normally carried by mother.   **Map** below

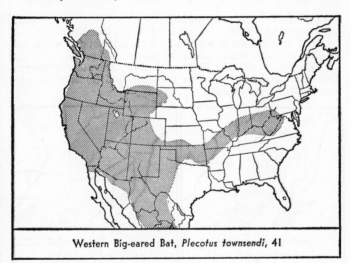

Western Big-eared Bat, *Plecotus townsendi,* 41

EASTERN BIG-EARED BAT *Plecotus rafinesquei*   p. 21
    Recognition: Forearm 1⅜–1⅘ in.; wt. ⅛–⅜ oz. Within its range, this bat may be distinguished from all others except the Western Big-eared Bat by the *tremendous ears* (over 1 in. high), which are *joined in the middle,* and 2 prominent lumps on top of nose. Color pale *brown;* ventral hairs black at bases with white tips. Skull has 36 teeth. There are 2 mammae.
    Formerly known as *Corynorhinus macrotis.*
    Similar species: Western Big-eared Bat — bases of ventral hairs gray or brown, tips brown or buff.
    Habitat: Caves, mine tunnels, buildings.
    Habits: Colonial. Some hibernate, especially in North.
    Young: Born May or June; 1.   Map p. 44

MEXICAN BIG-EARED BAT *Plecotus phyllotis*
    Recognition: Forearm 1⅘ in.; wt. ⅓–½ oz. Large ears with

lappets or *small lobes* on inner edge near base; *ears joined* by membrane across forehead. Skull has 36 teeth.

Also known as *Idionycteris* and *Corynorhinus*.
Similar species: (1) Western Big-eared and (2) Pallid Bats — no lappets at inner edge of ears.
Habitat: Caves in pine-oak forests.
Habits: Late flier. Flies rapidly; folds ears back over shoulders or coils them in ram's horn fashion when resting.
Young: Born probably June or July.   Map below

PALLID BAT   *Antrozous pallidus*   p. 21
     Recognition: Forearm 2–2⅖ in.; wt. 1–1⅛ oz. This *large-eared* (over 1 in. high) *pallid* bat has a simple muzzle; ears *not joined.* Color yellowish drab (palest in desert, darkest along North Pacific Coast). Skull (p. 244) has 28 teeth. There are 2 mammae.
Similar species: (1) Western Big-eared and (2) Mexican Big-eared Bats — ears joined.

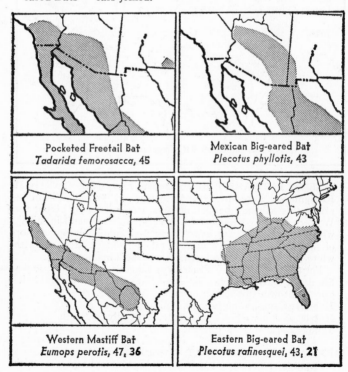

Pocketed Freetail Bat
Tadarida femorosacca, 45

Mexican Big-eared Bat
Plecotus phyllotis, 43

Western Mastiff Bat
Eumops perotis, 47, 36

Eastern Big-eared Bat
Plecotus rafinesquei, 43, 21

Habitat: Caves, mine tunnels, crevices in rocks, buildings, trees for roosts.
Habits: Late flier. Colonial. Night roost, for feeding, different from day roost. Feeds low, near ground; often lands to pick up beetles, Jerusalem crickets, other large insects; wingbeats, 10–12 per second. Hibernates in winter. Sexes segregate in summer.
Young: Born April–June; normally 2, occasionally 1 or 3. Naked; eyes closed. Fly at 6 or 7 weeks.   Map p. 46

Freetail Bats: Molossidae

MEMBERS of this family have the tail extending *well beyond edge of tail membrane.* All have short, dense, *dark brown* fur; they give off a *musty odor.* Primarily cave bats, but also found in buildings. Colonial in habits. The Carlsbad Caverns house one of the largest colonies (of Mexican Freetail Bat) in this country. Known from Lower Oligocene as fossils.

MEXICAN FREETAIL BAT *Tadarida brasiliensis*   p. 36
(Guano Bat)
   Recognition: Forearm 1⅗–1⅘ in. This is the common freetail bat of s. U.S. Short *velvety fur* is usually *chocolate-brown.* Smallest of the freetails within its range. Ears separate. Skull (p. 244) has 32 teeth.
   Formerly known as *T. mexicana.*
   Similar species: (1) Pocketed Freetail and (2) Big Freetail Bats — ears connected at base. (3) Eastern, (4) Underwood, and (5) Western Mastiff Bats — larger.
   Habitat: Caves and buildings for roosts.
   Habits: Usually in large colonies. Some, as those in the Carlsbad Caverns, New Mexico, and Nye Cave, near Bandera, Texas, are made up of thousands of individuals. Flies high and fast. Emerges from roosting site at dusk and flies to feeding grounds, sometimes several miles distant. Feeds mostly on moths, but takes other insects also. Known to have migrated 800 mi. Migrates south for winter. Has lived 4 years, 5 months in captivity.
   Young: Born late June; usually 1. Weaned in July or Aug.
                                                       Map p. 46

POCKETED FREETAIL BAT *Tadarida femorosacca*
   Recognition: Forearm 1⅘–2 in. Ears connected at base. Skull has 30 teeth. This rare bat barely ranges into the U.S. in the Southwest.
   Similar species: (1) Mexican Freetail Bat — ears separate. (2) Big Freetail, (3) Underwood Mastiff, and (4) Western Mastiff Bats — larger.

Habitat: Caves and crevices in rocks for roosts.
Habits: Little known; may be similar to those of other freetail bats.   Map p. 44

BIG FREETAIL BAT *Tadarida molossa*
Recognition: Forearm 2⅓–2½ in. Ears connected at base. Skull has 30 teeth.
Similar species: (1) Mexican Freetail Bat — ears separate. (2) Pocketed Freetail Bat — smaller. (3) Underwood and (4) Western Mastiff Bats — larger.
Habitat: Caves, crevices in cliffs, and buildings for roosts.
Habits: Leaves roost when nearly dark. Colonial.
Young: Born late May or early June; 1.   Map below

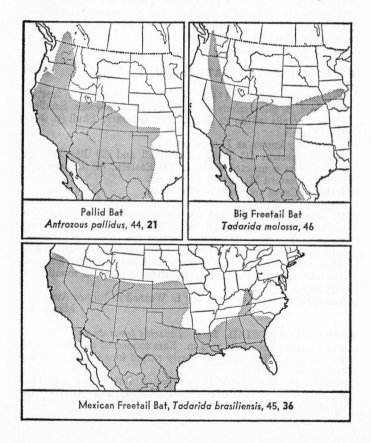

Pallid Bat
Antrozous pallidus, 44, **21**

Big Freetail Bat
Tadarida molossa, 46

Mexican Freetail Bat, *Tadarida brasiliensis*, 45, **36**

WESTERN MASTIFF BAT *Eumops perotis* p. 36

Recognition: Forearm 2⅞–3⅛ in. This is the *largest* of the bats here considered. Chocolate-brown. The *free tail*, extending well beyond the membrane, and *large size* serve to distinguish it. Skull (p. 244) has 30 teeth.

Similar species: (1) Underwood Mastiff and (2) Freetail Bats — smaller.

Habitat: This bat roosts on or in buildings, crevices in cliffs, in trees, and in tunnels.

Habits: Emerges at late dusk. Normally colonial, but may roost singly. Feeds on various insects, mostly hymenopterous kinds.

Young: Born May–July; usually 1, occasionally 2. Map p. 44

UNDERWOOD MASTIFF BAT *Eumops underwoodi*

Recognition: Forearm 2⅗–2⅘ in.; wt. 1⅗–2⅓ oz. Similar to Western Mastiff Bat but slightly smaller. Skull has 30 teeth.

Similar species: (1) Western Mastiff Bat — larger. (2) Freetail Bats — smaller.

Habitat: Roosting sites not known.

Habits: Flies late, in fairly straight course; makes high-pitched peeps while flying.

Young: Born July; 1.

Range: In U.S. known only from Pima Co., Arizona.

EASTERN MASTIFF BAT *Eumops glaucinus*

Recognition: Forearm 2⅓–2⅖ in. Similar to Western Mastiff Bat (above) but smaller. Skull has 30 teeth.

Similar species: Mexican Freetail Bat — smaller.

Range: In U.S. known only from vicinity of Miami, Florida.

Flesh-eaters: Carnivora

THIS order includes those mammals that are primarily *meat-eaters.* Many of them eat berries, nuts, and fruits also, but usually their main diet is flesh. They vary in size from the small Least Weasel (wt. about ⅒ lb.) to the Big Brown Bear (which may weigh more than 1500 lb.). All have *5 toes on front foot;* some have the inner toe high on foot, so that only 4 toes touch the ground. Can have 4 or 5 toes on hind foot. Large *canine teeth* are present in all.

Bears: Ursidae

IN this family we have the *largest* living carnivores. They walk on the entire foot, as does man, have 5 toes on front and back feet, and have *short tails* that are almost concealed in the long fur. Ears are relatively small and rounded. Date from Middle Miocene as fossils.

BLACK BEAR (Cinnamon Bear) *Ursus americanus* p. 37
 Recognition: Head and body 5–6 ft.; height at shoulders 2–3 ft.;
 wt. 200–475 + lb. Color varies from *black* (in East) to *cinnamon*
 or black (in West) to *nearly white* (on Gribble I., B.C.). The
 "Blue" or "Glacier" Bear from near Yakutat Bay, Alaska, is
 probably a color phase of the Black Bear. Face in profile,
 straight or Roman, always *brown*. There is usually a small patch
 of *white* on breast. Commonest and most widely distributed of
 the bears; also the smallest. Skull (p. 260) has 42 teeth. There
 are 6 mammae.
 Similar species: (1) Grizzly and (2) Big Brown Bears — larger;
 hump above shoulders; dish-faced profile.
 Habitat: In East, primarily forests and swamps; in West, chiefly
 mountainous areas.
 Habits: Primarily nocturnal, but occasionally out at midday.
 Usually solitary, except female with cubs. Eats berries, nuts,
 tubers, insects and their larvae, small mammals, eggs, honey,
 carrion, garbage. Dens beneath down tree, in hollow log or tree,
 beneath roots, or wherever there is shelter. Semihibernates in
 winter in North. Males may range 15 mi. or more, females less.
 Speed of more than 30 mph for short distances. Sight poor;
 hearing moderate; sense of smell good. Voice varies — loud
 growl when fighting, *woof-woof* to warn cubs of danger, and a
 whimper to call cubs. May live 30 years or more.
 Young: Born in winter den, Jan. or Feb.; normally 2, occasionally
 1 or 3; maximum of 6 reported; gestation period 7–7½ months;
 1 litter every other year; wt. 7–12 oz. Eyes open at 25–30 days;
 weaned in Aug. but may stay with mother for 1 year; first mate
 at 3½ years.
 Economic status: An important game animal; occasionally
 attacks young domestic animals and does damage to apiaries
 and fruit trees where man's activities border on wilderness areas.
 May be seen in most of the parks within its range, particularly
 in West. Map p. 51

GRIZZLY BEAR *Ursus horribilis* p. 37
 Recognition: Head and body 6–7 ft.; height at shoulders 3–3½
 ft.; wt. 325–850 lb. Color ranges from pale *yellowish* to dark
 brown, *nearly black;* usually *white tips* on hairs, especially on the
 back — giving it the *frosted* or grizzly effect. Dish-faced in
 profile. Claws on front feet long (about 4 in.) and curved. A
 noticeable hump is present above shoulders. Skull has 42 teeth.
 There are 6 mammae.
  There are about 74 "species" of Grizzly Bears recognized by
 some authors, 1 species recognized by others. Obviously, 74 is
 too many, and to try to treat them separately would lead only
 to confusion. These are all treated as Grizzly Bears here, but
 this does not imply that all belong to the species *horribilis.*

Most of them probably do. *U. inopinatus*, the Yellow Bear, from Rendezvous Lake, Mackenzie, Canada, may be distinct.

Similar species: (1) Big Brown Bear — larger. (2) Black Bear — smaller; profile of face not dished; no distinct hump in shoulder region.

Habitat: High mts. of West and onto tundra in the Far North; wilderness areas.

Habits: Prefers twilight hours, but may be abroad any time of day or night. Mostly solitary or in small family groups. Eats meat, fruit, grass, grubs, or any edible material; digs small rodents from dens and gorges on salmon during runs. May dig own den on slope. Hibernates in North and in high mts. in winter. Home range may be 50 mi., but usually less than half that. Uses trails over and over, steps in same footprints. Lives 25 years or more in captivity. Breeds first when 3 years old, then in alternate years or at 3-year intervals. Mates May–July.

Young: Born Jan.; usually 2, sometimes 3, rarely 4; gestation period about 6 months; wt. 10–24 oz. Nearly naked; eyes open at about 10 days.

Economic status: A magnificent game animal that should be preserved; now restricted to wilderness areas where there is little

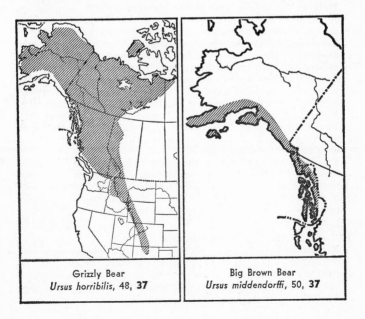

Grizzly Bear
Ursus horribilis, 48, **37**

Big Brown Bear
Ursus middendorffi, 50, **37**

competition with man. Occasionally seen in Glacier, Yellowstone, Banff, Jasper, or Mt. McKinley Natl. Parks. Map p. 49

BIG BROWN BEAR *Ursus middendorffi*   p. 37
(Kodiak Bear)

Recognition: Head and body about 8 ft.; height at shoulders 4–4½ ft.; wt. up to 1500 lb. *Largest* of the bears. Dish-faced in profile. A *noticeable hump* is present above shoulders. Claws relatively smaller than Grizzly's, but size is the best character separating the two. Color ranges from *yellowish to dark brown*, often with white-tipped hairs. Skull (p. 260) has 42 teeth.

According to some authors there are 9 species of Big Brown Bears; others would place them in the species *arctos*. All are included under one general heading here. Those from the islands off Alaska are: *arctos* from St. Lawrence I. (1 reported); *sitkensis*, Baranof and Chichagof Is.; *shirisi*, Admiralty I.; *nuchek*, Hinchinbrook I. and mainland; *middendorffi*, Kodiak I.; and *sheldoni*, Montague I. Mainland forms are: *gyas*, *dalli*, and *kenaiensis*.

Similar species: (1) Grizzly Bear — smaller. (2) Black Bear — smaller, not dish-faced.

Habitat: Coast and adjacent islands, Alaska; forests and open country, but near the sea.

Habits: Active day and night; usually solitary. Emerges in April, when it feeds primarily on seaweed and carrion; in spring and early summer grazes on grasses, forbs, and sedges; turns to fish during salmon run, then to berries in fall; eats mice whenever available, also stranded whales; omnivorous in diet, but eats more plant than animal food; many of the salmon eaten have spawned. Dens up in late autumn, but may appear in midwinter. Unprovoked attacks on man rare; dangerous if wounded or if cubs or food threatened. Lives 20 years or more in captivity. Mates in July. In captivity has crossed with Polar Bear.

Young: Born Jan.; 1–4; usually 2, probably every 3rd year; wt. about 1½ lb. Naked; eyes open at about 6 weeks; remain with mother for year or more.

Economic status: One of the most prized of the big game mammals. Eats some salmon on their way up streams, but many that it consumes have already spawned. We should be able to spend a few salmon for this largest of all carnivores. It would be tragic if it were to disappear from the Alaskan wilderness.

                                                        Map p. 49

POLAR BEAR *Thalarctos maritimus*   p. 37

Recognition: Head and body 6½–7½ ft.; height at shoulders 3–4 ft.; wt. 600–1100 lb. or more. By its large size and *white* or pale *yellowish-white* fur it may be distinguished from all other bears within its range. Eyeshine pale silvery blue. Skull has 42 teeth.

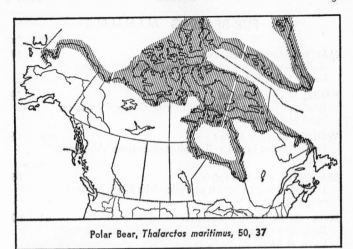

Polar Bear, *Thalarctos maritimus*, 50, **37**

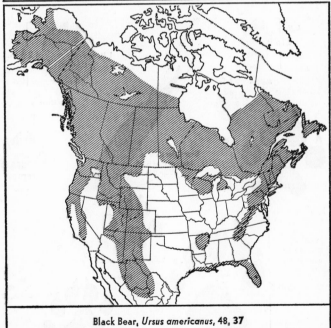

Black Bear, *Ursus americanus*, 48, **37**

FUR-BEARING MAMMALS

	Map	Text
MARTEN, *Martes americana*	58	57

Yellowish brown to dark brown; pale buff on breast;
bushy tail. N.

	Map	Text
FISHER, *Martes pennanti*	58	59

Blackish brown; frosted with white-tipped hairs on
head and shoulders. N.

	Map	Text
WOLVERINE, *Gulo luscus*	66	65

Dark brown; broad yellowish stripes from shoulders
to rump. N.

	Map	Text
SEA OTTER, *Enhydra lutris*		65

Head and neck grayish or yellowish; floats on back;
seacoast. W.

	Map	Text
RIVER OTTER, *Lutra canadensis*	64	62

Rich brown upperparts, silvery underparts; tail
thick at base. N, S, E, W.

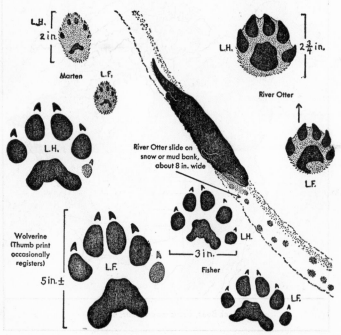

L.H.
2 in.

Marten   L.F.

L.H.   2¾ in.

River Otter

River Otter slide on
snow or mud bank,
about 8 in. wide

L.F.

L.H.

Wolverine
(Thumb print
occasionally
registers)

5 in. ±

L.F.

3 in.

L.H.

Fisher

L.F.

MARTEN

FISHER

WOLVERINE

SEA OTTER

RIVER OTTER

LEAST WEASEL

Winter

SHORTTAIL WEASEL

Summer Male

LONGTAIL WEASEL

Northeast Female

Southwest

BLACK-FOOTED FERRET

MINK

Plate 6 53

WEASELS AND MINK

| | Map | Text |

LEAST WEASEL, *Mustela rixosa*   60   61
No black tip on short tail. N.

SHORTTAIL WEASEL, *Mustela erminea*   60   59
Winter: White; medium-sized; tail with black tip.
Summer: Brown; white down hind leg to foot.
N.

LONGTAIL WEASEL, *Mustela frenata*   63   61
Hind legs brownish; black tip on long tail. N, S,
E, W.
Northeast: No white on face.
Southwest: White on face.

BLACK-FOOTED FERRET, *Mustela nigripes*   64   62
Yellowish-brown to buffy body; black forehead and
feet. W Central.

MINK, *Mustela vison*   63   62
Rich dark brown; white on chin. E, NW.

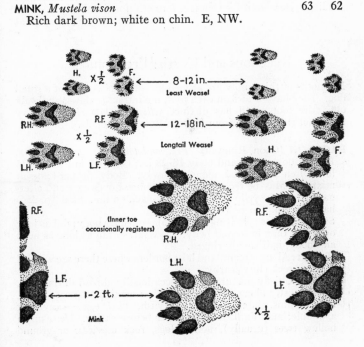

Polar Bears on the eastern coast of Greenland and along coast
of Labrador are usually listed as distinct species (*T. eogroen-
landicus* and *T. labradorensis*).

Habitat: Ice floes and barren rocky shores and islands.

Habits: Solitary, except during mating season in midsummer or
when mother is with cubs. A strong swimmer, keeps head and
neck out of water; readily takes to water when endangered, and
will float if killed there. Feeds mostly on seals, but feasts on
stranded whales or other dead animals on shore; also eats birds
and their eggs as well as vegetation if available. Dens in deep
snowbank in winter; emerges in late March. Apparently has
good sense of smell and sight. Lives 30 years or more in captivity. Breeds in alternate years. In captivity has crossed with
Big Brown Bear.

Young: Born in winter den; normally 2, sometimes 1; gestation
period probably 7–8 months. Stay with mother at least until
next winter.

Economic status: In Canada, an important food animal for
Eskimos and their dogs; protected from trophy hunters. Liver
toxic because of concentration of vitamin A, but remainder
edible. Hide used for bedding, formerly for clothing.

Map p. 51

Raccoons and Coatis: Procyonidae

MEMBERS of this family are of medium size, about that of a small
dog. They have 5 toes on each foot, nonretractile claws, and walk
on entire foot. Tail has distinct *yellowish-white rings* or very
indistinct rings. Date from Lower Miocene as fossils.

RACCOON (Coon, Ringtail)   *Procyon lotor*   p. 100
  Recognition: Head and body 18–28 in.; tail 8–12 in.; wt. 12–35
  lb. Often seen dead along highway. Body pepper-and-salt
  mixture. May be recognized by *black mask* over eyes and alter-
  nating *rings* of yellowish white and black on tail. Skull (p. 256)
  has 40 teeth. There are 6 mammae.
  Similar species: (1) Ringtail (p. 56) — slender body; tail as long
  or longer than head and body. (2) Coati — tail as long as head
  and body, indistinctly ringed.
  Habitat: Along streams and lake borders where there are wooded
  areas or rock cliffs nearby.
  Habits: Chiefly nocturnal, but occasionally abroad during day.
  Feeds mostly along streams and lakes; omnivorous; eats fruits,
  nuts, grains, insects, frogs, crayfish, bird eggs — anything
  available; may dunk food in water before eating. Dens up in
  hollow trees (usually), hollow logs, rock crevices, or ground

burrows during cold spells in North, but does not hibernate.
Home range up to 2 mi. across, normally less than 1 mi.; young
known to disperse up to 165 mi. from birth place, mostly less
than 30 mi. Recorded population of 1 per acre (highest) to 1
per 15 acres (considered high). Captives live to 14 years. Voice
variable — low twittering sound from mother assures young,
growls and snarls denote anger. Some females mate 1st year;
mate Feb.–March in North, earlier in South.

Young: Born April or May; 2–7, average 4; gestation period
63 days; 1 litter a year; wt. 2½ oz. Eyes open in about 3 weeks.
Abroad with mother at 2 months; leave mother in fall.

Economic status: May damage roasting-ear corn and raid
poultry yards; for many, value of pelts and pleasure of seeing
them in the wild outweighs harm done; meat edible.

Map below

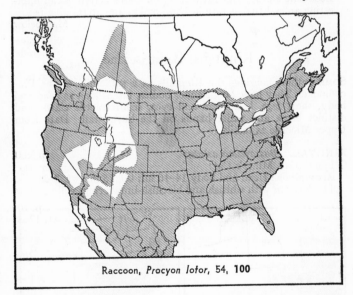

Raccoon, *Procyon lotor,* 54, **100**

COATI   *Nasua narica*   p. 100
  Recognition: Head and body 20–25 in.; tail 20–25 in.; wt. 15–25
lb. This *long-snouted* grizzled-brown invader from the tropics
barely enters s. U.S. The *long tail*, which is often carried erect,
is indistinctly ringed. There are *white spots above and below each
eye.* Has 5 toes on each foot, and walks on entire foot. *Nose
whitish.* Eyeshine blue-green to gold. Skull (p. 256) has 40 teeth.
There are 6 mammae.

Similar species: (1) Raccoon and (2) Ringtail (below) — tail distinctly ringed.

Habitat: Open forests in U.S.

Habits: More active by day than at night. Usually runs in bands of up to a dozen, but old males may be solitary. An excellent climber; uses tail to balance on branches, also as brake by wrapping it around small branches or vines when descending headfirst; when on ground, tail held nearly vertical. Omnivorous; a tough nose pad aids in rooting for grubs and tubers; also eats fruits, nuts, bird eggs, lizards, scorpions, and tarantulas; rolls poisonous and other arthropods on ground with front paws to remove scales, wings, etc., before eating them.

Young: Born probably July in this area; 4–6; gestation period about 2½ months.

Economic status: Has little effect on man's activities; an interesting animal that is rare in U.S.; makes an entertaining pet.

Map below

Ringtails: Bassariscidae

SOME authors consider the Ringtails as a subfamily of the Procyonidae. They have long slender bodies, tail as long as head and body, short legs, large ears and eyes, semiretractile claws, and distinct black and white bands on the bushy tail. Date from Upper Miocene as fossils.

RINGTAIL *Bassariscus astutus*   p. 100
(Ringtail Cat, Miner's Cat)

Recognition: Head and body 14–16 in.; tail 15 in.; wt. 2–2½ lb. The *long tail* with whitish and blackish-brown rings will identify

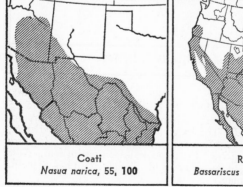

Coati
Nasua narica, 55, **100**

Ringtail
Bassariscus astutus, 56, **100**

the Ringtail. Body pale yellowish gray. Has thick fur between pads on feet. Eyeshine red to yellowish green. The only species of this family occurring north of the Mexican border. Skull (p. 257) has 40 teeth. There are 6 mammae.

Similar species: (1) Raccoon (p. 54) — shorter tail, black mask. (2) Coati (p. 55) — tail not distinctly ringed.

Habitat: Chaparral, rocky ridges and cliffs; near water.

Habits: Nocturnal. May be partially colonial, usually 2 (a pair) together. Feeds chiefly on small mammals, insects, birds, and fruits; also eats lizards and various invertebrates. Dens in caves or crevices along cliffs, in hollow trees, under rock piles, or in unused buildings. Populations of 5–10 per sq. mi. considered high. Has lived 8 years in captivity. When agitated, makes a coughing bark similar to that of a fox; also whimpers.

Young: Born May or June; 3–4; 1 litter a year. Covered with white fuzz; eyes open in 4–5 weeks. Go abroad at 2 months; leave mother in Aug. or Sept.

Economic status: Fur occasionally of some value; a good mouser; probably wholly beneficial.   Map opposite

Weasels, Skunks, etc.: Mustelidae

MEMBERS of this family are varied in size and color. Usually they have long slender bodies and short legs, short, rounded ears, and anal scent glands. In many species, males are distinctly larger than females. Date from Lower Oligocene as fossils.

MARTEN *Martes americana*   p. 52

Recognition: Head and body: males, 16–17 in.; females, 14–15 in. Tail: males, 8–9 in.; females, 7–8 in. Wt.: males, 1⅔–2¾ lb.; females, 1½–1⅞ lb. This graceful furbearer has soft, dense *yellowish-brown* fur shading to *dark brown* on bushy tail and on legs. Has a *pale buff patch* on throat and breast, and belly is paler than back. Skull (p. 256) has 38 teeth. There are 8 mammae.

Similar species: (1) Mink — white patch on chin. (2) Fisher — larger, dark brown; grizzled on head and back. (3) Red Fox (p. 77) — white tip on tail.

Habitat: Fir, spruce, and hemlock forests preferred in West; cedar swamps in East.

Habits: Chiefly nocturnal. Spends much time in trees, but also forages and moves on ground. Eats chiefly red squirrels and other small mammals, but varies diet with insects, birds, fruits, and nuts. Dens in hollow tree or log. Normal home range 1 sq. mi. for male, ¼ sq. mi. for female; may range as far as 15 mi. Population of 2 per sq. mi. probably high. Has lived 17 years in captivity. Mates in late July or early Aug.

Young: Born April; 2–4; gestation period 8½–9 months; wt. 1 oz. Covered with fine yellowish hair; eyes open at 5–6 weeks; weaned at 6–7 weeks. May breed 1st year.

Economic status: Valuable as a furbearer; lives in areas remote from civilization, so does not interfere with man's activities.

Map below

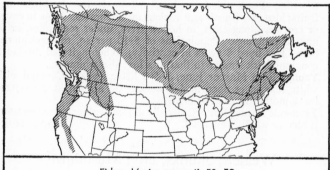

Fisher, *Martes pennanti*, 59, **52**

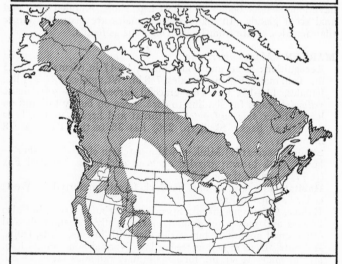

Marten, *Martes americana*, 57, **52**

FISHER (Pekan) *Martes pennanti* p. 52
  Recognition: Head and body 20–25 in.; tail 13–15 in. Wt.: males, 6–12 lb.; females, 3–7 lb. This magnificent furbearer is *dark brown to nearly black, with white-tipped hairs* over most of its body, giving it a *frosted* appearance. Long, slim body and bushy tail. Skull has 38 teeth. There are 4 mammae.
  Similar species: (1) Marten — smaller; buffy patch on throat and breast. (2) Wolverine — yellowish stripes on sides and rump. (3) Red Fox (p. 77) — white tip on tail.
  Habitat: Extensive mixed hardwood forests, cutover wilderness areas.
  Habits: Active day and night. At home both on ground and in trees. Feeds primarily on small mammals, birds, carrion, fruits, and fern tips; one of few predators that feed on Porcupines. Dens in hollow tree or in ground. Home range about 10 sq. mi.; males range farther than females. Has lived more than 9 years in captivity. Mates soon after young are born.
  Young: Born late March or early April; 1–4; gestation period 11–12 months.
  Economic status: A valuable furbearer; also beneficial to forests by destroying Porcupines.   Map opposite

SHORTTAIL WEASEL (Ermine) *Mustela erminea* p. 53
  Recognition: Head and body: males, 6–9 in.; females, 5–7½ in. Tail: males, 2¼–4 in.; females, 2–3 in. Wt.: males, 2½–6 oz.; females, 1–3 oz. Largest in East and North, smallest in West. Males are ⅕ to ¼ larger than females. *Dark brown*, with *white underparts and feet* in summer; *white in winter*, except along Pacific Coast, where it is light brown; always has *black tip on tail*. In summer, has a *white line down hind leg*, connecting the white of underparts with that of toes. Skull has 34 teeth. There are 8–10 mammae.
  Similar species: (1) Longtail Weasel — respective sexes larger; tail longer; no white line on hind leg. (2) Least Weasel — no black tip on tail. (3) Mink — uniform color.
  Habitat: Brushy or wooded areas, usually not far from water.
  Habits: Chiefly nocturnal, but also hunts during day. Climbs trees, but more at home on ground. Food mostly small mammals (mice) and a few birds, but other animals also consumed; kills by piercing skull with canine teeth. Dens in ground burrows, under stumps, rock piles, or old buildings; nest usually contains fur of mice. Home range probably 30–40 acres; may move 3 mi. or more; returned 2 mi. to homesite. Population high of 20 per sq. mi. in good habitat. Voice a shrill shriek when agitated or seizing prey.
  Young: Born April–May; 4–8; gestation period 8½–10 months; 1 litter a year. Definite mane on neck; eyes open at 30–45 days.
  Economic status: Beneficial; an expert mouser. Winter pelts

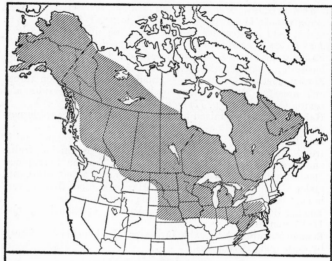

Least Weasel, *Mustela rixosa*, 61, **53**

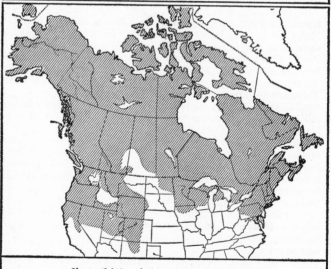

Shorttail Weasel, *Mustela erminea*, 59, **53**

(ermine) of some value when fur prices are high; rarely destroys poultry. Map opposite

LEAST WEASEL *Mustela rixosa* p. 53
Recognition: Head and body: males, 6–6½ in.; females, 5½–6 in. Tail: males, 1⅛–1½ in.; females, 1–1⅛ in. Wt.: males, 1⅖–2¼ oz.; females, 1⅓–1⅖ oz. The *smallest* living carnivore. Brown above, whitish below in summer; white all over in winter except in South, where it may be partially white. Sometimes a few black hairs, but *no black tip*, at end of short tail. Rare throughout most of its range. Skull has 34 teeth. There are 8 mammae.
Similar species: (1) Shorttail and (2) Longtail Weasels — both have black tips on tails.
Habitat: Meadows, fields, brushy areas, and open woods.
Habits: Most active at night. Feeds almost entirely on mice; often caches several near nest. Kills by biting through base of skull; death of prey nearly instantaneous. May take over revamped mouse nest. Normal home range about 2 acres. Voice a shrill shriek when agitated.
Young: May be born any month of year; 3–10, usually 4–5; may be more than 1 litter a year.
Economic status: Entirely beneficial; a very effective mouser.
Map opposite

LONGTAIL WEASEL *Mustela frenata* p. 53
Recognition: Head and body: males, 9–10½ in.; females, 8–9 in. Tail: males, 4–6 in.; females, 3–5 in. Wt.: males, 7–12 oz.; females, 3–7 oz. Distinguished by its long slender body, long neck (head slightly larger than neck), *yellowish-white underparts*, black tip on tail, and *no whitish line down inside of hind leg*. In winter, in North, white except for black tip on tail. In some parts of its range (Southwest) has a white bridle across face, and head is usually of a darker brown than body. Most widely distributed weasel. Skull (p. 256) has 34 teeth. There are 8 mammae.
Similar species: (1) Shorttail Weasel — respective sexes smaller; white line down inside of hind leg. (2) Least Weasel — smaller; no black tip on tail. (3) Mink — nearly uniform dark brown.
Habitat: Not restricted; it is found in all land habitats that are near water.
Habits: Chiefly nocturnal, but also active by day. Climbs trees, but spends most of time on ground. Feeds mostly on small mammals up to rabbit size; also takes a few birds and other animals; kills by piercing skull with canines. Usually nests in old burrows of other animals, sometimes under wood or rock piles. Home range normally 30–40 acres. Population of 15–20 per sq. mi. is probably high. Voice a high-pitched shriek. Mates in July or Aug.

Young: Born late April or early May; 4–8; gestation period 205–337 days. Eyes open at 35 days; males mate at 1 year, females at 3–4 months.
Economic status: Beneficial; kills many small rodents and seldom kills poultry. Fur (ermine) of some value.   Map opposite

BLACK-FOOTED FERRET *Mustela nigripes*   p. 53
  Recognition: Head and body 15–18 in.; tail 5–6 in.; wt. (2 males) 2⅛, 2⅜ lb. This large weasel-like mammal may be recognized by its *yellowish-brown to buffy* body, *black forehead*, black-tipped tail, and *black feet*. Skull has 34 teeth.
  Similar species: Kit Fox (p. 79) — bushy tail, feet not black.
  Habitat: Prairies.
  Habits: Has been seen in prairie dog towns, where it apparently preys on the inhabitants; undoubtedly preys on any animal that it can overpower. Nests in prairie dog burrows. Practically nothing is known about this, one of our rarest mammals.
  Young: Born June; at least 2, probably more.   Map p. 64

MINK *Mustela vison*   p. 53
  Recognition: Head and body: males, 13–17 in.; females, 12–14 in. Tail: males, 7–9 in.; females, 5–8 in. Wt.: males, 1½–3 lb.; females, 1¼–2⅔ lb. The Mink is usually *rich dark brown* with a *white chin patch*, and sometimes with scattered small white spots on its belly. Tail is slightly bushy. Eyeshine yellowish green. Skull (p. 256) has 34 teeth. There are 8 mammae.
  Similar species: (1) Weasels — white or yellowish underparts. (2) Marten — buffy patch on throat and breast. (3) River Otter — larger.
  Habitat: Along streams and lakes.
  Habits: Chiefly nocturnal; solitary except for family groups. An excellent swimmer. Feeds primarily on small mammals, birds, eggs, frogs, crayfish, and fish. Dens along stream or lake banks. Males may range several miles along a stream. Mates Jan.–March.
  Young: Born April or May; usually 2–6, occasionally as many as 10; gestation period 39–76, normally about 42, days. Eyes open at 25 days. May breed 1st year.
  Economic status: One of the most valuable fur animals; occasionally raids a poultry yard.   Map opposite

RIVER OTTER *Lutra canadensis*   p. 52
  Recognition: Head and body 26–30 in.; tail 12–17 in.; wt. 10–25 lb. A large weasel-like mammal, *rich brown above*, with a *silvery sheen below*, and with small ears and *broad snout;* feet *webbed*, tail thick at base, tapering toward tip. Eyeshine pale amber. Skull (p. 256) has 36 teeth. There are 4 mammae.
  Similar species: (1) Beaver (p. 157) — tail flat and scaly. (2)

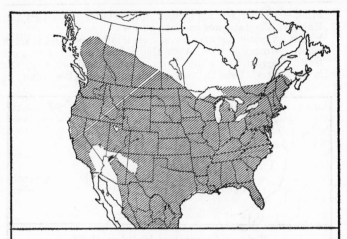

Longtail Weasel, *Mustela frenata*, 61, **53**

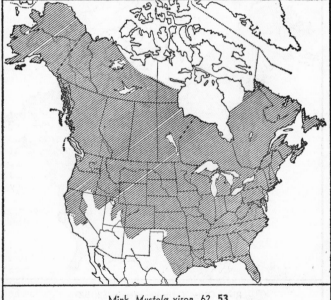

Mink, *Mustela vison*, 62, **53**

Mink — smaller; feet not webbed.　(3) Sea Otter — head grayish.
Habitat: Along streams and lake borders.
Habits: Aquatic, but may travel several miles over land to reach
another stream or lake.　A sociable animal, usually 2 or more
travel together.　Eats fish, frogs, crayfish, and other aquatic
invertebrates.　Dens in banks, with entrance below water, or

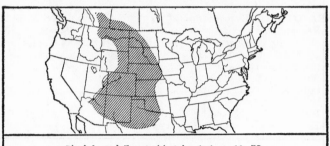

Black-footed Ferret, *Mustela nigripes*, 62, **53**

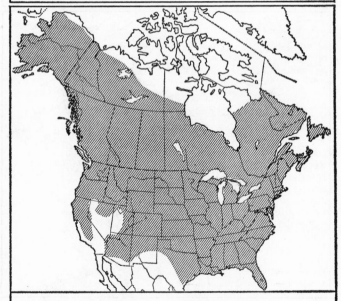

River Otter, *Lutra canadensis*, 62, **52**

other suitable places. Home range 15 mi. or more. Has lived 14½ years in captivity.

Young: Born April or May; 1–5, usually 2; gestation period 9½–10 months. Covered with dark brown fur; blind.

Economic status: Fur valuable. Eats some trout, but mostly rough fish.   Map opposite

SEA OTTER *Enhydra lutris*   p. 52

Recognition: Head and body 30–36 in.; tail 11–13 in.; wt. 30–85 lb. *Brownish black, glossy*, with white-tipped hairs, giving it a frosted effect; head and neck grayish or yellowish; feet completely *webbed and flipperlike*. Skull has 32 teeth.

Similar species: (1) Seals and (2) Sea Lions (p. 86) — shorter tails, well-developed flippers, shorter fur. (3) River Otter — head dark brown.

Habitat: Kelp beds and rocky shores.

Habits: Spends most of time resting and feeding among kelp beds. Hauls out onto shore during severe storms. Gregarious. Floats, feeds, and swims on back when not hurried. Brings abalones, sea urchins, and other marine animals to surface and uses chest for table; may bring rock from bottom to break sea urchin on.

Young: Born probably June; 1; body furred, eyes open; wt. about 3 lb. Brown, head and shoulders paler than remainder of body.

Economic status: The Sea Otter is fully protected. Fur formerly extremely valuable and ruthlessly sought after. Once thought to be extinct, it is now increasing in numbers. Abalone fishermen begrudge the few abalones eaten by this interesting mammal.

Range: From California to Aleutian Is. Most likely to be seen off Pt. Lobos, California, and Amchitka I., Alaska.

WOLVERINE (Glutton)   *Gulo luscus*   p. 52

Recognition: Head and body 29–32 in.; tail 7–9 in.; wt. 35–60 lb. In general appearance, except for the bushy tail, the Wolverine looks like a small bear. *Dark brown, paler on the head*, and with *2 broad yellowish stripes* that start at shoulders and join on rump. Feet are large for its size. Skull (p. 256) has 38 teeth.

Considered by some to belong to Old World species (*G. gulo*).

Similar species: Fisher (p. 59) — without yellowish stripes.

Habitat: High mts. of West, near timberline, and onto tundra in the North; a wilderness mammal.

Habits: Active day or night. Solitary. Feeds on anything available in the form of meat, also larvae, eggs, berries; has reputation for robbing traps and destroying food caches of trappers; travels many miles in search of food. Dens in any sheltered place. Has lived more than 15 years in captivity. Probably territorial. Mates April–Aug.

Wolverine, *Gulo luscus*, 65, **52**

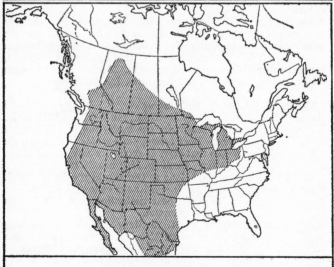

Badger, *Taxidea taxus*, 67, **100**

Young: Born Feb.–April; 2–3; probably 1 litter every 2–3 years. Yellowish white, blind.

Economic status: Apparently does damage to traplines; fur used primarily for trimming parkas. One of the few remnants of true wilderness, and should be preserved.   Map opposite

BADGER *Taxidea taxus*   p. 100
  Recognition: Head and body 18–22 in.; tail 4–6 in.; wt. 13–25 lb. Sometimes seen along highway in early morning. This heavy-bodied, short-legged, *yellowish-gray* mammal has a *median white stripe* from nose over the top of its head, *white* cheeks, and a *black spot* in front of each ear. Feet *black*, front claws extremely long. Belly and short tail yellowish. No other N. American mammal has above characters. Skull (p. 256) has 34 teeth. There are 8 mammae.
  Habitat: Open grasslands and deserts.
  Habits: Mostly nocturnal, but often abroad during day, especially early morning. A great digger; digs out small rodents, its chief food; dens in burrows of own making. Has lived 12 years in captivity.
  Young: Born Feb.–May, depending on altitude and latitude; 2–5.
  Economic status: Destroys many rodents; fur of little value; open burrows may be hazardous to livestock.   Map opposite

SPOTTED SKUNK *Spilogale putorius*   p. 73
(Civit, Hydrophobia Cat)
  Recognition: Head and body 9–13½ in.; tail 4½–9 in. Wt.: males, 1–2⅕ lb.; females, ⅘–1¼ lb. Smallest in West, largest in Midwest and East. This handsome little carnivore is *black*, with a *white spot on the forehead, 1 under each ear*, and with *4 broken white stripes along neck, back, and sides*. Tail has a white tip. Relative proportions of white and black vary considerably. There is no other mammal with a similar color pattern. Eyeshine pale amber. Skull (p. 256) has 34 teeth. There are 8 mammae.
  Habitat: Brushy or sparsely wooded areas, along streams, among boulders; prairies.
  Habits: Nocturnal. Will climb trees to escape danger, but normally stays on ground. Stands on front feet and discharges scent directly over its head; does this only in defense. Feeds on mice, birds, eggs, insects, carrion, and some vegetable matter. Nests in burrows, beneath buildings, or rock piles. Several may den together in winter. Home range 160 acres or less, males may wander farther. Populations to 13 or more per sq. mi.
  Young: Born May or June; 4–7; gestation period, 120+ days. Weaned at 50 days.
  Economic status: Beneficial as destroyer of rats and mice, especially around farm buildings; occasionally kills poultry. Fur of some value. Rabies occasionally detected in these skunks.
                                                                  Map **p. 71**

DOGLIKE MAMMALS

	Map	Text

RED FOX, *Vulpes fulva*   78   77
  White tip on bushy tail. N, S, E, W.
  Red phase: Reddish yellow; feet black.
  Black phase: Black with white-tipped hairs.
  Cross phase: Reddish yellow to brown; dark cross
  over shoulders.

GRAY FOX, *Urocyon cinereoargenteus*   80   81
  Black stripe down top of tail; feet and legs rusty.
  S, E, W.

ARCTIC FOX, *Alopex lagopus*   80   79
  Blue phase: Bluish brown; no white tip on tail.
  White phase: White.
  Arctic, Subarctic.

SWIFT FOX, *Vulpes velox*   78   79
  Black tip on tail. W Central.

COYOTE, *Canis latrans*   74   73
  Rusty legs, feet, and ears; nose pad less than 1 in.
  wide; tail down when running. W, NE.

GRAY WOLF, *Canis lupus*   76   75
  Usually gray; nose pad more than 1 in. wide; tail
  high when running. N, W.

RED WOLF, *Canis niger*   76   77
  Reddish or blackish; tail high when running. SE.

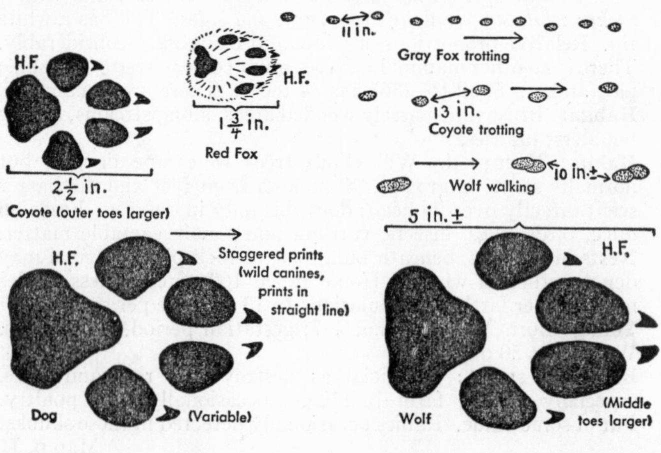

H.F.

11 in.
Gray Fox trotting

H.F.

1¾ in.
Red Fox

13 in.
Coyote trotting

2½ in.
Coyote (outer toes larger)

Wolf walking   10 in.

5 in. ±

H.F.

Staggered prints
(wild canines,
prints in
straight line)

H.F.

Dog   (Variable)

Wolf   (Middle
toes larger)

Red phase

Black phase

Cross phase

RED FOX

Blue phase

GRAY FOX

White phase

ARCTIC FOX

SWIFT FOX

COYOTE

GRAY WOLF

RED WOLF

LYNX

BOBCAT

Young

MOUNTAIN LION

Adult

Red phase

Gray phase

OCELOT

JAGUARUNDI CAT

JAGUAR

CATS

	Map	Text
LYNX, *Lynx canadensis*	85	85

Short tail with tip black all way around. N.

BOBCAT, *Lynx rufus*   85   86
Short tail with tip black only on top. N, S, E, W.

MOUNTAIN LION, *Felis concolor*   82   82
Young: Spotted.
Adult: Tawny to grayish; large; long tail with dark brown tip.
W, SE.

OCELOT, *Felis pardalis*   83   84
Spots arranged in rows; long tail; small size. S.

JAGUARUNDI CAT, *Felis yagouaroundi*   83   84
Long tail; short legs. SW.
Red phase: Reddish.
Gray phase: Bluish gray.

JAGUAR, *Felis onca*   83   81
Spots in form of rosettes; large size. SW.

9 in.
Bobcat walking slowly

13 in.   L.H.
Bobcat walking rapidly

R.F.
2 in.   8 in. to next track   1 in.
House Cat walking

Mountain Lion
(R. F. foot in snow)

4 in.
R.H.   R.F.

22 in.
Mountain Lion walking slowly
(Lynx smaller, Jaguar larger)

STRIPED SKUNK   *Mephitis mephitis*   p. 73
   Recognition: Head and body 13–18 in.; tail 7–10 in.; wt. 6–14 lb.
   Often seen dead along highway. Probably the best-known
   mammal in this *Field Guide*. About size of a House Cat, it may
   be recognized by its *black body, narrow white stripe* up middle of
   forehead, and *broad white area* on nape, which usually divides
   into a V at about the shoulders. The resulting 2 white lines may
   continue back to base of bushy tail, which may or may not have
   a white tip. Much variation in length and width of side stripes.
   Scent glands well developed. Often the presence of a skunk is
   first detected by *odor*. Eyeshine deep amber. Skull (p. 256) has
   34 teeth. There are 10–14 mammae.
   Similar species: (1) Hooded Skunk — tail longer; white V on
   back rarely present. (2) Hognose Skunk — white back stripe
   not divided.
   Habitat: Semi-open country; mixed woods, brushland, and open
   prairie preferred; normally within 2 mi. of water.
   Habits: Chiefly nocturnal; starts hunting shortly after sundown
   and retires at about sunrise. Omnivorous; feeds on mice, eggs,
   insects, grubs, berries, and carrion. Dens in ground burrows,
   beneath abandoned buildings, boulders, or wood or rock piles.
   Several females may den together in winter; males tend to be
   solitary. Does not hibernate; often appears abroad on warm
   nights in middle of winter in North; active all winter in South.
   Population of 1 skunk to 10 acres in good areas is high. Mates
   Feb.–March.
   Young: Born early May; up to 10, usually 5 or 6; gestation
   period 63 days. Blind. Accompany mother late June or July;
   follow in single file.
   Economic status: One of our most valuable fur animals; single
   pelt not very valuable, but tremendous numbers are taken.
   Rarely eats poultry; destroys many small rodents and insects.
   Makes fair pet if descented; sometimes carries rabies.
   Map opposite

HOODED SKUNK   *Mephitis macroura*   p. 73
   Recognition: Head and body 12–16 in.; tail 14–15 in. This is a
   southern skunk that barely enters s. U.S. There are 2 general
   color patterns, with intermediate variants, in this species. In
   one, entire back is chiefly *white*, including tail; in the other, back
   is nearly all-*black* and there are 2 white side stripes — the belly
   being *black*. Hair on neck usually spreads out into a *ruff*. Tail
   as long as head and body. Skull has 34 teeth.
   Similar species: (1) Striped Skunk — white V on back, tail
   shorter. (2) Hognose Skunk — long, bare snout; entire back
   and tail white, with no black hairs; tail shorter.
   Habitat: Along streams, rocky ledges.
   Habits: Probably similar to those of Striped Skunk.

Young: Born May–June; 5 embryos reported from 1 female.
Economic status: Probably beneficial; fur of little value; destroys
insects and small rodents. Map p. 72

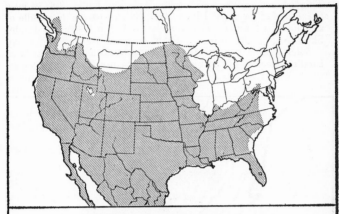

Spotted Skunk, *Spilogale putorius,* 67, **73**

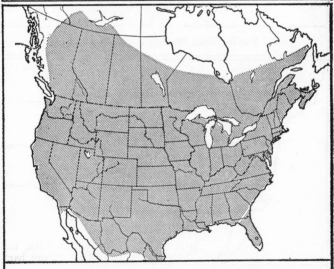

Striped Skunk, *Mephitis mephitis,* 70, **73**

HOGNOSE SKUNK   *Conepatus leuconotus*   p. 73
(Rooter Skunk)
  Recognition: Head and body 14–19 in.; tail 7–12 in.; wt. 2–6 lb.
This 2-toned skunk is well named. It has a long *piglike snout*
that is *naked* for about 1 in. *on top. Entire back and tail are white*
and lower sides and belly are black. Fur is short and coarse.
Skull (p. 256) has 32 teeth. There are 6 mammae.
  Some authors recognize another species, *C. mesoleucus.*
Similar species: (1) Striped Skunk — white blaze on forehead.

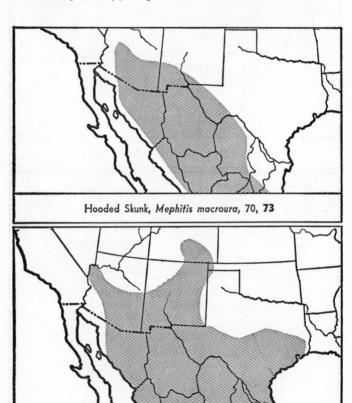

Hooded Skunk, *Mephitis macroura*, 70, **73**

Hognose Skunk, *Conepatus leuconotus*, 72, **73**

Striped Skunk

Spotted Skunk

Hognose Skunk

Hooded Skunk

(2) Hooded Skunk — if white on back, usually mixed with black; tail longer.

Habitat: Partly wooded, brushy, rocky areas.

Habits: Primarily nocturnal, but active also by day. Usually solitary. Feeds on insects, mollusks, and other invertebrates; also small mammals, reptiles, and vegetation; roots for much of its food. Dens in crevices in rock cliffs. Mates in Feb.

Young: Born April–May; 2–4; gestation period about 2 months.

Economic status: Fur of little value; does no appreciable damage; destroys small rodents and insects.   Map opposite

Dogs, Wolves, and Foxes: Canidae

MEMBERS of this family are all *doglike* in general appearance. They have 5 toes on each front foot (inside toe is high) and 4 on each back foot (some domestic dogs have a 5th toe). All have a scent gland at base of tail, on top; its position revealed by black-tipped hairs without underfur. Rabies occurs sporadically in all members of the family. Known as fossils back to Upper Eocene.

COYOTE (Brush Wolf)   *Canis latrans*   p. 68
  Recognition: Head and body 32–37 in.; tail 11–16 in.; wt. 20–50 lb. The Coyote looks like a medium-sized dog; it is *gray or reddish gray, with rusty legs, feet,* and *ears;* throat and belly whitish. Nose is more pointed and tail is bushier than normal in dogs; tail *held down* between hind legs *when running.* Pupil of eye round; nose pad less than 1 in. wide. In evening a series of high-pitched *yap*'s may be heard, especially on desert. Eye-

shine greenish gold. Skull (p. 257) has 42 teeth. There are 8 mammae.

Similar species: (1) Red Wolf — usually larger; darker color. (2) Gray Wolf — larger; holds tail high when running; nose pad 1 in. or more wide. (3) Foxes — smaller; hold tails out straight when running.

Habitat: Prairies, open woodlands, brushy or boulder-strewn areas.

Habits: Chiefly nocturnal, but may be abroad at any time. A true scavenger, Coyote will eat almost anything animal or vegetable; food predominantly small rodents and rabbits; sometimes hunts in pairs; will cache uneaten food; hunting route normally about 10 mi., may move up to 100 mi.; kills large animals by attacking at throat. Normally dens in ground, but

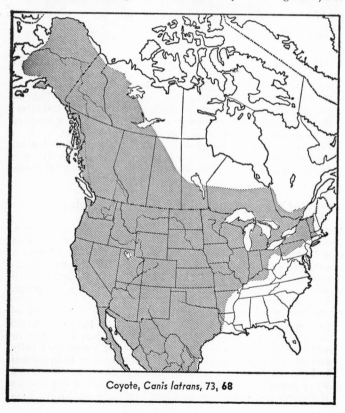

Coyote, *Canis latrans*, 73, **68**

often uses other shelter, usually not more than 6 mi. from water. Has lived more than 18 years in captivity; can run more than 40 mph for short distances. Mates Jan.–Feb.; will cross with domestic dog; females breed at 1 year.

Young: Born April–May; 5–10; gestation period 60–63 days. Eyes open at 9–14 days. Pups brown all over.

Economic status: Somewhere there has always been a bounty on the Coyote since this country was settled. The bounty has not reduced its numbers. Much of damage to livestock attributed to Coyote is probably done by wild dogs. Coyotes kill many rodents and rabbits, and in this way do a real service to the rancher. But they may also kill sheep and calves at times. May they never cease to yap on moonlight nights in the desert. Can be seen, or heard, in most western parks.   Map opposite

GRAY WOLF (Timber Wolf) *Canis lupus*   p. 68

Recognition: Head and body 43–48 in.; tail 12–19 in.; height at shoulders 26–28 in.; wt. 70–120 lb. Largest of our wild dogs and found only in wilder parts of its range. Color varies from *nearly white* (in Arctic) *to nearly black,* usually gray. When running, *tail is carried high;* ears more rounded and relatively smaller than those of Coyote; also, more doglike in appearance. Nose pad more than 1 in. wide. Eyeshine greenish orange. Skull has 42 teeth. There are 10 mammae.

Similar species: Coyote — smaller; carries tail low when running; nose pad less than 1 in.

Habitat: Wilderness forests and tundra.

Habits: Most active at night, but may be abroad during day; hunts in packs of up to 12 or more during nonbreeding season. Both parents bring food to pups. Feeds on anything available, primarily birds and mammals; deer and caribou constitute most of big game prey. Hunting area may be 60 mi. or more in diam.; leaves scent posts along trails; often travels single file in snow. Population estimates range from 1 wolf for 40 sq. mi. to 1 for 100 or more sq. mi. Voice a deep howl; other whimpers, whines, and growls normally not heard by man. May breed in 2nd year; mates for season, Jan.–March.

Young: Born April–May; 3–14, usually 6–7; gestation period 9 weeks. Pups sooty black with dirty gray on head.

Economic status: The wolf kills some big game (deer, caribou, sheep, Moose), but mostly it is the old, the weak, the diseased that are taken. Actually, this is beneficial to the species. For millions of years there was a natural relation between predators and prey, to the advantage of both. Now man enters the picture and thinks that all predators should be exterminated. Local control may be necessary in some instances, but extermination — no. May be seen, or heard, in Mt. McKinley and Isle Royale Natl. Parks and Algonquin Provincial Park.   Map p. 76

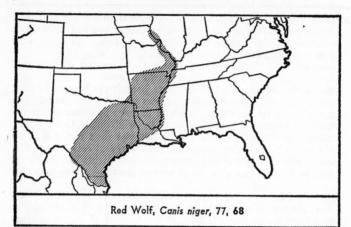

Red Wolf, *Canis niger*, 77, **68**

Gray Wolf, *Canis lupus*, 75, **68**

RED WOLF *Canis niger* p. 68

Recognition: Head and body 42–49 in.; tail 13–17 in.; wt. 30–80 lb. This southern wolf varies in color from *reddish gray to nearly black*, with tawny muzzle, ears, and outer parts of legs. Small individuals in light-color phase are difficult to distinguish from Coyote. Runs with *tail held high*, not down between legs. Eyeshine gold to bluish green. Skull has 42 teeth.

Similar species: Coyote — usually smaller and reddish gray; runs with tail between legs; nose pad less than 1 in. wide.

Habitat: Brushy and forested areas, river bottoms.

Habits: Probably similar to Coyote's (p. 74). Feeds primarily on small mammals and birds, also crabs along Gulf Coast.

Young: Born April or May; 4–7 pups.

Economic status: Undoubtedly kills some domestic animals and game species, but also destroys rodents and rabbits that compete with grazing livestock. Map opposite

RED FOX *Vulpes fulva* p. 68

Recognition: Head and body 22–25 in.; tail 14–16 in.; wt. 10–15 lb. Appearance of small dog; normally *reddish yellow*, darkest on back; belly white; *bushy tail* mixed with black hairs and *tipped with white;* legs and feet *black*. There are many color variations: cross, with dark area (cross) over shoulders and down middle of back; black phase (silver), black with white-tipped body hairs and white tip on tail; intermediates between above. Skull (p. 257) has 42 teeth. There are 8 mammae.

Some authors consider this and the Old World Red Fox as one species (*V. vulpes*).

Similar species: (1) Coyote, (2) Swift Fox, (3) Kit Fox, (4) Gray Fox, (5) Marten (p. 57), and (6) Fisher (p. 59) — no white tip on tail. (7) Arctic Fox — all-white or without white tip on tail.

Habitat: Mixture of forest and open country preferred.

Habits: Most active at night, early morning, and late evening; often active during day. Food consists of available animals ranging in size from insects to hares; berries and other fruits round out diet; often cache rabbits, mice, or other animals near trails, especially when there is a cover of snow. Male brings food to vixen for a few days after pups are born; later both bring food to young in den; usually one or more spare dens so pups may be moved on short notice if home den is disturbed; dens normally on slopes in porous soil. Home range, 1 to 2 sq. mi., but often travels greater distances, especially in winter. Known to have moved 126 mi. from birth den. Male and female probably mate for the year.

Young: Born March or April, depending on latitude; 4–9; gestation period about 51 days; 1 litter a year. Dark brown with white tip on tail; eyes closed. Pups remain in den for about a month, then come to entrance to play and feed; leave parents in fall and shift for themselves.

Economic status: In much of its range the Red Fox has a bounty on its head. Whether it is beneficial or harmful depends on circumstances. If it kills a few pheasants, grouse, or rabbits, the hunter will consider it harmful, but if it kills hundreds of

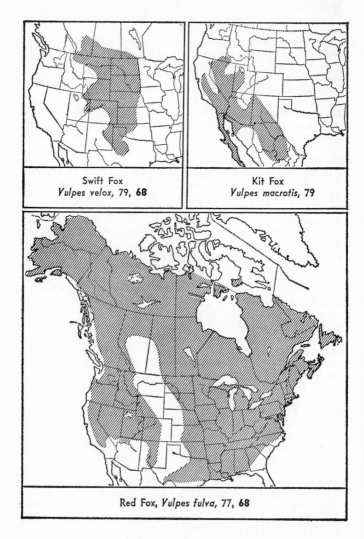

Swift Fox
Vulpes velox, 79, **68**

Kit Fox
Vulpes macrotis, 79

Red Fox, *Vulpes fulva,* 77, **68**

mice and rats the farmer might consider it beneficial. Many sportsmen enjoy hunting the fox when other seasons are closed. Actually foxes do more good than harm, as shown by many food studies. All bounties should be removed. May be seen in most parks within its range.   Map opposite

SWIFT FOX *Vulpes velox*   p. 68
Recognition: Head and body 15–20 in.; tail 9–12 in.; wt. 4–6 lb. This small, large-eared, pale *buffy-yellow* fox with a blackish spot on either side of its snout and a *black tip* on its *bushy tail* is now rare over much of its range. Skull has 42 teeth.
Similar species: (1) Red Fox — white tip on tail. (2) Gray Fox — black streak along top of tail. (3) Coyote — larger.
Habitat: Open desert and plains.
Habits: Feeds mostly on small mammals, also insects; dens in ground burrows. Less wary than other foxes; easily trapped.
Young: Born Feb.–April; 4–7 pups.
Economic status: Probably wholly beneficial; has suffered from poison campaigns for other predators; should be protected.
                                                                  Map opposite

KIT FOX *Vulpes macrotis*
Recognition: Head and body 15–20 in.; tail 9–12 in.; wt. 3–6 lb. A small, slender fox with exceptionally *large ears;* body pale gray washed with rusty; belly whitish; *black tip* on tail. Skull has 42 teeth.
  This may be a subspecies of *V. velox.*
Similar species: (1) Red Fox — larger; white tip on tail. (2) Gray Fox — larger; black streak along top of tail. (3) Coyote — larger. (4) Black-footed Ferret (p. 62) — feet black, tail not bushy.
Habitat: Open, level, sandy ground preferred; low desert vegetation, junipers.
Habits: Remains in burrow during day and forages at night; feeds on small desert rodents.
Young: Born Feb.–April; 4–7 pups.
Economic status: Beneficial; destroys many rodents; now rare because of poison campaigns.   Map opposite

ARCTIC FOX *Alopex lagopus*   p. 68
Recognition: Head and body 20± in.; tail 11± in.; wt. 7–15 lb. This far-northern fox has *short, rounded ears* and heavily furred feet, as becomes an arctic mammal. There are 2 color phases, *blue* and *white.* Both phases are similar in summer — dull *brownish* to slate with yellowish white on belly, sides of neck, and flanks; in winter, white phase is *white* throughout; the blue phase is *slate-blue*, sometimes with brownish on head and feet. No white tip on tail. On Pribilof I. they are all-blue. Skull has 42 teeth.

Similar species: (1) Red Fox — reddish yellow with white tip on tail. (2) Coyote — larger.

Habitat: Tundra of Far North, mostly near shores.

Habits: Scavenger in the true sense; follows Polar Bear in winter and eats scraps from his table; dead marine mammals, fish, or other animals on shore are eaten; also eats lemmings, hares, birds, and eggs, as well as berries in season. Dens on well-drained slopes. Home range limited until pups are able to take care of themselves; wanders widely throughout winter. Populations fluctuate, highs and lows follow those of lemmings by about 1 year. Has lived 14 years in captivity. Not as shy as most other foxes. Voice a sharp bark, heard especially during breeding season.

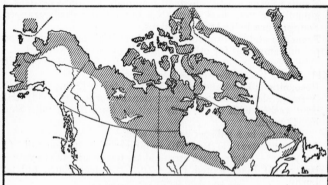

Arctic Fox, *Alopex lagopus*, 79, **68**

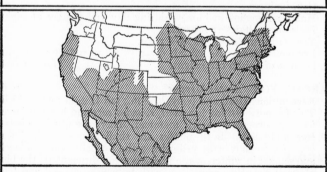

Gray Fox, *Urocyon cinereoargenteus*, 81, **68**

Young: Born April–June; 1–14 (usually 5–6); gestation period 51–54 days. Pups dark brown, blind.

Economic status: The economy of the Eskimo is closely tied to Arctic Fox abundance; this little fox had a large share in building the Hudson's Bay Company; definitely valuable to the Far North country; ranches established on some islands. Flesh edible.   Map opposite

GRAY FOX   *Urocyon cinereoargenteus*   p. 68
Recognition: Head and body 21–29 in.; tail 11–16 in.; wt. 7–13 lb. The *pepper-and-salt* coat with buffy underfur, long *bushy tail* with a *median black stripe* down its total length (and *tipped with black*), and the rusty-yellowish sides of neck, backs of ears, legs, and feet will serve to distinguish it. Skull (p. 257) has 42 teeth. There are 6 mammae.

The Gray Foxes on the Santa Barbara Is., California (*U. littoralis*), and along the Pacific Coast (*U. californicus*) have been considered as separate species by some authors. One occurrence at Lake Athabaska, not shown on map.

Similar species: (1) Red Fox — white tip on tail. (2) Swift and (3) Kit Foxes — black of tail only at tip. (4) Coyote — larger; black of tail only at tip.

Habitat: Chaparral, open forests, rimrock country.

Habits: Chiefly nocturnal, secretive. Will climb trees to escape enemies. Omnivorous; eats chiefly small mammals, but adds insects, fruits, acorns, birds, and eggs. Dens in hollow logs, beneath boulders, or sometimes in ground burrows. Has moved over 50 mi. from place of release. Has lived 10 years in captivity. Speed of 28 mph for short distances. Mates in Feb. or March.

Young: Born April–May; 3–7; gestation period 51± days. Pups dark brown, blind.

Economic status: Fur of some value. A wonderful mouser; rarely invades poultry yards; probably wholly beneficial. May be seen in most of the western parks.   Map opposite

Cats: Felidae

THIS family, to which the House Cat belongs, is familiar to most people. Except for color and size, cats all look about alike. They have *short faces*, relatively small rounded ears, and *retractile claws*. They have 5 toes on each front foot, 4 on each back foot. Known as fossils first in Lower Pliocene.

JAGUAR   *Felis onca*   p. 69
Recognition: Head and body 44–58 in.; tail 21–26 in.; height at shoulder 27–30 in.; wt. 150–225 lb. This large tawny cat is uniformly spotted with black. *Spots* on sides and back *form*

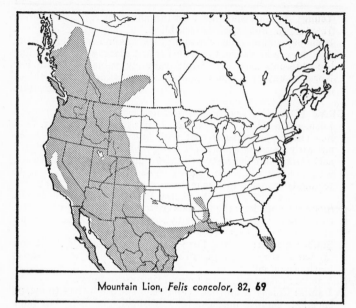

Mountain Lion, *Felis concolor,* 82, **69**

rosettes, a ring of black with a small black spot in the center; belly white with black spots. Eyeshine golden. Skull has 30 teeth. Rare in s. U.S.

Similar species: (1) Ocelot and (2) Margay Cat — small; spots do not form rosettes. (3) Mountain Lion — uniform color.

Habitat: Low mts., chaparral, open forests.

Habits: Not well known. Feeds on Peccaries and other mammals, also turtles and fish; preys on livestock when available. Breeds in Jan.

Young: Born April–May; 2–4; gestation period 99–105 days.

Economic status: Of little importance in U.S. because of its rareness; does destroy domestic stock.   Map opposite

MOUNTAIN LION   *Felis concolor*   p. 69
(Cougar, Puma, Panther)

   Recognition: Head and body 42–54 in.; tail 30–36 in.; height at shoulders 26–31 in.; wt. 80–200 lb. This large, *tawny to grayish* cat, with *dark brown on tip of long tail* and on backs of ears and sides of nose, is fast disappearing from the scene. Eyeshine greenish gold. Skull (p. 257) has 30 teeth. There are 8 mammae (6 functional).

   Similar species: (1) Jaguarundi Cat — smaller. (2) Jaguar — spotted.

Habitat: Rugged mts., forests, swamps.
Habits: Chiefly nocturnal, but may be abroad during day. Secretive, seldom seen. Most at home on ground, but climbs trees, especially to evade dogs. Feeds largely on deer, but also takes hares, rodents, and occasionally domestic animals; caches uneaten portions of kills; won't eat tainted meat. Dens in any sheltered spot that is concealed. Roams widely except when cubs are small; may move 75–100 mi. from place of birth. Has lived 18 years in captivity. Voice like ordinary tomcat, but much magnified. Breeds first at 2 or 3 years, then every 2 or 3 years; mates for season.
Young: May be born any month of year; 1–6, usually 2; gestation period 88–97 days. Cubs spotted; eyes open at about 10 days.
Economic status: Now inhabits mostly wilderness areas; kills

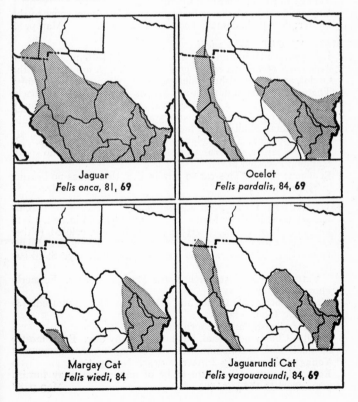

Jaguar
Felis onca, 81, **69**

Ocelot
Felis pardalis, 84, **69**

Margay Cat
Felis wiedi, 84

Jaguarundi Cat
Felis yagouaroundi, 84, **69**

some domestic animals, but mainly deer; a few Mountain Lions are good for the deer herd, but few sportsmen see it this way.   Map p. 82

OCELOT *Felis pardalis*   p. 69
Recognition: Head and body 27–35 in.; tail 13–15 in.; wt. 20–40 lb. This small, *spotted* cat with a long tail does not have the rosettes of the Jaguar. Some of the *dark markings* are *elongate*, more nearly stripes than spots. Eyeshine golden. Skull has 30 teeth. There are 4 mammae.
Similar species: (1) Margay Cat — smaller. (2) Jaguar — larger, with rosettes. (3) Jaguarundi Cat — no spots.
Habitat: Thick thorn scrub, rocky areas.
Habits: Probably similar to those of other cats; little known; said to kill some domestic stock.
Young: Born in autumn; normally 2.
Economic status: Skins valuable as trophies; offers sport to the hunter; does little damage because of rareness.   Map p. 83

MARGAY CAT *Felis wiedi*
Recognition: Head and body 20–23 in.; tail 14–16 in.; wt. 5–7 lb. This *small spotted* cat rarely gets into s. U.S. A miniature of the Ocelot, and distinguished chiefly by size. Ground color is buffy. There are 4 broken dark brown stripes on neck and 1 on back; brown spots on sides irregular in shape; some have dark buffy centers, giving a rosette-like appearance. Belly white, with dark brown spots. Skull has 30 teeth.
Similar species: (1) Ocelot — larger, coloration similar. (2) Jaguar — larger, with rosettes. (3) Jaguarundi Cat — no spots.
Habitat: Forested areas.
Economic status: This cat so rare in U.S. that it has no bearing on the economy.   Map p. 83

JAGUARUNDI CAT *Felis yagouaroundi*   p. 69
Recognition: Head and body 22–30 in.; tail 13–24 in.; wt. 15–18 lb. This long-bodied, short-legged, uniformly colored (either *reddish* or *bluish-gray*) cat is about twice the size of an ordinary House Cat. Tail is nearly as long as head and body. Skull has 30 teeth.
   Extremely rare just north of the Mexican border. Formerly known as *F. eyra*.
Similar species: (1) Ocelot and (2) Margay Cat — spotted. (3) Mountain Lion — larger.
Habitat: Brushy areas, thorn thickets.
Habits: Chiefly nocturnal, but hunts also by day. Feeds mostly on small birds and mammals.
Young: 2–3; probably 2 litters a year. Not spotted.
Economic status: Too rare to be of importance; may furnish some sport to the hunter.   Map p. 83

LYNX (Canada Lynx)   *Lynx canadensis*   p. 69
Recognition: Head and body 32–36 in.; tail 4 in.; wt. 15–30 lb.
This *bob-tailed* cat of the north country is distinguished by the
short tail, with a *completely black tip*, and tufted ears. Skull has
28 teeth. There are 4 mammae.

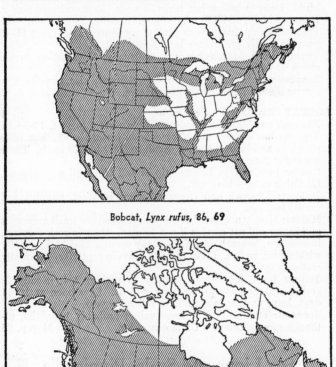

Bobcat, *Lynx rufus*, 86, **69**

Lynx, *Lynx canadensis*, 85, **69**

Similar species: Bobcat — tip of tail black only on top.
Habitat: Forested areas, swamps.
Habits: Primarily nocturnal and solitary. Extremely large feet enable it to travel easily over deep snow. Feeds for the most part on Snowshoe Hares; diet supplemented with rodents and birds. Dens in hollow log, beneath roots, other sheltered places. Ranges widely, up to 50 mi. or more. Breeding range about 5 mi. Populations fluctuate, with peak every 9–10 years. Lives 15–18 years in captivity. Mates Jan.–Feb.
Young: Born March–April; 1–4, usually 2; gestation period about 62 days.
Economic status: A valuable fur mammal; also benefits new forests by eliminating Snowshoe Hares.   Map p. 85

BOBCAT (Bay Lynx)   *Lynx rufus*   p. 69
Recognition: Head and body 25–30 in.; tail 5 in.; wt. 15–35 lb. This cat has a short tail *black only on top at the tip.* Ear tufts are short and inconspicuous. Skull (p. 257) has 28 teeth. There are 6 mammae.
Similar species: (1) Lynx — tip of tail black all way around. (2) Other cats — long tail.
Habitat: Rimrock and chaparral areas in West, swamps and forests in East.
Habits: Mostly nocturnal and solitary. Feeds on small mammals and birds; will eat carrion if not tainted. Dens in rock crevices, hollow logs, beneath downfalls. May wander 25–50 mi., usually within 2-mi. radius. Lives 15 to 25 years in captivity. Normally mates in spring.
Young: Born any month, mostly in spring; 2–4, usually 2; gestation period 50–60 days; wt. 4–8 oz. Eyes open at 10–11 days; leave mother in autumn or following year.
Economic status: Fur of some value; probably beneficial, although some sportsmen think otherwise.   Map p. 85

Sea Lions and Seals: Pinnipedia

MOSTLY marine mammals with front and hind limbs developed into *flippers*. They haul out onto land or ice to rest and to give birth to young. Usually seen only *along shores*, although they may go far out to sea when in migration.

Sea Lions and Fur Seals: Otariidae

MEMBERS of this family have external ears (eared seals); hind foot (flipper) can be turned forward so they can "walk" on land. Males are distinctly larger than females (as much as 4½ times). Skull has 34–38 teeth (variable). There are 4 mammae. Known as fossils from Lower Miocene.

Similar species: Sea Otter (p. 65) — smaller; longer tail; usually in kelp bed.

Habitat: Haul out onto rocky beaches and offshore rocks.

Young: Born on land, June–July; normally 1. Pup does not enter water for 2 weeks or more.

NORTHERN SEA LION *Eumetopias jubata*   p. 90
(Steller Sea Lion)

    Recognition: Head and body: males to 10½ ft.; females to 7 ft. Wt.: males to 2000 lb.; females to 600 lb. *Large yellowish-brown* to brown sea lions; *low forehead.* Usually fairly *quiet* when not molested.

    Similar species: (1) California Sea Lion — smaller, darker; high forehead; usually barking. (2) Alaska Fur Seal — much smaller; reddish below; face brown. (3) Harbor Seal — smaller, spotted.

    Habits: Gregarious; chiefly marine, but sometimes goes up rivers; able to dive to 80 fathoms. Feeds mostly on fish and squids. Estimated population for Pacific Coast, N. America (1955), 54,500; for Pribilofs only (1961), 5700–6700. Polygamous, harems of 10–15 cows. Breeds soon after pups are born.

    Economic status: Robs fishermen of some fish; hides used by Eskimos to cover boats.

    Range: Pacific Coast, Santa Rosa I., California, northward. Seen off coast at San Francisco.

CALIFORNIA SEA LION *Zalophus californianus*   p. 90

    Recognition: Head and body: males to 8 ft.; females to 6 ft. Wt.: males to 600 lb.; females to 200 lb. This is a *small brown* (blackish when wet) sea lion with a *high forehead.* Has small, pointed ears and large eyes. *Continual honking bark* is also characteristic. This is the circus "seal."

    Similar species: (1) Northern Sea Lion — larger, paler; low forehead; seldom barks when not molested. (2) Guadalupe Fur Seal — forehead low, nose pointed, silvery on neck and head. (3) Elephant Seal — much larger; no external ears; usually quiet. (4) Harbor Seal — spotted.

    Habits: Gregarious; marine, occasionally seen on sandy beaches. Can swim 10 mph when after food. Principal food, fish and squids. Estimated population for N. America (1955), 50,000–100,000. Has lived 23 years in captivity. Polygamous; females breed at 3 years, males at 5. Breeds shortly after pups are born.

    Economic status: Does some damage to fishnets; eats fish. Valuable as a trained show mammal.

    Range: Pacific Coast; occasionally as far north as B.C.; normally to Monterey Bay, California. May be seen off coast of s. California.

GUADALUPE FUR SEAL *Arctocephalus philippi*
Recognition: Head and body: males to 5½ ft.; females to 4½ ft. Wt.: males to 300± lb. This rare fur seal has a *pointed muzzle;* it is dark brown, with a *silvery grizzling of head and neck.* Sides of snout are rusty.
Formerly known as *A. townsendi.*
Similar species: (1) California Sea Lion — larger; high forehead. (2) Elephant Seal — much larger; male has proboscis. (3) Harbor Seal — spotted.
Habits: Marine; now on offshore islands; formerly thought to be extinct; estimated total population, mostly off Mexican coast (1955), 200–500.
Range: Pacific Coast, north to San Nicolas I., California.

ALASKA FUR SEAL *Callorhinus ursinus*   p. 90
Recognition: Head and body: males to 6 ft.; females to 4½ ft. Wt.: males to 600 lb.; females to 135 lb. Males *blackish above, reddish on belly,* and gray on shoulders and front of neck; face *brownish.* Females gray above, reddish below.
Similar species: (1) Northern Sea Lion — larger; not reddish below. (2) Harbor Seal — spotted.
Habits: Gregarious; spends 6–8 months of each year at sea. Top swimming speed 17 mph; can dive to 30 fathoms. Feeds on 30 or more kinds of marine animals, mostly fish and squids; males can fast for over 2 months. Estimated population for N. America (1960), 5700–6700 adults. Polygamous; harems of 40 or more. Females breed at 3 years. Breeds soon after pups are born, on land.
Economic status: The Alaskan herd is now managed, and about ⅘ of the 3- and 4-year bachelors are harvested each year, pelts for fur and meat for oil and meal. The original purchase price of Alaska ($7,200,000) has been returned severalfold to the U.S. Treasury over the years through the fur-seal operations.
Range: Pacific Coast, south to California. Seen principally on the *Pribilof Is.* and at other localities in the Bering Sea. In winter, may be seen as far south as California.

Walrus: Odobenidae

HIND feet (flippers) can be turned forward; both sexes have large tusks projecting downward from upper jaw; males larger than females; nearly nude; 18–24 teeth; 4 mammae. Known as fossils from Upper Miocene.

WALRUS *Odobenus rosmarus*   p. 90
Recognition: Head and body: males to 12 ft.; females to 9 ft. Wt.: males to 2700 lb.; females to 1800 lb. A huge seal with 2

large, white tusks; bay color when dry, black when wet. No other marine mammal has these characters.

Habitat: Ice floes and islands in Arctic.

Habits: Usually found in groups. Bottom-feeder in fairly shallow water (50 fathoms or less); grubs mollusks and other marine life from bottom with tusks; rarely swallows any shell; occasionally eats seals. Estimated total population (1955), 45,000–90,000. Lives 35 years or more. When killed, will sink. Females first breed at 5 or 6 years, then every 2 or 3 years.

Young: Born April–June; 1; gestation period 11–12 months. Wt. to 130 lb.; length 48 in. Calf remains with mother 2 years.

Economic status: One of the most important marine mammals for the Eskimo economy; hide used for lines, boats, etc., meat for dogs as well as Eskimos; meat should be cooked, may contain *Trichinella*. Ivory carvings bring additional income to the Eskimo.

Range: Arctic waters, south into Hudson Bay and northeastern coast of Ungava Pen., and Bering Sea, Alaska.

Hair Seals: Phocidae

HIND flippers cannot be turned forward; must wriggle to move on land; no great disparity in sizes of two sexes; ears indicated by openings in skin, no pinnae. Known as fossils from Middle Miocene.

HARBOR SEAL *Phoca vitulina*   p. 90

Recognition: Head and body to 5 ft.; wt. to 255 lb. A small seal; iron-gray with brown spots, brown with gray spots, or uniform silver-gray or brownish black. Skull has 34–36 teeth (variable). There are 2 mammae.

Similar species: (1) Sea Lions and (2) Fur Seals (p. 86) — no spots; external ears; can rotate hind flippers forward. (3) Elephant Seal — larger; no spots. (4) Ringed Seal — both spots and streaks along back.

Habitat: Coastal waters, mouths of rivers, and inland lakes; it spends much time on shore.

Habits: Often seen at mouths of rivers and in shallow harbors. Has limited seasonal movements. Can remain 20 min. underwater. Feeds on fish, shellfish, and squids. Populations in N. America estimated (1955), 40,000–100,000. Females first breed at 2 years.

Young: Born on land, early summer; 1, rarely 2; gestation period more than 9 months. Pup bluish gray above, whitish below when born; first whitish pelage usually shed before birth, except possibly in Far North.

Economic status: Eats some commercial fish and damages some

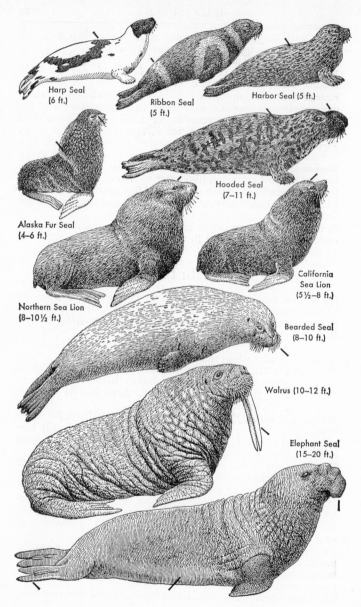

Harp Seal
(6 ft.)

Ribbon Seal
(5 ft.)

Harbor Seal (5 ft.)

Alaska Fur Seal
(4–6 ft.)

Hooded Seal
(7–11 ft.)

California
Sea Lion
(5½–8 ft.)

Northern Sea Lion
(8–10½ ft.)

Bearded Seal
(8–10 ft.)

Walrus (10–12 ft.)

Elephant Seal
(15–20 ft.)

fishnets; is utilized as food in Far North; skin of slight value.
Range: Pacific; Atlantic, south to Carolinas; Arctic; Hudson
Bay; Seal Lakes (freshwater) on Ungava Pen.

RINGED SEAL   *Pusa hispida*
Recognition: Head and body to 4½ ft.; wt. to 200 lb. This small,
dull *yellowish* to *brownish* seal has *dark spots* and *streaks* that
are usually continuous *along the back.* There are pale buffy rings
on the sides. Belly is yellowish, sometimes spotted. Skull has
34–36 teeth. There are 2 mammae.
   Formerly known as *Phoca.*
Similar species: Harbor Seal — no streaks.
Habitat: Cold waters, usually near ice, not far from shore.
Habits: Not gregarious, but occasionally found in small groups.
Either finds open water or keeps hole open in ice in winter.
Can remain underwater 20 min.; normally hauls out onto ice
to rest and sleep. Feeds mostly on marine invertebrates. Esti-
mated population for N. America (1955), 2–5 million. May live
40 years or more. Females breed in 5th year.
Young: Born on ice; 1; gestation period about 9 months. Woolly,
white pup sheds to darker coat in 2 weeks.
Economic status: An important item in the economy of the
Eskimo; both skin and meat are utilized. Known to carry
Trichinella; meat should be cooked.
Range: Arctic Ocean, south to Labrador, Hudson Bay, and
Bristol Bay, Alaska; also found in freshwater lake (Nettilling)
on Baffin I.

RIBBON SEAL   *Histriophoca fasciata*   p. 90
Recognition: Head and body to 5 ft. Wt.: males to 200 lb.;
females to 170 lb. This small, brown seal has *bands of yellowish
white* around *neck,* around *front flipper,* and around *rump.*
Females less brightly colored than males. The only seal with
above markings. Skull has 34–36 teeth. There are 2 mammae.
   Formerly known as *Phoca.*
Habitat: Ice packs of Arctic.
Habits: Occurs singly or in small groups; a rare, little-known
seal. Total population estimate (1955), 20,000–50,000.
Young: Born on ice in spring; 1. Pup covered with white fur;
eyes open.
Economic status: Of little importance because of rarity.
Range: Pacific-Arctic, south to Alaska Pen.

HARP SEAL   *Pagophilus groenlandicus*   p. 90
(Saddleback Seal)
Recognition: Head and body to 6 ft.; wt. to 400 lb. This northern seal is grayish or yellowish, with a *dark brown or black face*
and a dark, irregular band that crosses the shoulders and extends
back along sides, sometimes over rump. Smaller spots may be

present on flippers and neck. Females less distinctly marked or without dark markings; young *yellowish white*. No other seal has the above markings. Skull has 34–36 teeth. There are 2 mammae.

Formerly known as *Phoca groenlandica*.

Habitat: Deep seas with drifting pack ice.

Habits: Makes long migrations; can dive 100 fathoms. Feeds on macroplankton and fish. Populations on pack ice nearly 2000 per sq. mi.; total N. American population estimate (1955), 3 million. Lives 30 years or more. Females breed in 5th year.

Young: Born on pack ice; 1 (occasionally 2). Pup covered with white fur; eyes open.

Economic status: More than 200,000 seals are harvested annually in w. North Atlantic. Skins of pups are used for clothing, skins of adults for leather. Oil is extracted from the carcasses.

Range: Atlantic-Arctic; west to mouth of Mackenzie River, south to Hudson Bay and Gulf of St. Lawrence; rarely south to Virginia.

GRAY SEAL   *Halichoerus grypus*

Recognition: Head and body: males to 10 ft.; females to 7½ ft. Wt.: males to 640 lb.; females to 550 lb. A *large* black or grayish seal with a Roman nose; *size* and *plain color* characterize it. Skull has 34–36 teeth. There are 2 mammae.

Habitat: Rocky shores, temperate waters, strong currents.

Habits: Dives to 80 fathoms; can remain underwater 20 min. Canadian population estimated at about 5000; a fairly rare seal. Lives 40 years or more. Polygamous; harems of about 10.

Young: Born on land in early winter; 1. Pup covered with white fur; eyes open.

Economic status: Of little importance because of small numbers.

Range: Labrador, south to St. Lawrence River, rarely to New Jersey.

BEARDED SEAL   *Erignathus barbatus*   p. 90
(Square Flipper)

Recognition: Head and body: males to 10 ft.; females to 8 ft. Wt.: males to 875 lb. This seal is uniformly dark *grayish to yellowish*. Has a prominent *tuft* of long flattened *bristles* on *each side of muzzle*, characteristic of this, and no other, seal. Skull has 34–36 teeth. There are 4 mammae.

Habitat: Shallow waters (15–25 fathoms) at edge of ice; mouths of creeks, small bays.

Habits: Solitary except during breeding season, when up to 50 may be seen on ice; occasionally goes up rivers some distance. Swims with head out of water; entire body breaks surface as it loops to dive. Feeds on bottom. Total population estimate (1955), 50,000–100,000.

Young: Born on ice; 1. Pup covered with dark fur; eyes open.
Economic status: A fairly important seal in the economy of the Eskimo. Its thick hide makes good boot bottoms and harpoon lines. Meat should be cooked because of possible *Trichinella* infection.
Range: Arctic waters, south to Bering Sea, Hudson Bay, and Ungava Bay.

CARIBBEAN MONK SEAL *Monachus tropicalis*
Recognition: Head and body to 10 ft. Uniformly brown, slightly paler below; no spots. Skull has 32–34 teeth. There are 4 mammae. Only seal in Caribbean.
Habitat: Tropical waters.
Habits: Supposedly monogamous; rather sluggish.
Young: Pups black; eyes open.
Range: Rarely north to s. Texas and Key West.

HOODED SEAL (Bladdernose) *Cystophora cristata* p. 90
Recognition: Head and body to 11 ft.; wt. to 900 lb. A *dark gray to slaty-black* seal with *paler sides*, which are *spotted with whitish*. On top of head of male is an inflatable bag. When male is angry this is "blown up" and makes the animal appear more formidable. Skull has 26–34 teeth.
Habitat: Deep waters with thick ice.
Habits: Nomadic. Occurs in small numbers except during breeding and molting times. Total population estimated (1955) at more than 300,000. Monogamous.
Young: Born on ice, late Feb.; 1. Pup white or covered with dark fur (white embryonic coat may be shed before birth); eyes open.
Economic status: Numbers have been reduced to where they are of minor importance.
Range: Arctic-Atlantic waters, south to St. Lawrence River; accidentally as far south as Florida.

ELEPHANT SEAL *Mirounga angustirostris* p. 90
Recognition: Head and body: males to 20 ft.; females to 11 ft. Wt.: males to 8000 lb.; females to 2000 lb. These large seals are pale *brown to grayish*, lighter on belly; nearly nude. Old males have large, overhanging, *proboscis-like snouts*. Largest of the seals where they occur. Skull has 26–34 teeth.
Similar species: (1) Sea Lions and (2) Fur Seals (p. 86) — much smaller; have external ears; can rotate hind flippers forward. (3) Harbor Seal — smaller; usually spotted.
Habitat: Warm waters, sandy beaches.
Habits: Gregarious. Lie close together on sandy beaches and sleep by day. Feed on small sharks, squid, rays during night;

can fast 3 months. Total population estimate (1955), 8000–
10,000. Polygamous.
Young: Born on land; 1. Pup covered with dusky brown fur;
eyes open.
Economic status: Now fully protected; once nearly extinct.
Range: Pacific, north to San Miguel and San Nicolas Is., California; accidentally to B.C.

Gnawing Mammals: Rodentia

THE order of rodents is made up of small to medium-sized mammals. All are characterized by having only *2 incisors* (gnawing
teeth) *above* and *2 below.* There is a distinct *space* between these
teeth and the grinding (or cheek) teeth. Most, but not all, have 4
toes on each front foot, 5 on each hind foot. Earliest rodents
known as fossils are from Late Paleocene.
Similar kinds: Rabbits and Hares. These have a small pair of
incisors immediately behind the large upper incisors, not apparent
from the outside. They also have short, cottony tails.

Aplodontia: Aplodontiidae

THIS family of rodents, now restricted to a small strip along the
western coast of N. America, contains but 1 species. It is presumed
to be the most primitive living rodent. It has 5 toes on each foot,
but the thumb is much reduced and without a claw. Skull (p. 249)
has 22 teeth. There are 6 mammae. Known as fossils from Upper
Eocene.

APLODONTIA (Mountain Beaver)   *Aplodontia rufa*   p. 196
   Recognition: Head and body 12–17 in.; tail 1–1⅛ in.; wt. 2–3
   lb. This dark brown rodent, the size of a small House Cat but
   chunkier, has small rounded ears and small eyes. By size, color,
   and apparent absence of a tail, it may be distinguished from all
   other mammals in the area. It looks like a tailless Muskrat.
   Habitat: Forests and dense thickets, usually moist situations.
   Habits: More active at night than during day. Makes extensive
   tunnels, runways, and burrows beneath dense streamside vegetation; in diam. burrows are 6–10 in. Rarely climbs trees. Feeds
   on herbaceous plants and shrubs of many kinds; builds hay
   piles along runways in late summer and early autumn. Home
   range not known, but probably less than 400 yds. Females first
   breed at 2 years.
   Young: Born March–April; usually 2–3; gestation period 28–30
   days; 1 litter a year. Young slate-brown.

Economic status: In the wild areas the Aplodontia is of little importance, but it can be a nuisance in reforestation projects; also, it may raid truck gardens and cause general damage by its persistent burrowing. Meat is strong and the hide is worthless. It is an interesting element in the biological world, probably its only asset.   Map below

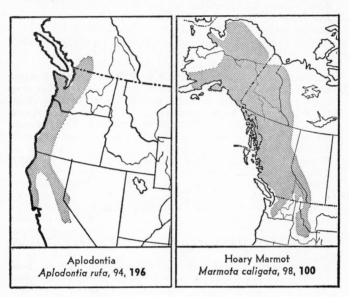

Aplodontia
Aplodontia rufa, 94, **196**

Hoary Marmot
Marmota caligata, 98, **100**

Squirrels: Sciuridae

THIS family includes a wide variety of mammals. Marmots, woodchucks, prairie dogs, ground squirrels, chipmunks, and tree squirrels all belong here. They have 4 toes on front foot, 5 on back. Tail is always covered with hair, is sometimes bushy. All are *active during the daytime* except the flying squirrels, which come out only at night. Marmots, ground squirrels, prairie dogs, and chipmunks all nest in burrows in the ground or beneath rocks or logs. Tree squirrels and flying squirrels nest in trees. Most of the ground-living species have a habit of sitting up "picket pin" fashion on their haunches. This enables them to see over low vegetation and avert danger. Ground squirrels and chipmunks have internal cheek pouches; most of them store food. Known as fossils from as far back as Miocene.

WOODCHUCK   *Marmota monax*   p. 100
(Ground Hog, Marmot)

Recognition: Head and body 16–20 in.; tail 4–7 in.; wt. 5–10 lb.
This heavy-bodied, short-legged, *yellowish-brown to brown* animal
is best known in the eastern part of its range. Belly paler than
the back; hairs on body have a slightly *frosted* appearance; feet
dark brown or black; no white except around nose. Skull (p. 249)
has 22 teeth. There are 8 mammae.

Similar species: (1) Hoary Marmot — black and white on head
and shoulders. (2) Arctic Ground Squirrel (p. 107) — smaller;
feet not black.

Habitat: Open woods, brushy and rocky ravines.

Habits: Diurnal for most part; may wander at night in early
spring. Feeds on tender, succulent plants. Dens in extensive
burrow with 2 or more openings; may be 4–5 ft. deep and 25–30
ft. long; known to have excavated dirt at 1 opening, others dug
from below, concealed. Hibernates Oct.–Feb. Home range,
40–160 acres. Voice a shrill whistle. Lives 4–5 years. Mates in
March or April; breeds at 1 year.

Young: Born April–May; 2–6; gestation period 31–32 days;
1 litter a year. Naked; blind.

Economic status: In an agricultural area the Woodchuck can
do considerable damage to crops; in other areas it is probably
beneficial, since its burrows are refuges and homes for many
other mammals — game and furbearers.   Map opposite

YELLOWBELLY MARMOT   *Marmota flaviventris*   p. 100
(Rockchuck)

Recognition: Head and body 14–19 in.; tail 4½–9 in.; wt. 5–10
lb. This is a heavy-bodied, *yellowish-brown* marmot with *yellow
belly*, and usually with *white between the eyes*. Sides of neck have
conspicuous buffy patches. Feet are light buff to dark brown,
never black. Skull has 22 teeth. There are 10 mammae.

Similar species: Hoary Marmot — conspicuous white and black
head and shoulders.

Habitat: Rocky situations, talus slopes, valleys and foothills;
up to 12,000-ft. elevation.

Habits: Chiefly diurnal. Feeds on most grasses, relishes alfalfa.
Den usually near large boulder, which is used as lookout post.
Goes into estivation in late June, hibernation in Aug.; emerges
in late Feb. or March. High-pitched chirp at short intervals
warns of danger.

Young: Born March–April; 3–6. Emerge from den at about
30 days.

Economic status: Does serious damage to crops, especially
alfalfa, locally; away from agricultural areas, especially in parks,
has definite aesthetic value. Furnishes sport for some hunters.
It hosts the tick for Rocky Mountain spotted fever.

                                                  Map opposite

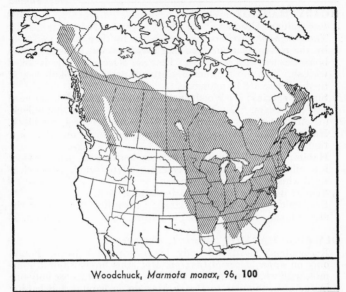

Woodchuck, *Marmota monax*, 96, **100**

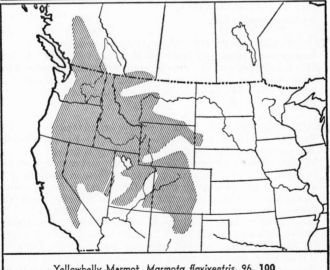

Yellowbelly Marmot, *Marmota flaviventris*, 96, **100**

HOARY MARMOT (Whistler) *Marmota caligata* p. 100
Recognition: Head and body 18–21 in.; tail 7–10 in.; wt. 8–20 lb.
These *high-mt.* dwellers may be known by their *shrill whistle* or
by the *black and white head and shoulders* and general grayish
body washed with yellowish. Feet are *black* and belly is soiled
whitish. Seen most commonly around *rockslides.* Skull has 22
teeth. There are 10 mammae.
Similar species: (1) Woodchuck — no black and white on head
and shoulders. (2) Yellowbelly Marmot — feet not black.
(3) Arctic Ground Squirrel (p. 107) — smaller; feet not black.
Habitat: Talus slopes, alpine meadows, high in mts. near
timberline.
Habits: Diurnal. Feeds on various herbaceous plants. Goes
into hibernation in Sept. and emerges in late spring. Issues clear
shrill whistle from lookout post.
Young: Born late spring or early summer; 4–5.
Economic status: Does no damage; furnishes pleasure for the
alpine hiker who is interested in nature. Map p. 95

OLYMPIC MARMOT *Marmota olympus*
Recognition: Head and body 18–21 in.; tail 7–10 in. Found
only on *upper slopes* of *Olympic Mts.,* this brownish-drab marmot, with white intermixed, and with brown feet, is the only one
in the area. Similar to Hoary Marmot in habitat and habits;
may belong to same species.
Range: Olympic Pen.

VANCOUVER MARMOT *Marmota vancouverensis*
Recognition: Head and body 16–18 in.; tail 8–12 in. A dark
brown marmot, not likely to be confused with any other kind
of mammal on Vancouver I. Similar to Hoary Marmot in
habitat and habits (above); may belong to same species.
Range: Vancouver I.

BLACKTAIL PRAIRIE DOG *Cynomys ludovicianus* p. 101
Recognition: Head and body 11–13 in.; tail 3–4 in.; wt. 2–3 lb.
The presence of the Blacktail Prairie Dog is usually revealed
by a group of bare mounds 25–75 ft. apart and each mound 1–2
ft. high. If, sitting erect on top of one of these mounds, there is
a *yellowish* animal slightly smaller than a cat, it is probably a
Blacktail. On closer inspection, it will be found to have the
terminal ⅓ of its short tail *black.* Ears are small and belly is
pale buff or whitish. Skull has 22 teeth. There are 8 mammae.
Similar species: (1) Whitetail Prairie Dog — tip of tail white.
(2) Rock Squirrel — smaller, with longer tail.
Habitat: Dry upland prairies.
Habits: Diurnal; gregarious; lives in "towns." Within the town
are small groups that display territorial behavior toward adja-

cent groups. At least one is on alert while others feed; danger signal is a 2-syllable bark, issued at about 40 per min. Feeds mostly on grasses, but may eat grasshoppers and other insects. Digs own deep burrows; may be dormant for short periods of cold weather, but not true hibernators. Populations vary from 5 to 35 per acre. Has lived 8½ years in captivity. Mating begins last week in Jan. and continues 2–3 weeks; breeds first at 2 years.

Young: Born March–April; 3–5, rarely 8; gestation period 28–32 days. Naked; eyes open at 5 weeks. Come aboveground at 6 weeks.

Economic status: Competes with grazing stock for food; once numerous on prairies, now reduced to few towns through poisoning operations. Colonies are being preserved in Wind Cave Natl. Park, Devils Tower Natl. Monument, and near Lubbock, Texas.   Map p. 102

WHITETAIL PRAIRIE DOG *Cynomys gunnisoni*   p. 101
  Recognition: Head and body 11–12 in.; tail 1¼–2½ in.; wt. 1½–2½ lb. Usually found in *high country*, this small prairie dog is similar in general to the Blacktail Prairie Dog (above). Tail is white-tipped. Skull (p. 249) has 22 teeth. There are 10 mammae.
  Two other species (*C. leucurus* and *C. parvidens*) are recorded in the literature. Subsequent study may show them to belong to this species. All are included on the one map.
  Similar species: (1) Blacktail Prairie Dog — black tip on tail; low country. (2) Rock Squirrel — smaller; longer tail.
  Habitat: Mt. valleys, 5000–8500 ft.; open or slightly brushy country, scattered junipers and pines.
  Habits: Similar to those of the Blacktail Prairie Dog (above), but less likely to be colonial. Estivates in July, and young of the year hibernate with adults from Oct. or Nov. to March in the North and in high mt. valleys. Mates in March or April; young born early May.   Map p. 102

CALIFORNIA GROUND SQUIRREL *Citellus beecheyi* p. 101
  Recognition: Head and body 9–11 in.; tail 5–9 in.; wt. 1–2⅛ lb. Head brownish; body brown, flecked with buffy white or buff; sides of *neck and shoulders whitish;* a conspicuous dark triangle on back between shoulders; belly buff; tail somewhat bushy. Skull has 22 teeth. There are 11–14 (usually 12) mammae. Found also on Santa Catalina I.
  Similar species: (1) Other ground squirrels — all smaller, with shorter, less bushy tails. (2) Western Gray Squirrel (p. 123) — white belly; no buff; tail very bushy.
  Habitat: Pastures, grainfields, slopes with scattered trees; rocky ridges. It avoids thick chaparral and dense woods.

MEDIUM-SIZED MAMMALS

	Map	*Text*
WOODCHUCK, *Marmota monax* Yellowish brown or brown, frosted; feet dark brown or black. NW, E.	97	96
YELLOWBELLY MARMOT, *Marmota flaviventris* Belly yellow; white between eyes. W.	97	96
HOARY MARMOT, *Marmota caligata* Head and shoulders black and white; feet black. NW.	95	98
RINGTAIL, *Bassariscus astutus* Yellowish gray; long tail with rings. SW.	56	56
RACCOON, *Procyon lotor* Black mask; tail with rings. N, S, E, W.	55	54
COATI, *Nasua narica* Grizzled brown; white spots above and below each eye; long tail; long snout. SW.	56	55
BADGER, *Taxidea taxus* Yellowish gray; white stripe on forehead; feet black. W, N Central.	66	67

WOODCHUCK

YELLOWBELLY MARMOT

HOARY MARMOT

RINGTAIL

RACCOON

COATI

BADGER

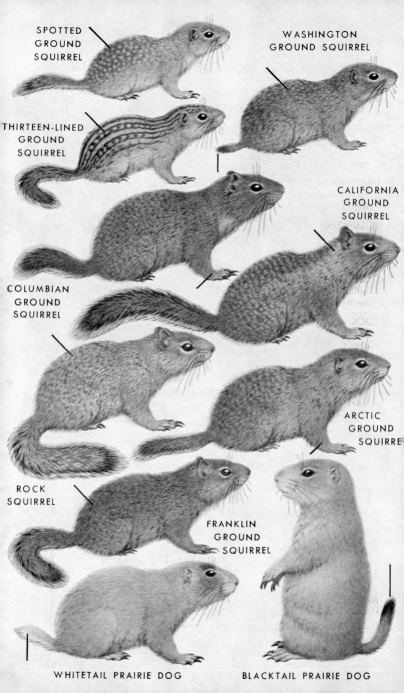

SPOTTED GROUND SQUIRREL

WASHINGTON GROUND SQUIRREL

THIRTEEN-LINED GROUND SQUIRREL

CALIFORNIA GROUND SQUIRREL

COLUMBIAN GROUND SQUIRREL

ARCTIC GROUND SQUIRREL

ROCK SQUIRREL

FRANKLIN GROUND SQUIRREL

WHITETAIL PRAIRIE DOG

BLACKTAIL PRAIRIE DOG

Plate 10   101

GROUND SQUIRRELS AND PRAIRIE DOGS

	Map	*Text*

SPOTTED GROUND SQUIRREL, *Citellus spilosoma*   110   108
 Indistinct squarish spots not in rows. S Central.

WASHINGTON GROUND SQUIRREL   102   104
Citellus washingtoni
 Smoke-gray dappled with whitish; blackish tip on
 short tail. NW.

THIRTEEN-LINED GROUND SQUIRREL   109   107
Citellus tridecemlineatus
 Broken stripes on sides and back. Central.

COLUMBIAN GROUND SQUIRREL   106   105
Citellus columbianus
 Upperparts mottled gray; feet and legs dark rufous.
 NW.

CALIFORNIA GROUND SQUIRREL, *Citellus beecheyi*   102   99
 Sides of neck and shoulders whitish; dark on back
 between shoulders. W.

ROCK SQUIRREL, *Citellus variegatus*   102   103
 Mottled grayish; large; tail slightly bushy; rocky
 areas. SW.

ARCTIC GROUND SQUIRREL, *Citellus undulatus*   106   107
 Top of head reddish; back flecked with white; feet
 and legs tawny. NW.

FRANKLIN GROUND SQUIRREL, *Citellus franklini*   110   111
 Dark gray; large; open prairies. N Central.

WHITETAIL PRAIRIE DOG, *Cynomys gunnisoni*   102   99
 Body yellowish; tip of tail white. W Central.

BLACKTAIL PRAIRIE DOG, *Cynomys ludovicianus*   102   98
 Body yellowish; tip of tail black. W Central.

Prairie dog town

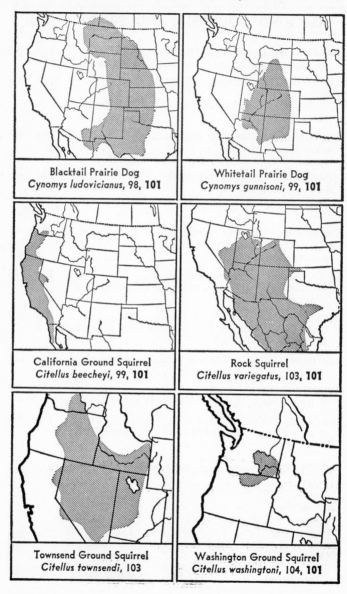

Blacktail Prairie Dog
Cynomys ludovicianus, 98, **101**

Whitetail Prairie Dog
Cynomys gunnisoni, 99, **101**

California Ground Squirrel
Citellus beecheyi, 99, **101**

Rock Squirrel
Citellus variegatus, 103, **101**

Townsend Ground Squirrel
Citellus townsendi, 103

Washington Ground Squirrel
Citellus washingtoni, 104, **101**

Habits: Diurnal; colonial. Eats green vegetation, seeds, acorns, mushrooms, fruits, berries, birds, eggs, and insects; stores food in dens. Burrows 5–200 ft. long, on gentle slopes, may have many openings; used for several years; runways from hole to hole. Nest of dried vegetation. Most adults estivate in July or Aug.; young and adults hibernate in Oct. or Nov.; always a few aboveground; emerge in Jan. Home range normally less than 150 yds. across. A loud chirp warns others of danger. Breeding population of 2–3 per acre is fairly high. Lives 5 years or more in wild.

Young: Born throughout spring, summer, and fall; usually March–April; 4–15 (av. 7); gestation period 25–30 days. Remain underground 6 weeks.

Economic status: Does considerable damage to crops and pastureland; has been host to the plague. Considered detrimental where man's interests are concerned.   Map opposite

ROCK SQUIRREL *Citellus variegatus*   p. 101

Recognition: Head and body 10–11 in.; tail 7–10 in.; wt. 1½–1⅘ lb. Largest of the ground-living squirrels within its range; may be seen foraging in the open or *sitting on top of a boulder* on the watch for danger. Usual color is *grayish* (sometimes nearly black) mixed with cinnamon or brown, sometimes with head and back blackish; tail nearly as long as head and body and somewhat bushy; a slightly *mottled* effect over body. Skull has 22 teeth. There are 10 mammae.

Similar species: (1) Other ground squirrels — smaller; shorter tails. (2) Prairie Dogs — tails short; found only on open prairies.

Habitat: Rocky canyons and boulder-strewn slopes.

Habits: Diurnal; not colonial. Climbs nearly as well as tree squirrels. Feeds on seeds, fruits, nuts, eggs, meat; stores food in den. Den usually beneath a boulder. Hibernates for short periods, if at all. A clear whistle warns of danger. Has lived 10 years in captivity. Mates March–July.

Young: Born April–Aug.; 5–7; gestation period not known, probably 30± days.

Economic status: Harmful in agricultural areas; in foothills, probably neutral; young are edible.   Map opposite

TOWNSEND GROUND SQUIRREL *Citellus townsendi*

Recognition: Head and body 5½–7 in.; tail 1⅓–2⅛ in.; wt. 6–9 oz. Tail *short*, fulvous beneath; body *smoke-gray* washed with *pinkish buff;* belly and flanks whitish. Skull has 22 teeth. There are 10 mammae.

Similar species: (1) Washington Ground Squirrel — dappled. (2) Belding Ground Squirrel — larger; tail reddish beneath. (3) Uinta Ground Squirrel — brownish down middle of back; black in tail. (4) Columbian Ground Squirrel — larger; feet and legs rufous. (5) Whitetail Antelope Squirrel (p. 112) — stripes on sides; underpart of tail white.

Habitat: Dry soil; sagebrush and grassland.

Habits: Colonial. Feeds on green vegetation and seeds. Burrow usually has small rim of dirt 4–6 in. high around opening. Becomes dormant May–July; emerges Jan.–Feb. Voice, a faint peep; stands "picket pin" fashion at burrow entrance.

Young: Born March; usually 5–10, rarely 15.

Economic status: Damages green crops if nearby.   Map p. 102

WASHINGTON GROUND SQUIRREL   p. 101
Citellus washingtoni

Recognition: Head and body 6–7 in.; tail 1⅛–2½ in.; wt. 6–10 oz. A small, *dappled* ground squirrel; body *smoke-gray flecked with whitish spots;* short tail with *blackish tip.* Skull has 22 teeth. There are 10 mammae.

Similar species: (1) Townsend and (2) Belding Ground Squirrels — no spots. (3) Columbian Ground Squirrel — larger; feet and legs rufous.

Habitat: Sagebrush, grasslands, sandy flats, and rocky hillsides.

Habits: Similar to those of the Townsend Ground Squirrel (above).

Young: Born March; 5–11. Aboveground in April.

Economic status: Damages green crops if nearby.   Map p. 102

IDAHO GROUND SQUIRREL   *Citellus brunneus*

Recognition: Head and body 6½–7¾ in.; tail 2–2½ in. Ears relatively *large;* back distinctly *washed with cinnamon* or light brown and sprinkled with *small grayish-white spots;* tail rusty brown beneath; chin white. Skull has 22 teeth.

Similar species: Columbian Ground Squirrel — larger; feet and legs rufous.

Habitat: Dry, rocky ridges, grass and low herbs.

Habits: Burrows beneath logs and rocks; may estivate in July or Aug.

Range: Known only from Weiser and Payette Valleys, w. Idaho.

RICHARDSON GROUND SQUIRREL   *Citellus richardsoni*
(Picket Pin)

Recognition: Head and body 7¾–9½ in.; tail 2–4½ in.; wt. 11–18 oz. This plains ground squirrel is drab *smoke-gray,* washed with *cinnamon-buff,* sometimes dappled on back; belly pale buff or whitish; underside of tail clay color, buff, or light brown; tail *bordered with white or buff.* Skull has 22 teeth. There are 10 mammae.

Similar species: (1) Belding Ground Squirrel — median area of back usually brownish; tail reddish below. (2) Uinta Ground Squirrel — tail black mixed with buffy white above and below. (3) Columbian Ground Squirrel — larger; rufous feet and legs.

(4) Spotted Ground Squirrel — distinct spots. (5) Thirteen-lined Ground Squirrel — stripes on body. (6) Franklin Ground Squirrel — larger; long tail.

Habitat: Sagebrush, grassland; usually near green vegetation (water); up to 11,000-ft. elevation.

Habits: Feeds on green vegetation; fond of meat. Burrows may have several openings. Adults estivate in July, emerge late Jan. or Feb.

Young: Born May; 2–10.

Economic status: May damage green crops, but possibly destroys many insects. Map p. 106

UINTA GROUND SQUIRREL *Citellus armatus*

Recognition: Head and body 8¾–9 in.; tail 2½–3¼ in.; wt. 10–15 oz. Middle of back brownish; tail *black mixed with buffy white* above and below; belly hairs tipped with pale buff. Skull has 22 teeth. There are 10 mammae.

Similar species: (1) Townsend Ground Squirrel — tail not blackish. (2) Richardson Ground Squirrel — tail clay color beneath. (3) Belding Ground Squirrel — brownish streak down back. (4) Thirteen-lined Ground Squirrel — stripes.

Habitat: Meadows, edges of fields, near green vegetation; up to 8000-ft. elevation.

Habits: Colonial. Feeds primarily on green vegetation; hibernates in winter.

Young: Born April; 4–6 recorded; 1 litter a year.

Economic status: Of little importance because of limited range; harms green crops when nearby. Map p. 106

BELDING GROUND SQUIRREL *Citellus beldingi*

Recognition: Head and body 8–9 in.; tail 2⅕–3 in.; wt. 8–12 oz. A medium-sized ground squirrel with upperparts *grayish*, usually washed with buff, and usually with a definite *broad brownish streak down back*, contrasting with sides. Tail reddish beneath, tipped with black and bordered with buff or white. Skull has 22 teeth. There are 10 mammae.

Similar species: (1) Townsend Ground Squirrel — smaller; tail fulvous beneath. (2) Richardson Ground Squirrel — tail pale buff or clay color beneath. (3) Washington Ground Squirrel — dappled above. (4) Uinta Ground Squirrel — no brown streak down back.

Habitat: Meadows, edges of fields, near green vegetation.

Habits: Similar to those of Uinta Ground Squirrel.

Map p. 106

COLUMBIAN GROUND SQUIRREL p. 101
Citellus columbianus

Recognition: Head and body 10–12 in.; tail 3–5 in.; wt. ¾–1⅖

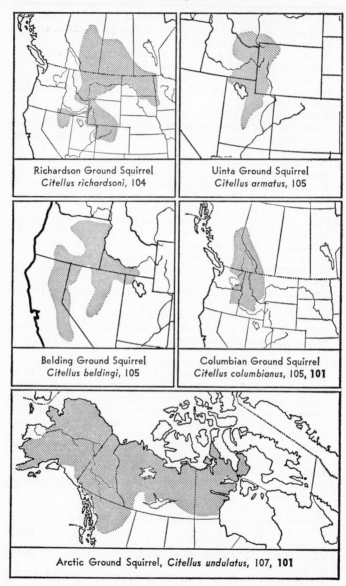

Richardson Ground Squirrel
Citellus richardsoni, 104

Uinta Ground Squirrel
Citellus armatus, 105

Belding Ground Squirrel
Citellus beldingi, 105

Columbian Ground Squirrel
Citellus columbianus, 105, **101**

Arctic Ground Squirrel, *Citellus undulatus,* 107, **101**

1b. This rather large, *bushy-tailed* ground squirrel may be distinguished from all others within its range by the *dark rufous feet* and *legs* and the *mottled gray upperparts*. Skull has 22 teeth. There are 10 mammae.

Similar species: (1) Townsend, (2) Washington, (3) Idaho, and (4) Richardson Ground Squirrels — all smaller; none has deep rufous feet and legs.

Habitat: Meadows, edges of open forests, cultivated fields.

Habits: Colonial. Feeds on green vegetation spring and early summer; stores some seeds in late summer. Dormant from July–Aug. to Feb.–March; males emerge 2 weeks earlier than females. Voice a high-pitched chirp or whistle.

Young: Born late March or early April; 2–7; gestation period about 24 days.

Economic status: Harmful near green crops; neutral in other areas.   Map opposite

ARCTIC GROUND SQUIRREL *Citellus undulatus* p. 101
(Parka Squirrel)

Recognition: Head and body 8½–13¾ in.; tail 3–6 in.; wt. 1–2½ lb. In the *Far North* lives this *large* ground squirrel. It is also found on a number of the islands off Alaska. Upperparts tawny to reddish brown or fuscous, abundantly flecked with white; sides gray; top of head reddish; feet and legs tawny; tail with some black. Only ground squirrel in its range. Skull has 22 teeth.

Formerly known as *C. parryi*.

Similar species: (1) Hoary Marmot (p. 98) and (2) Woodchuck (p. 96) — larger; black feet.

Habitat: Tundra and brushy meadows.

Habits: Eats variety of plants; also relishes meat. Hibernates for about 7 months, Oct.–May; may appear through snow for short periods. Highly vocal.

Young: Born June–July; 4–8; gestation period 25 days. Grow rapidly.

Economic status: Utilized by Eskimo for food and clothing; beneficial.   Map opposite

THIRTEEN-LINED GROUND SQUIRREL p. 101
(Gopher) *Citellus tridecemlineatus*

Recognition: Head and body 4½–6½ in.; tail 2½–5¼ in.; wt. 5–9 oz. This is the most widely ranging of the ground squirrels. Base color varies from light to dark brown. On sides and back are *13 whitish stripes*, some broken into rows of spots, others more or less continuous. Belly whitish. No other ground squirrel within its range has definite stripes on body. Skull (p. 248) has 22 teeth. There are 10 mammae.

Similar species: (1) Spotted Ground Squirrel — spots but not stripes. (2) Chipmunks (pp. 113–23) — stripes on sides of face. (3) Richardson, (4) Uinta, and (5) Franklin Ground Squirrels — no stripes.

Habitat: Shortgrass prairies, golf courses.

Habits: Solitary. Feeds on seeds, insects, and occasionally meat. Opening to burrow usually concealed, may be more than 1 opening; dirt thrown out at 1 opening only. Hibernates about 6 months of year, Oct.–March; prefers warm days. Home range 2–3 acres. Populations of 4–8 per acre probably high. Expanding general range north and east, following clearing of land for agriculture. Mates in April.

Young: Born May; usually 7–10, rarely 14; gestation period 28 days; possibly 2nd litter in late summer.

Economic status: May damage some crops, but does much good by eating weed seeds and harmful insects; probably does more good than harm.   Map opposite

MEXICAN GROUND SQUIRREL *Citellus mexicanus*

Recognition: Head and body 6¾–7½ in.; tail 4½–5 in.; wt. 7–12 oz. This is a medium-sized ground squirrel with a *long, slightly bushy tail,* the hairs of which are tipped with buff. Back and sides snuff-brown, with about *9 rows of light buff spots.* Skull has 22 teeth. There are 8–10 mammae.

Similar species: (1) Spotted Ground Squirrel — spots indistinct, not in rows. (2) Rock Squirrel — larger; no spots in rows.

Habitat: Grassland, brush, mesquite, creosote bush, and cactus; it prefers sandy or gravelly soil.

Habits: Probably similar to those of the Thirteen-lined Ground Squirrel (above). Feeds on green vegetation, seeds, insects, and meat. May be seen along highway eating dead animals. Most burrows without mound of earth; several refuge burrows to each den. Some hibernate, others may be active all winter. Home range about 100 yds. across. Mates in April.

Young: Born May; 4–10.   Map opposite

SPOTTED GROUND SQUIRREL *Citellus spilosoma*   p. 101

Recognition: Head and body 5–6 in.; tail 2¼–3½ in.; wt. 3–4½ oz. A small grayish-brown or reddish-brown squirrel with indistinct *squarish spots of white or buff* on back; tail pencil-like, *not bushy;* belly whitish. Skull has 22 teeth. There are 10 mammae.

Similar species: (1) Mexican Ground Squirrel — spots distinct and in rows. (2) Thirteen-lined Ground Squirrel — distinct stripes on body. (3) Richardson Ground Squirrel — no distinct spots.

Habitat: Open forests, scattered brush, grassy parks; sandy soil preferred.

Habits: Active throughout year. Shy and secretive; runs low to ground. Feeds on green vegetation, seeds, and insects. Burrows usually beneath bushes or rocks. Some may hibernate. Young: 5–7; probably 2 litters a year. Map p. 110

MOHAVE GROUND SQUIRREL *Citellus mohavensis*
Recognition: Head and body 6–6½ in.; tail 2–3½ in. This little squirrel, found only in the *Mohave Desert*, is *cinnamon-gray* with a *short tail* that is *fuscous above and white beneath*. There are *no stripes* on its sides. When running, holds tail over its back and exposes the white undersurface. Skull has 22 teeth. There are 10 mammae.
Similar species: Whitetail Antelope Squirrel — white stripes on body.
Habitat: Low desert with scattered brush; sandy or gravelly soil.

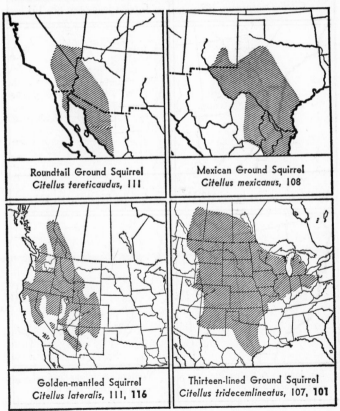

Roundtail Ground Squirrel
Citellus tereticaudus, 111

Mexican Ground Squirrel
Citellus mexicanus, 108

Golden-mantled Squirrel
Citellus lateralis, 111, **116**

Thirteen-lined Ground Squirrel
Citellus tridecemlineatus, 107, **101**

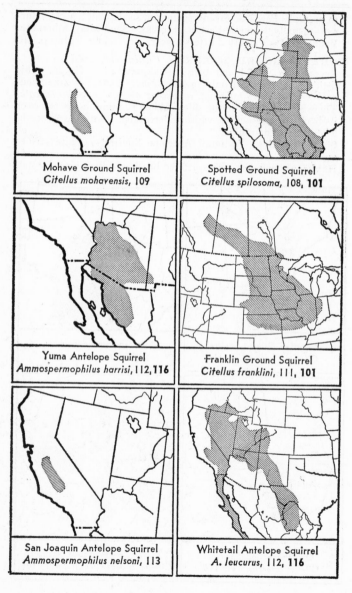

Mohave Ground Squirrel
Citellus mohavensis, 109

Spotted Ground Squirrel
Citellus spilosoma, 108, **101**

Yuma Antelope Squirrel
Ammospermophilus harrisi, 112, **116**

Franklin Ground Squirrel
Citellus franklini, 111, **101**

San Joaquin Antelope Squirrel
Ammospermophilus nelsoni, 113

Whitetail Antelope Squirrel
A. leucurus, 112, **116**

Habits: Most active on clear warm days. Solitary for most part. Feeds on tender green vegetation in spring. Openings to burrows (2 or more) without dirt mounds; several burrows used by each individual. Voice a shrill whistle, not very loud.

Young: March 29, 6 embryos reported; female suckling, April 12.

Map opposite

ROUNDTAIL GROUND SQUIRREL *Citellus tereticaudus*

Recognition: Head and body 5¾–6½ in.; tail 2½–4 in.; wt. 5–6½ oz. Upperparts *pinkish cinnamon* with a *grayish cast;* tail pencil-like, not bushy; belly slightly paler than back. There are *no contrasting markings*. Skull has 22 teeth. There are 8–10 mammae.

Similar species: Antelope Squirrels — with stripes.

Habitat: Low desert, mesquite, creosote bush, cactus.

Habits: Most active mornings and evenings; seeks shade or retires to burrow in heat of day; may be seen resting in shade of plant or post. Aboveground throughout year. Feeds on seeds and probably insects.

Young: Born April (possibly other months); 6–12 embryos reported. Map p. 109

FRANKLIN GROUND SQUIRREL *Citellus franklini* p. 101
(Gray Gopher)

Recognition: Head and body 9–10 in.; tail 5–6 in.; wt. 10–25 oz. A *large, gray* squirrel with a fulvous overwash on the back and rump. Belly nearly as dark as back; tail fairly long. Much larger and darker than any other ground squirrel in its range. Skull has 22 teeth. There are 10–12 mammae.

Similar species: (1) Richardson Ground Squirrel — smaller; short tail. (2) Thirteen-lined Ground Squirrel — spots or stripes.

Habitat: Fairly tall grass or herbs, borders of fields, open woods, edges of marshes.

Habits: Colonial, secretive. Climbs trees, but usually seen on ground. Prefers sunshine, little activity on cloudy days. Eats green vegetation, seeds, insects, meat, bird eggs. Burrows concealed in tall grass or weeds, some dirt at entrance. Hibernates in late Sept. and emerges in April or May; males appear first. Young often seen at edge of highway. Populations of 4–5 per acre are high.

Young: Born May–June; 4–11; gestation period 28 days.

Economic status: Destroys some grain and eggs of ground-nesting birds, but also destroys many insects; may be harmful in one place, beneficial in another. Map opposite

GOLDEN-MANTLED SQUIRREL *Citellus lateralis* p. 116
(Copperhead)

Recognition: Head and body 6–8 in.; tail 2½–4¾ in.; wt. 6–9¾ oz. A chipmunk-like ground squirrel; *head coppery*, a *white*

stripe bordered with black on each side of back; no stripes on sides of face; tail relatively short and fully haired, not bushy. Skull has 22 teeth. There are 8–10 mammae.

C. saturatus is included here; it may be a distinct species; found in the Cascades of Washington and B.C.

Similar species: (1) Chipmunks (below) — stripes on side of face. (2) Red Squirrel (p. 127) and (3) Chickaree (p. 128) — no contrast between color of head and body; no white stripe on side.

Habitat: Mountainous areas, chaparral, open pine, fir, and spruce forests; to above timberline.

Habits: Feeds on seeds, fruits, insects, eggs, meat; stores food. Burrows usually near bushes, trees, rocks, or logs. Hibernates Oct.–Nov., emerges March–May; sometimes comes up through snow in winter. Home range less than 200 yds. across. Populations of 2–5 per acre. Female may protect area near den. These squirrels become quite tame at camping areas.

Young: Born early spring; 2–8.

Economic status: Found principally in nonagricultural areas; affords pleasure to many campers and park visitors. Commonly seen in most western parks.   Map p. 109

YUMA ANTELOPE SQUIRREL   p. 116
Ammospermophilus harrisi

Recognition: Head and body 6–6¼ in.; tail 3–3¾ in.; wt. 4–5³⁄₁₀ oz. Body *pinkish cinnamon* to *mouse-gray;* a narrow *white line* on each side of the back. Tail gray above and below. Skull has 22 teeth. There are 10 mammae.

Similar species: (1) Chipmunks (below) — stripes on side of face; in mts. (2) Ground Squirrels (above) — no stripes on sides.

Habitat: Low arid desert with sparse vegetation.

Habits: Probably similar to those of the Whitetail Antelope Squirrel.   Map p. 110

WHITETAIL ANTELOPE SQUIRREL   p. 116
Ammospermophilus leucurus

Recognition: Head and body 5½–6½ in.; tail 2–3 in.; wt. 3–5½ oz. Body pale pinkish gray, a *white line on each side of the back; undersurface of tail white.* Runs with tail curled over its back, exposing the white undersurface. No other ground squirrel within its range has its color pattern. Skull has 22 teeth. There are 10 mammae.

Those in sw. Texas and central s. New Mexico are considered a distinct species (*A. interpres*) by some authors.

Similar species: (1) Chipmunks (below) — no white undertail. (2) Ground Squirrels (above) — no stripes on sides.

Habitat: Low desert and foothills, sparse vegetation, scattered junipers.

Habits: Active throughout year, even when snow on ground. Solitary for most part. Eats seeds, insects, meat; stores food; does not require drinking water. Some may hibernate. Often seen along highway.

Young: 6–10; possibly 2 litters a year.

Economic status: On irrigated land may do some damage to crops; also digs into banks of ditches.   Map p. 110

SAN JOAQUIN ANTELOPE SQUIRREL
Ammospermophilus nelsoni

Recognition: Head and body 6–6½ in.; tail 2½–3 in.; wt. 3–5½ oz. In the *San Joaquin Valley*, California, this pinkish-buff squirrel, with a creamy-*white line on each side* of back and a creamy-white underside of tail, is the only ground squirrel with stripes. Curls tail over back when running, exposing white undersurface. Skull has 22 teeth.

Habitat: Dry, sparsely vegetated areas.

Habits: Similar to those of Whitetail Antelope Squirrel (above).
Map p. 110

EASTERN CHIPMUNK   *Tamias striatus*   p. 116

Recognition: Head and body 5–6 in.; tail 3–4 in.; wt. 2³⁄₁₀–4½ oz. Squirrel-like; runs with bushy *tail straight up; facial stripes* distinguish it from all other mammals over most of its range; *side and back stripes end at reddish rump.* Often seen in trees, but mostly on ground. Its rather sharp *chuck-chuck-chuck* may be heard before the animal is seen. Skull (p. 248) has 20 teeth.

Similar species: (1) Least Chipmunk — smaller; side and back stripes continue to base of tail. (2) Thirteen-lined Ground Squirrel (p. 107) — yellowish; no stripes on face.

Habitat: Deciduous forests, brushy areas.

Habits: Solitary except for mother and young. Feeds on seeds, bulbs, fruits, nuts, insects, meat, eggs; stores food underground. Hibernates, but may come aboveground in middle of winter. Home range usually less than 100 yds. across. Populations of 2–4 per acre. Lives 3 years or more in wild, 8 years in captivity. Readily comes to feeding table. Displays territorial behavior. Mates in April and again July–Aug.

Young: 1st litter May; 2–8; 2nd litter Aug.–Sept.; gestation period 31 days. Appear aboveground when ⅔ grown. Breed 1st year.

Economic status: May destroy some garden fruit and bulbs; also digs many burrows; an attractive animal around camping areas.   Map p. 115

ALPINE CHIPMUNK   *Eutamias alpinus*

Recognition: Head and body 4¼–4½ in.; tail 2¾–3½ in.; wt. 1–1¾ oz. A small chipmunk. Head and body grayish, dark

side stripes on face and body tawny. Skull has 22 teeth.
Similar species: (1) Yellow Pine and (2) Lodgepole Chip-
munks — larger; dark stripes blackish or dark brown, and/or
clear white patches behind ears.
Habitat: Cliffs and talus slopes from timberline to 8000-ft.
elevation.
Range: High Sierra Nevada from Mt. Conness, Tuolumne Co.,
California, south to Olancha Peak, Inyo-Tulare Cos., California.

LEAST CHIPMUNK *Eutamias minimus*   p. 116
Recognition: Head and body 3⅔–4½ in.; tail 3–4½ in.; wt. 1–2
oz. This is the most widely ranging, geographically and alti-
tudinally, of the chipmunks. As a group, they are also the
smallest and most variable. Color ranges from a washed-out
yellowish gray with pale fulvous dark stripes (Badlands, S.
Dakota) to a *rich grayish fulvous* with black dark stripes (Wisconsin and Michigan). Stripes continue to *base of tail.* When
running, carry tail *straight up.* Skull has 22 teeth. There are 8
mammae.
Similar species: (1) Grayneck Chipmunk — larger; neck and
shoulders gray. (2) Yellow Pine Chipmunk — ears blackish in
front, whitish behind. (3) Panamint Chipmunk — rump gray,
contrasts with color of back and sides. (4) Townsend Chipmunk — larger; stripes indistinct. (5) Uinta, (6) Lodgepole, and
(7) Colorado Chipmunks — ears blackish in front, white behind.
(8) Cliff Chipmunk — side stripes indistinct. (9) Redtail Chipmunk — rump gray; tail dark rufous below. (10) Eastern Chipmunk — body stripes terminate at reddish rump.
Habitat: Low sagebrush deserts, high-mt. coniferous forests,
northern mixed-hardwood forests; varies with locality.
Habits: Active gathering and storing food during spring, summer, and fall. Climbs trees readily. Feeds on variety of vegetation, seeds, nuts, fruits; also insects and meat; readily adapts to
camps, especially if food is forthcoming. Nests beneath stumps,
logs, rocks; makes own burrow; hibernates.
Young: 2–6; possibly 2 litters a year.
Economic status: Affords pleasure to campers and tourists in
many of our parks. May be seen at the turnouts in Badlands
Natl. Monument, S. Dakota, and at most camping areas within
its range.   Map opposite

TOWNSEND CHIPMUNK *Eutamias townsendi*   p. 116
Recognition: Head and body 5⅓–6½ in.; tail 3⅘–6 in.; wt.
2½–4⅓ oz. This large, *dark brown* chipmunk, found on the
humid Pacific Coast, has indistinct dull yellowish or grayish
light stripes along its sides and back. Dark body stripes blackish; stripe below ear brownish. Backs of ears fuscous in front,
gray behind. Skull has 22 teeth. There are 8 mammae.

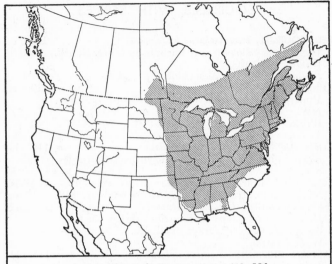

Eastern Chipmunk, *Tamias striatus*, 113, **116**

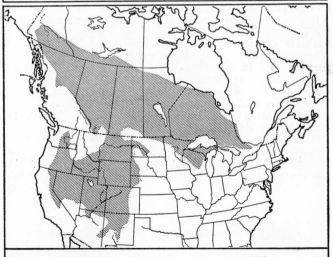

Least Chipmunk, *Eutamias minimus*, 114, **116**

SQUIRRELS WITH STRIPES

	Map	*Text*

RED SQUIRREL, *Tamiasciurus hudsonicus*   128   127
Upperparts yellowish or reddish; belly white. N, SW.
Winter: Ear tufts.
Summer: Black line along side.

CHICKAREE, *Tamiasciurus douglasi*   129   128
Upperparts reddish olive; belly yellowish or rusty.
NW.
Winter: Ear tufts.
Summer: Black line along side.

CLIFF CHIPMUNK, *Eutamias dorsalis*   118   119
Gray; indistinct dark stripes down back and sides.
SW.

COLORADO CHIPMUNK, *Eutamias quadrivittatus*   122   121
Bright colors; stripes distinct; white behind ear. SW.

LEAST CHIPMUNK, *Eutamias minimus*   115   114
East: Stripes on face; back stripes to base of tail.
West: Pale yellowish gray; small size.
W, N Central.

EASTERN CHIPMUNK, *Tamias striatus*   115   113
Stripes on face; body stripes end at reddish rump;
bushy tail. E.

TOWNSEND CHIPMUNK, *Eutamias townsendi*   118   114
Dark brown; stripes on face and body indistinct.
NW.

MERRIAM CHIPMUNK, *Eutamias merriami*   118   120
Stripes indistinct; stripe below ear brownish. SW.

YUMA ANTELOPE SQUIRREL   110   112
Ammospermophilus harrisi
Pinkish cinnamon to mouse-gray; white stripes on
body only. SW.

WHITETAIL ANTELOPE SQUIRREL   110   112
Ammospermophilus leucurus
Pinkish gray, with white stripes on body only; tail
white beneath. SW.

GOLDEN-MANTLED SQUIRREL, *Citellus lateralis*   109   111
Stripes on body only; coppery head. W.

Chipmunk,
front feet not together

1⅝ in.

6-12 in. to next print

Chipmunk at
food cache

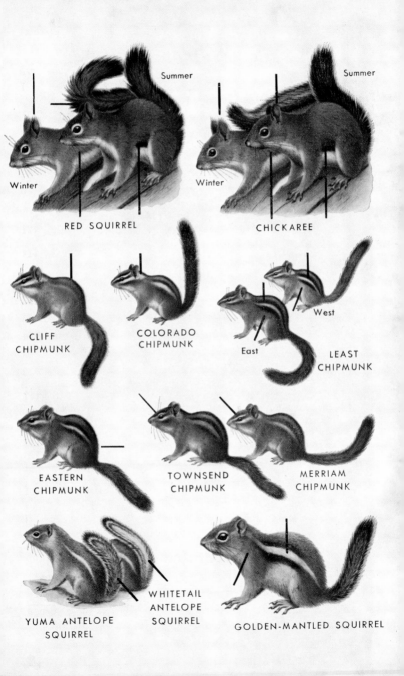

Summer

Winter

RED SQUIRREL

Summer

Winter

CHICKAREE

CLIFF CHIPMUNK

COLORADO CHIPMUNK

West

East

LEAST CHIPMUNK

EASTERN CHIPMUNK

TOWNSEND CHIPMUNK

MERRIAM CHIPMUNK

YUMA ANTELOPE SQUIRREL

WHITETAIL ANTELOPE SQUIRREL

GOLDEN-MANTLED SQUIRREL

EASTERN GRAY
SQUIRREL

Summer

Winter

WESTERN GRAY SQUIRREL

SOUTHERN
FLYING
SQUIRREL

TASSEL-EARED
SQUIRREL
South of Grand Canyon

North of Grand Canyon

South

North

East

EASTERN FOX SQUIRREL

Plate 12   117

TREE SQUIRRELS

	Map	Text

WESTERN GRAY SQUIRREL, *Sciurus griseus*   124   123
   Body gray, feet dusky; very bushy tail. W.

EASTERN GRAY SQUIRREL, *Sciurus carolinensis*   126   124
   Body gray, washed with fulvous in summer. E.
   Winter: White behind ears.
   Summer: Tail bordered with white.

SOUTHERN FLYING SQUIRREL, *Glaucomys volans*   129   129
   Fur soft; olive-brown above, white on belly; loose
   skin between front and hind legs. E.

TASSEL-EARED SQUIRREL, *Sciurus aberti*   124   124
   Ears tufted except in late summer. SW.
   South of Grand Canyon: Tail white beneath.
   North of Grand Canyon: Tail all-white.

EASTERN FOX SQUIRREL, *Sciurus niger*   126   125
   South: Head blackish, body grayish.
   North: Rusty; tail bordered with fulvous.
   East: Steel-gray; no fulvous.
   E.

Leaf nest of
Tree Squirrel

Flying Squirrel gliding
from den-tree hole

Gray Squirrel
bounding

Fox Squirrel,
H. F. 2⅞ in.

2¼ in.

(Front feet paired)

Red Squirrel
H. F. 1¾ in.

24 in.

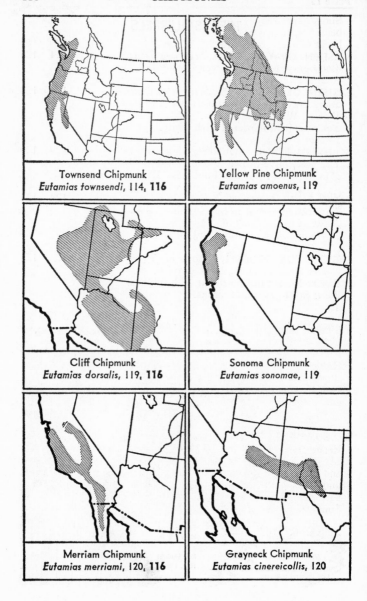

Townsend Chipmunk
Eutamias townsendi, 114, **116**

Yellow Pine Chipmunk
Eutamias amoenus, 119

Cliff Chipmunk
Eutamias dorsalis, 119, **116**

Sonoma Chipmunk
Eutamias sonomae, 119

Merriam Chipmunk
Eutamias merriami, 120, **116**

Grayneck Chipmunk
Eutamias cinereicollis, 120

CHIPMUNKS

Similar species: (1) Long-eared Chipmunk — large white patch behind ear, black line below ear. (2) Sonoma Chipmunk — backs of ears 1 color. (3) Least, (4) Yellow Pine, (5) Lodgepole, and (6) Uinta Chipmunks — smaller; distinct stripes contrast with body colors.
Habitat: Coniferous forests and adjacent chaparral.
Habits: Climbs trees. Feeds mostly on forest floor and in nearby chaparral; food habits probably similar to those of other chipmunks. Hibernates for short periods. Mates in April. May be seen at Mt. Rainier and Olympic Natl. Parks.
Young: Born May; 3–6.   Map opposite

CLIFF CHIPMUNK   *Eutamias dorsalis*   p. 116
Recognition: Head and body 5–6 in.; tail 3½–4⅕ in.; wt. 2–3 oz. Gray with indistinct dark stripes down middle of back and along sides. Lower sides and feet washed with yellow. Skull has 22 teeth. There are 8 mammae.
Similar species: (1) Least, (2) Uinta, (3) Panamint, and (4) Gray-neck Chipmunks — all with distinct dark and light stripes.
Habitat: Piñon pine–juniper slopes and lower edge of pines.
Map opposite

SONOMA CHIPMUNK   *Eutamias sonomae*
Recognition: Head and body 4⅘–6 in.; tail 4–5 in. A *large dark* chipmunk. Backs of ears uniform color; body stripes indistinct, the light ones yellowish. Skull has 22 teeth.
Similar species: (1) Yellow Pine Chipmunk — stripes bright, black and white. (2) Townsend Chipmunk — backs of ears bicolored, fuscous in front and gray behind.
Habitat: Chaparral, brushy clearings, streamside thickets; warm slopes, sea level to 6000-ft. elevation.
Habits: Sits on limb, stump, or rock while eating. Forages among small branches of bushes as well as on ground.
Map opposite

YELLOW PINE CHIPMUNK   *Eutamias amoenus*
Recognition: Head and body 4½–5⅕ in.; tail 3–4¼ in.; wt. 1⅓–2½ oz. Colors bright; black and white (or grayish) back and side stripes *distinct;* ears blackish in front, whitish behind; underside of tail fulvous, as are the sides. Skull has 22 teeth. There are 8 mammae.
Similar species: (1) Least Chipmunk — fronts of ears fulvous. (2) Alpine Chipmunk — dark side stripes fulvous. (3) Redtail Chipmunk — underside of tail dark rufous. (4) Lodgepole and (5) Uinta Chipmunks — side stripes dark brown. (6) Townsend, (7) Merriam, (8) Long-eared, and (9) Sonoma Chipmunks — larger; stripes indistinct.
Habitat: Open coniferous forests, chaparral, rocky areas with

brush or scattered pines, burned-over areas with stumps and brush.

Habits: Strictly diurnal. Climbs trees. Eats great variety of plant material, mostly seeds, and a few insects; eats meat in captivity. Nests in ground burrows up to 3 ft. long; no loose soil at entrances; stores food in nest chamber. Hibernates Nov.–March in North. Lives 5 years or more in wild. Mates in April.

Young: Born May; 5–7; 1 litter a year. Naked; blind. Aboveground in June; weaned at 6 weeks. Breed following spring.

Economic status: Found usually in nonagricultural country; an attractive animal in several parks. May be seen at Craters of the Moon Natl. Monument (larger and darker of 2 species), Mt. Rainier and Olympic Natl. Parks (smaller and brighter-colored of 2 kinds). Map p. 118

MERRIAM CHIPMUNK *Eutamias merriami* p. 116

Recognition: Head and body 4⅔–6½ in.; tail 3½–5⅗ in.; wt. 2½–4 oz. A large, grayish-brown chipmunk with *indistinct stripes.* Stripe below ear brownish. Skull has 22 teeth. There are 8 mammae.

Similar species: (1) Long-eared Chipmunk — black stripe under ear; white patch behind ear. (2) Yellow Pine and (3) Lodgepole Chipmunks — distinct white stripes.

Habitat: Chaparral slopes, mixed oak and digger pine forests, streamside thickets, rock outcroppings, foothills. Map p. 118

GRAYNECK CHIPMUNK *Eutamias cinereicollis*

Recognition: Head and body 4¾–5½ in.; tail 3⅗–4⅗ in.; wt. 2–3 oz. Body *dark gray* washed on sides with fulvous and with *pale gray neck and shoulders;* lateral dark stripes dark brown, median one black. Skull (p. 248) has 22 teeth. There are 8 mammae.

Similar species: (1) Least Chipmunk — smaller; neck not noticeably gray. (2) Cliff Chipmunk — side stripes indistinct.

Habitat: Coniferous forests, high mts. Map p. 118

LONG-EARED CHIPMUNK *Eutamias quadrimaculatus*

Recognition: Head and body 5–6 in.; tail 3½–4⅔ in.; wt. 2½–3½ oz. This *large, high-Sierra* chipmunk is grayish or tawny, with indistinct body stripes. Behind each ear is a large, clearly defined *white patch;* stripe below ear black. Skull has 22 teeth.

Similar species: (1) Yellow Pine, (2) Lodgepole, and (3) Uinta Chipmunks — smaller; stripes distinct. (4) Townsend and (5) Merriam Chipmunks — stripe below ear brownish.

Habitat: Forests and brush thickets; 3600–7300-ft. elevation.

Map p. 122

REDTAIL CHIPMUNK *Eutamias ruficaudus*

Recognition: Head and body 4⅗–5⅘ in.; tail 4–4⅘ in. *Large;*

brilliantly colored; shoulders and sides bright fulvous; rump gray; underside of tail dark rufous. Skull has 22 teeth. There are 8 mammae.

Similar species: (1) Yellow Pine Chipmunk — underside of tail fulvous. (2) Least Chipmunk — smaller; rump does not contrast with sides and head.

Habitat: Coniferous forests talus slides, mts. up to timberline.

Map p. 122

COLORADO CHIPMUNK *Eutamias quadrivittatus*   p. 116
Recognition: Head and body 4½–5 in.; tail 3⅓–4½ in.; wt. 2–3 oz. Head, rump, and sides gray with an overwash of fulvous on sides; color bright; side stripes dark brown; ears blackish in front, white behind. Tail fulvous beneath, tipped with black, and bordered with white or pale fulvous. Skull has 22 teeth. There are 8 mammae.

Similar species: Least Chipmunk — smaller; dorsal stripes continue to base of tail.

Habitat: Coniferous forests, rocky slopes and ridges.

Map p. 122

UINTA CHIPMUNK *Eutamias umbrinus*
Recognition: Head and body 4½–5 in.; tail 3½–4⅜ in.; wt. 2–3 oz. Characters as in Colorado Chipmunk. Skull has 22 teeth. There are 8 mammae.

Some authors have included this with *E. quadrivittatus*.

Similar species: (1) Least Chipmunk — front of ear fulvous. (2) Yellow Pine Chipmunk — side stripes black. (3) Lodgepole Chipmunk — top of head brown; subterminal black area on underside of tail more than ½ in. long. (4) Panamint Chipmunk — shoulders and sides bright fulvous; ears fulvous in front. (5) Townsend, (6) Long-eared, and (7) Cliff Chipmunks — side stripes indistinct.

Habitat: Coniferous forests (yellow pine zone) up to timberline; rocky slopes; 6000–11,000-ft. elevation.   Map p. 122

PANAMINT CHIPMUNK *Eutamias panamintinus*
Recognition: Head and body 4½–4⅔ in.; tail 3½–4 in.; wt. 1½–2⅛ oz. Brightly colored; head and rump gray; sides, back, and front of ears fulvous; median line fuscous. Skull has 22 teeth. There are 8 mammae.

Similar species: (1) Least Chipmunk — rump similar to back. (2) Lodgepole and (3) Uinta Chipmunks — ears blackish in front, white behind. (4) Charleston Mountain Chipmunk — in yellow pine belt and above. (5) Cliff Chipmunk — no white side stripe.

Habitat: Piñon pines and junipers; semi-arid areas.

Map p. 122

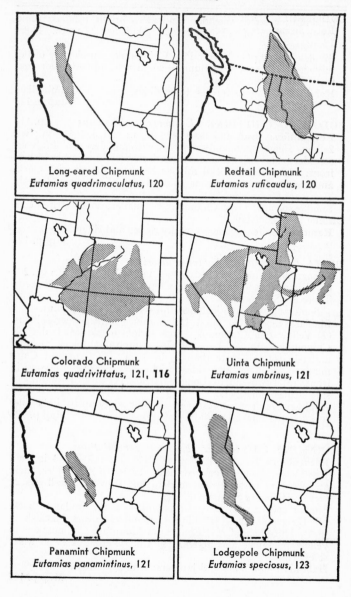

Long-eared Chipmunk
Eutamias quadrimaculatus, 120

Redtail Chipmunk
Eutamias ruficaudus, 120

Colorado Chipmunk
Eutamias quadrivittatus, 121, **116**

Uinta Chipmunk
Eutamias umbrinus, 121

Panamint Chipmunk
Eutamias panamintinus, 121

Lodgepole Chipmunk
Eutamias speciosus, 123

LODGEPOLE CHIPMUNK *Eutamias speciosus*

Recognition: Head and body 4⅗–5⅓ in.; tail 2⅘–4 in.; wt. 1⅘–2⅕ cz. Brightly colored; light and dark colors contrast; *top of head brown* sprinkled with gray; side stripes white and dark brown, distinct; median dorsal stripe *black;* ears blackish in front, whitish behind; *subterminal black area* on underside of tail ½–⅘ in. long. Skull has 22 teeth. There are 8 mammae.

Similar species: (1) Uinta Chipmunk — top of head gray; subterminal black area on underside of tail less than ½ in. long. (2) Yellow Pine Chipmunk — side stripes black. (3) Panamint Chipmunk — smaller, shoulders and sides bright fulvous; ears fulvous in front. (4) Least and (5) Alpine Chipmunks — smaller. (6) Merriam, (7) Townsend, and (8) Long-eared Chipmunks — larger; side stripes indistinct.

Habitat: Lodgepole pine forests and adjacent chaparral.

Map opposite

CHARLESTON MOUNTAIN CHIPMUNK *Eutamias palmeri*

Recognition: Head and body 5 in.; tail 3½–4 in. Skull has 22 teeth.

Similar species: Panamint Chipmunk — smaller; piñon-juniper belt.

Habitat: Coniferous forest, rocky slopes, yellow pines and above.

Range: Charleston Mts., Nevada.

WESTERN GRAY SQUIRREL *Sciurus griseus* p. 117

Recognition: Head and body 9–12 in.; tail 10–12 in.; wt. 1¼–1¾ lb. A *large, gray* tree squirrel with a long, very *bushy tail, white belly,* and *dusky feet.* Skull has 22 teeth. There are 8 mammae.

Similar species: (1) California Ground Squirrel (p. 99) — tail less bushy; shoulders whitish. (2) Chickaree (p. 128) — belly yellowish or rusty. (3) Eastern Fox Squirrel —rusty yellowish, not gray.

Habitat: Oak and pine-oak forests; fairly open.

Habits: Most active during mornings. Arboreal, but often seen on the ground. Feeds mostly on acorns and seeds of conifers. Nests in cavities in trees or in tree nest made of sticks and shredded bark; nest usually 20 ft. or more from ground. Home range ½–2 acres. Populations vary from 2 squirrels per acre to 1 squirrel for 10 acres. Has lived 11 years in captivity. Voice, a rather rapid barking sound. Female displays territorial behavior when young are in nest.

Young: Born Feb.–June; 3–5; gestation period probably more than 43 days; 1 litter a year.

Economic status: A fair game mammal; also attractive to visitors of parks such as Yosemite Natl. Park and several state and city parks. Walnut and almond crops are often damaged by these squirrels.

Map p. 124

TASSEL-EARED SQUIRREL *Sciurus aberti* p. 117
(Abert Squirrel, Kaibab Squirrel)

Recognition: Head and body 11–12 in.; tail 8–9 in.; wt. 1½–2 lb.
This is the most colorful of our tree squirrels. Tail either *all-white* or *white beneath* and broadly bordered with white; belly
either *white or black;* prominent black, or blackish, *ear tufts*
except late summer; sides gray; back reddish. Skull has 22
teeth. The only squirrel with the above markings.
    Some authors consider the squirrels north of the Grand Canyon
(*S. kaibabensis*) as a distinct species; they have *all-white tails.*
Habitat: Yellow pine forests, 7000–8500-ft. elevation.
Habits: Feeds primarily on pinecones and the cambium layer of
small pine twigs; also eats fungi. Builds bulky nest high in pines;
may be heard barking when excited, but usually rather quiet.
Mates March–April.
Young: Born April–May; 3–4.
Economic status: Does not interfere with man's activities; a
wonderful tourist attraction in Grand Canyon Natl. Park,
especially on North Rim. Quite rare, seen by few visitors.

Map below

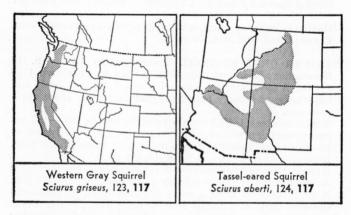

Western Gray Squirrel
Sciurus griseus, 123, **117**

Tassel-eared Squirrel
Sciurus aberti, 124, **117**

EASTERN GRAY SQUIRREL *Sciurus carolinensis* p. 117
Recognition: Head and body 8–10 in.; tail 7¾–10 in.; wt. ¾–
1⅗ lb. Its general *grayish* color, washed with fulvous in summer, and *very bushy tail bordered with white-tipped hairs* will
usually serve to distinguish this squirrel. Black squirrels (a
melanistic color phase) are common in some parts of its range.
Skull has 22 teeth. There are 8 mammae. Introduced in Seattle,
Washington, and Stanley Park, Vancouver, B.C.
Similar species: (1) Eastern Fox Squirrel — yellowish; tail

bordered with fulvous-tipped hairs; or body with distinct white or black markings, or steel-gray all over. (2) Red Squirrel — small; yellowish or reddish.

Habitat: Hardwood forests with nut trees, river bottoms.

Habits: Primarily arboreal, rarely ventures far from trees. Apparently has homing instinct. Feeds on a great variety of nuts, seeds, fungi, fruits, and often the cambium layer beneath the bark of trees; stores nuts and acorns singly in small holes in ground, many are never recovered and some sprout to grow into trees. Nests in holes in trees or builds leaf nest in branches, usually 25 ft. or more from ground. Home range 2–7 acres. Populations of 2–20 per acre. Formerly emigrated in great masses when populations were high. May be detected by a series of short barks when excited. Has lived 15 years in captivity. Mates Jan.–Feb., and July in North, Dec. and June in South.

Young: 3–5; gestation period 44 days; 2 litters a year. Naked, blind. Weaned at 2 months.

Economic status: In some parts of range one of the most important small game mammals; important as a reforestation agent by planting many nuts; an attractive mammal in many towns; does little harm to crops.   Map p. 126

ARIZONA GRAY SQUIRREL *Sciurus arizonensis*

Recognition: Head and body 10–11 in.; tail 10–12 in.; wt. 1⅛–1⅔ lb. The common tree squirrel in the mts. of se. Arizona. A large *gray* squirrel, sometimes washed with yellowish on the back; *belly* and *tail fringe white*. Skull has 20 teeth. There are 8 mammae.

Similar species: (1) Tassel-eared Squirrel — prominent tufts (except late summer) on ears. (2) Apache Fox Squirrel — yellowish brown. (3) Red Squirrel — smaller; yellowish or reddish on sides and back.

Habitat: Oak and pine forests.

Habits: Chiefly arboreal. Feeds on acorns, nuts, seeds; behavior similar to that of Eastern Gray Squirrel (above) as far as known.

Economic status: Probably neutral; not found in large numbers; range restricted.   Map p. 126

EASTERN FOX SQUIRREL *Sciurus niger*   p. 117

Recognition: Head and body 10–15 in.; tail 9–14 in.; wt. 1⅛–3 lb. Wherever there are nut trees in its range there are Eastern Fox Squirrels. Over most of its extensive range, this squirrel is *rusty* yellowish with a pale *yellow to orange belly*, and with the bushy tail *bordered with fulvous-tipped hairs*. In Southeast, body may be variously sprinkled with mixtures of yellow, white, and black, and the head more or less black with white on nose and ears. In a small area on Atlantic Coast (Delaware, Maryland) and adjoining parts of Virginia, West Virginia, and Pennsylvania, they may be pure steel-gray with no fulvous. Skull (p. 248) has 20 teeth. There are 8 mammae.

Similar species: (1) Eastern Gray Squirrel — smaller; gray with slight overwash of fulvous (summer) and with white border on tail. (2) Western Gray Squirrel — gray, not rusty or yellowish. (3) Red Squirrel — smaller; whitish belly.

Habitat: Open hardwood woodlots in North and pine forests in South, both with clearings interspersed.

Habits: Spends much time on ground foraging, sometimes in open several rods from trees. Feeds on great variety of nuts, acorns, seeds, fungi, bird eggs, and cambium beneath bark of small branches of trees; buries nuts singly, many of which are not retrieved. Nests in cavities in trees or builds twig and leaf nest in crotch or branches, usually 30 ft. or more from ground. Home range 10–40 acres. Populations of 1 squirrel per 2 acres

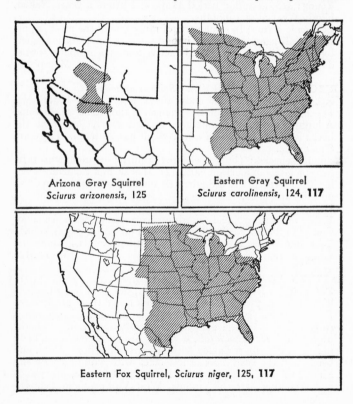

Arizona Gray Squirrel
Sciurus arizonensis, 125

Eastern Gray Squirrel
Sciurus carolinensis, 124, **117**

Eastern Fox Squirrel, *Sciurus niger,* 125, **117**

to 3 squirrels per acre. Lives 10 years or more. Mates Jan.–
Feb. and June–July in North, about 1 month earlier in South;
females breed at 1 year.

Young: Born Feb.–April and Aug.–Sept. in North, a month
earlier in South; 2–5; gestation period 44 days; yearling females
have 1 litter, old females 2 litters. Weaned at 2–3 months.

Economic status: An important small game mammal; does some
damage to grain crops near woodlots; an attractive mammal in
many small cities and parks. Introduced in several western
cities — i.e., Seattle, Washington, and Fresno, Sacramento, and
San Francisco, California.   Map opposite

APACHE FOX SQUIRREL *Sciurus apache*

Recognition: Head and body 10½–11½ in.; tail 10½–11½ in.;
wt. 1⅛–1⅘ lb. Barely enters U.S. in mts. of se. Arizona. A
large, *yellowish-brown* squirrel with an *ochraceous belly*. Skull
has 20 teeth. The only tree squirrel in the area with above
characters.

Habitat: Thickets of canyon bottoms.

Range: Known only from Chiricahua Mts., se. Arizona, in U.S.

RED SQUIRREL *Tamiasciurus hudsonicus* p. 116
(Spruce Squirrel)

Recognition: Head and body 7–8 in.; tail 4–6 in.; wt. 7–8⅘ oz.
This *noisy* little squirrel is usually heard before seen. Its *ratchet-
like call* reveals it, usually sitting on a branch 10 or 20 ft. aboveground. Color uniformly *yellowish or reddish*, paler on back in
winter (ear tufts), a *black line* along side in summer; whitish
belly. Tail is bushy. Smallest of the tree squirrels in its range.
Skull (p. 248) has 20 teeth (rarely 22). There are 8 mammae.

Similar species: (1) Eastern Gray Squirrel — larger; gray or
black. (2) Eastern Fox Squirrel — larger; no black line on side
in summer; no ear tufts in winter. (3) Arizona Gray Squirrel —
gray. (4) Tassel-eared Squirrel — gray sides; tail white or gray.
(5) Golden-mantled Squirrel (p. 111) — head copper color;
white stripe on side.

Habitat: Pine and spruce or mixed hardwood forests, swamps.

Habits: Active throughout year. Primarily diurnal, but occasionally out after dark. Tunnels in snow. Feeds on great variety
of seeds, nuts, eggs, fungi; stores conifer cones and nuts in
caches, not singly; fungi may be stored in crotches of trees,
singly; usually has favorite feeding stump where shucks from
pinecones or nuts may accumulate in piles of a bushel or more.
Nest either in cavity in tree or outside in branches, built of
leaves, twigs, and shredded bark, usually near tree trunk.
Home range less than 200 yds. across. Populations of 2 squirrels to 3 acres probably average, may be as high as 10 per
acre. May live 10 years. Displays territorial behavior by pro-

tecting food supply. Mates Feb.–March and again June–July.
Young: Born April–May and Aug.–Sept.; 2–7; gestation period 38 days.
Economic status: May damage cabins while unattended; affords pleasure to campers and hikers; too small for a game species.

Map below

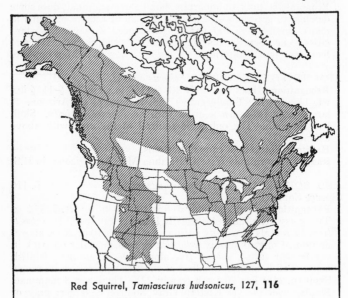

Red Squirrel, *Tamiasciurus hudsonicus*, 127, **116**

CHICKAREE *Tamiasciurus douglasi* p. 116
(Douglas Squirrel)

Recognition: Head and body 6–7 in.; tail 4¾–5 in.; wt. 6–7⅛ oz. This *noisy* little squirrel of the *evergreen forests* of the West is a counterpart of the Red Squirrel. It is dark *reddish olive*, grayer in winter, with a *yellowish or rusty belly*. Distinct *black line* along each side in summer, absent or indistinct in winter. Skull has 20 teeth. There are 8 mammae.
Similar species: (1) Western Gray Squirrel (p. 123) — larger; gray with white belly. (2) Golden-mantled Squirrel (p. 111) — head copper color, white stripe on side.
Habitat: Coniferous forests.
Habits: Similar to those of the Red Squirrel (above).
Young: Born June and Oct.; 4–8.
Economic status: Does little if any harm; affords pleasure to campers and visitors of parks within its range. Map opposite

SOUTHERN FLYING SQUIRREL *Glaucomys volans*   p. 117
  Recognition: Head and body 5½–5⅔ in.; tail 3½–4½ in.;
  wt. 1¾–2⅖ oz. Flying squirrels are seldom seen. Thick soft
  fur is glossy *olive-brown above, white to the skin below.* A folded
  layer of *loose skin along each side* of body, from front leg to hind
  leg, is found in no other mammals (except bats) here considered.
  When outstretched, this skin supports body as animal glides
  from tree to tree. Eyeshine is a reddish orange. Skull has 22
  teeth. There are 8 mammae.
  Similar species: Northern Flying Squirrel — larger; hairs of
  belly lead color at bases near skin.
  Habitat: Woodlots and forests of deciduous or mixed deciduous-
  coniferous trees.
  Habits: This and the next species are the only strictly nocturnal
  squirrels. Appears in open at deep dusk. Gregarious in winter.
  Apparently has homing instinct. Feeds on variety of seeds,
  nuts, insects, bird eggs; will eat meat if available; stores some
  food in nest chamber, also in crotches in trees. Makes nest in
  an old woodpecker hole, or builds outside nest of leaves, twigs,
  and bark; also occupies attics of buildings; 20 or more may den
  together in winter. Home range about 4 acres. Populations of
  1–2 per acre in summer. Has lived 13 years in captivity; makes
  good pet. Voice, a high-pitched twitter. Mates Feb.–March and
  June–July.
  Young: Born April–May and Aug.–Sept.; 2–6; gestation period
  about 40 days.
  Economic status: Unless its home is in the attic of a house, does
  not interfere with man's activities.   Map below

NORTHERN FLYING SQUIRREL *Glaucomys sabrinus*
  Recognition: Head and body 5½–6⅖ in.; tail 4⅛–5½ in.;

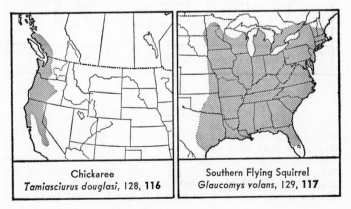

Chickaree
Tamiasciurus douglasi, 128, **116**

Southern Flying Squirrel
Glaucomys volans, 129, **117**

wt. 4–6½ oz. Characters similar to those for Southern Flying
Squirrel (above) except that it is larger and belly hairs are *white*
only at tips, lead color at bases near skin. Skull (p. 248) has 22
teeth. There are 8 mammae.

Similar species: Southern Flying Squirrel — belly hairs white
to bases near skin.

Habitat: Coniferous and mixed forests.

Habits: Probably similar to those of the Southern Flying Squirrel (above); not too well known.

Young: Born May–June; 2–5.

Economic status: Serves as food for some furbearers; may enter
traps set for furbearers with meat bait.   Map below

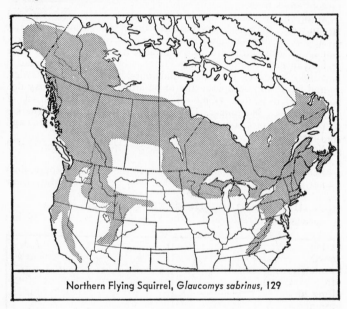

Northern Flying Squirrel, *Glaucomys sabrinus,* 129

Pocket Gophers: Geomyidae

MEMBERS of this family are small to medium-sized; head and body,
4¾–9 in.; they have external *cheek pouches* (pockets) which are
fur-lined and reversible and open on either side of mouth. Their
large, yellowish incisor teeth are *always exposed* in front of the
mouth opening; skin, with hair, extends behind the incisors and
the teeth are exposed when mouth is closed. Front claws large

and curved for efficient digging tools; tail *always shorter than head and body* and naked or scantily haired. Eyes and ears small. Presence of pocket gophers is easily detected by *mounds* of earth which they push out as they excavate their subterranean tunnels. Mounds characteristically *fan-shaped;* indication of position of opening is a round earth plug, the last of the dirt to be pushed to surface. They never leave their burrows open for long.

Some of the species are difficult to distinguish without resorting to internal structures. Rarely are 2 kinds found in the same field, but the general ranges of some interdigitate. If in doubt, specimens should be sent to a museum for positive identification. Color varies from nearly white to nearly black; mostly they are some shade of brown. Strictly N. American family of rodents. Known as fossils from Middle Oligocene.

Habits: General habits of all members of this family similar, as far as known. Solitary for much of their lives, they are active day and night throughout the year. All are burrowers, seldom seen aboveground. Prefer soil that is slightly moist and easy to work, but some are found in rocky situations, especially in mts. In winter, particularly in mts., they tunnel through snow and push loose dirt into tunnels. When snow melts, long ropelike cores of dirt settle to surface of ground. Pocket gophers feed largely on roots and tubers as well as some surface vegetation. Sometimes come aboveground to forage, but often pull plants down through surface soil into burrow system. Home range about 2200 sq. ft. for males and 1300 sq. ft. for females of *T. bottae.* In some at least, territorial behavior is displayed. They are polygamous and may breed once a year in the North and 2 or more times a year in the South.

Economic status: Considered harmful wherever they occur in cultivated areas; particularly bad in alfalfa fields, where not only do they consume some of the vegetation but their mounds hinder harvesting the crop. Root crops also suffer from their depredations. In wilderness areas pocket gophers are probably important as soil-forming agents; they bring subsoil to the surface and aid in water conservation and aeration of the soil. Biologically they are interesting animals. If control is necessary, it is best to consult a farm agent.

VALLEY POCKET GOPHER *Thomomys bottae* p. 148
 Recognition: Head and body 4⅘–7 in.; tail 2–3¾ in.; wt. 2½–8⅘ oz. Throughout its range this pocket gopher is extremely variable in size and coloration: small on some of the southern desert mts., large in the valleys; nearly white in the Imperial Desert, nearly black along parts of Pacific Coast. Usually some shade of brown. Best identified by where it lives. Differences given below apply to those parts of the population where ranges interdigitate. A single indistinct groove near inner border of

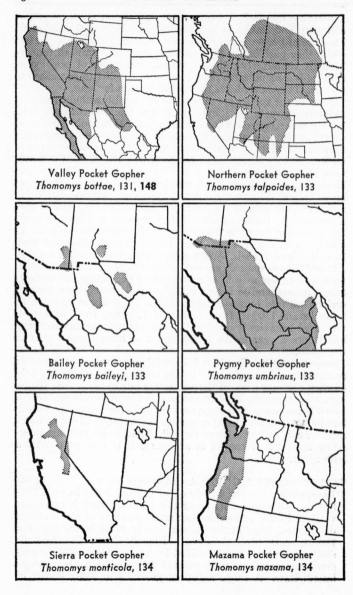

Valley Pocket Gopher
Thomomys bottae, 131, **148**

Northern Pocket Gopher
Thomomys talpoides, 133

Bailey Pocket Gopher
Thomomys baileyi, 133

Pygmy Pocket Gopher
Thomomys umbrinus, 133

Sierra Pocket Gopher
Thomomys monticola, 134

Mazama Pocket Gopher
Thomomys mazama, 134

each upper incisor. Skull has 20 teeth. There are 8 mammae.
Similar species: (1) Bailey Pocket Gopher — smaller; in mts.
(2) Northern Pocket Gopher — smaller, grayish; female has 10
mammae; high in mts. (3) Sierra Pocket Gopher — smaller;
high in mts. (4) Townsend Pocket Gopher — larger, grayish.
(5) Pygmy Pocket Gopher — smaller; in mts. (6) Mexican
Pocket Gopher — larger, yellowish; a deep groove down middle
of each upper incisor. (7) Plains Pocket Gopher — larger; 2
grooves down front of each upper incisor.
Habitat: Valleys and mt. meadows; it prefers a loam soil, but
some occur in sandy or rocky situations.
Young: Born Oct.–June; usually 5–7 (extremes, 3–13); gestation
period about 19 days; peaks in breeding activity, Nov. 1 and
April 1. Map opposite

BAILEY POCKET GOPHER *Thomomys baileyi*
Recognition: Head and body 6 in.; tail 2½ in. Wt.: males,
6⅛–8⅘ oz.; females, 5–6⅛ oz. This fulvous pocket gopher,
found in the *foothills*, is similar to the Valley Pocket Gopher.
It may be the same species, but is treated separately here.
Skull has 20 teeth. There are 8 mammae.
Similar species: (1) Valley Pocket Gopher — difficult to distinguish; lowlands. (2) Pygmy Pocket Gopher — 6 mammae;
high in mts. (3) Mexican and (4) Plains Pocket Gophers —
prominent grooves in upper incisors.
Habitat: Hard, clayey soils. Map opposite

PYGMY POCKET GOPHER *Thomomys umbrinus*
Recognition: Head and body 4⅜–5 in.; tail 2–2⅖ in. This small
pocket gopher, *yellowish brown* to deep *chestnut* in color, is found
only in the *mts.* Other pocket gophers with which it might be
confused are usually found in valleys. A single indistinct groove
near inner border of each upper incisor. Skull has 20 teeth.
There are 6 mammae.
Similar species: (1) Valley Pocket Gopher — larger; lowlands.
(2) Bailey Pocket Gopher — females with 8 mammae. (3) Mexican Pocket Gopher — larger, yellowish; deep groove down
middle of each incisor; lowlands.
Habitat: Oaks and pines, sometimes rocky soil. Map opposite

NORTHERN POCKET GOPHER *Thomomys talpoides*
Recognition: Head and body 5–6½ in.; tail 1¾–3 in.; wt. 2¾–
4⅜ oz. Males are larger than females. This gopher, where it
occurs close to ranges of others, is usually found in the *high mts.*
Grayish, sometimes washed with brown; nose brown or blackish;
black patches behind rounded ears. A single indistinct groove
near inner border of each upper incisor. Skull (p. 248) has 20
teeth. There are 10 mammae.

Similar species: (1) Valley Pocket Gopher — usually not grayish; female has 8 mammae; foothills and valleys. (2) Sierra Pocket Gopher — brown, not grayish; ears pointed. (3) Townsend Pocket Gopher — larger; along river valleys. (4) Giant Pocket Gopher — larger; lowlands. (5) Plains Pocket Gopher — larger; prominent groove in each upper incisor; lowlands.
Habitat: Grassy prairies, alpine meadows, brushy areas, and open pine forests.
Young: Born Feb.–June; usually 4–7; 1 or 2 litters a year.
Map p. 132

SIERRA POCKET GOPHER *Thomomys monticola*
Recognition: Head and body 5⅗–6 in.; tail 2–3 in.; wt. 2½–3⅕ oz. Small; *mummy-brown to yellowish brown;* nose black or blackish, as are patches behind the pointed ears; tail with some white; feet and wrists often white. A single indistinct groove near inner border of each upper incisor. Skull has 20 teeth. There are 8 mammae.
Similar species: (1) Northern Pocket Gopher — grayish; female has 10 mammae. (2) Valley Pocket Gopher — low foothills and valleys. (3) Giant Pocket Gopher — larger; lowlands.
Habitat: Mt. meadows.
Habits: In wet meadows, tunnels through snow; builds winter nest aboveground in snow; length of burrow system, 20–120 ft. Populations of 4–14 per acre. May live 4 years in wild.
Young: Born July–Aug.; 3–4; 1 litter a year. Map p. 132

MAZAMA POCKET GOPHER *Thomomys mazama*
Recognition: Head and body 5½–6⅗ in.; tail 2⅛–2⅞ in.; wt. 2⅘–4½ oz. Males slightly larger than females; similar in external appearance to Northern Pocket Gopher (above); ranges separate. Skull has 20 teeth.
Similar species: Giant Pocket Gopher — larger; in valleys.
Map p. 132

TOWNSEND POCKET GOPHER *Thomomys townsendi*
Recognition: Head and body 7–7½ in.; tail 2–3⅘ in.; wt. 8½–10¼ oz. Largest pocket gopher within its range; *grayish,* faintly washed with buff; tail, feet, and area around mouth may be white. A single indistinct groove near inner border of each upper incisor. Skull has 20 teeth. There are 8 mammae.
Similar species: (1) Valley Pocket Gopher — smaller, usually brownish. (2) Northern Pocket Gopher — smaller; high mts.
Habitat: Deep soils of river valleys.
Young: Born March–April; 3–8; 2 litters a year. Map opposite

GIANT POCKET GOPHER *Thomomys bulbivorus*
Recognition: Head and body 7⅗–8½ in.; tail 3¼–3⅗ in. This is by far the *largest* pocket gopher in Oregon. It is sooty brown.

A single indistinct groove near inner border of each upper incisor. Skull has 20 teeth. There are 8 mammae.

Similar species: (1) Sierra, (2) Mazama, and (3) Northern Pocket Gophers — all smaller and all mt. dwellers.

Habitat: Deep soils of Willamette Valley, Oregon; does not enter pines.

Young: Born April–July; 3–5; 1 litter a year. Map below

PLAINS POCKET GOPHER *Geomys bursarius* p. 148

Recognition: Head and body 5½–9 in.; tail 2–4½ in.; wt. 4½–12½ oz. Largest in the North, smallest in the South; males larger than females. Color varies from yellowish tawny to browns; nearly black in Illinois. Spotted and albino individuals fairly common. May be distinguished from other pocket gophers (except South Texas Pocket Gopher) by the *2 distinct grooves down* front of each upper incisor. Skull (p. 248) has 20 teeth. There are 6 mammae.

The species *G. arenarius*, from w. Texas and s. New Mexico, is considered a distinct species by some authors; it is included with *G. bursarius* on the distribution map.

Similar species: (1) South Texas Pocket Gopher — slightly larger; ranges separate for most part. (2) Mexican Pocket Gopher — 1 distinct groove in middle (front) of each upper incisor. (3) Bailey, (4) Northern, and (5) Valley Pocket Gophers — 1 indistinct groove near inner border of each upper incisor.

Habitat: Grassland, alfalfa fields, pastures, roadsides, and railroad rights-of-way.

Habits: Burrows up to 300 ft. long; nests in underground tunnels in North; in South some nest, in winter, in large mounds that they build up on surface. Breeds April–July in North, Feb.–Aug. in South.

Young: Usually 3–5 (1–8); 1 litter a year in North, 2 or more in South; gestation period 18–19 days. Map p. 136

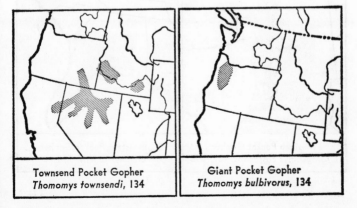

Townsend Pocket Gopher
Thomomys townsendi, 134

Giant Pocket Gopher
Thomomys bulbivorus, 134

SOUTH TEXAS POCKET GOPHER *Geomys personatus*
　Recognition: Head and body 7–8⅕ in.; tail 2½–4⅘ in.; wt.
10–14 oz. Pale, grayish brown; tail scantily haired; belly whitish
to dusky. Similar to Plains Pocket Gopher (above).
　Similar species: Plains Pocket Gopher — similar, but smaller
where they meet; ranges separate for most part.
　Habitat: Deep, sandy soils.　　　　　　　　　　Map below

SOUTHEASTERN POCKET GOPHER *Geomys pinetis*
(Salamander)
　Recognition: Head and body 6½–8 in.; tail 3–4 in. This is the
only mammal in its area that has *fur-lined external cheek pouches*.
Skull has 20 teeth.
　Formerly known as *G. tuza*.
　In current literature, 3 other species are recognized (all occur-

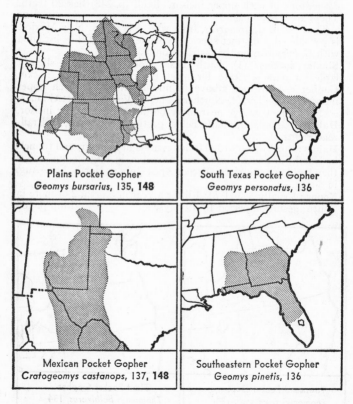

Plains Pocket Gopher
Geomys bursarius, 135, **148**

South Texas Pocket Gopher
Geomys personatus, 136

Mexican Pocket Gopher
Cratogeomys castanops, 137, **148**

Southeastern Pocket Gopher
Geomys pinetis, 136

ring in Georgia). They are: *G. colonus* in Camden Co., *G. fontanelus* in Chatham Co., and *G. cumberlandius* on Cumberland I., Camden Co. In this *Field Guide* they are treated together on the distribution map for *G. pinetis*.

Habitat: Pine woods and fields.

Young: May appear in any month; 1–3; at least 2 litters a year.

Map opposite

MEXICAN POCKET GOPHER   p. 148
Cratogeomys castanops

    Recognition: Head and body 7¼–8 in.; tail 3–4 in.; wt. 7½–11⁷⁄₁₀ oz. This *large, yellowish* pocket gopher may be distinguished from other pocket gophers by the distinct *single groove down middle* (front) *of each upper incisor.* Skull (p. 248) has 20 teeth.

    Similar species: (1) Plains Pocket Gopher — 2 grooves on front of each upper incisor. (2) Bailey, (3) Pygmy, and (4) Valley Pocket Gophers — smaller; an indistinct groove down front of each upper incisor, near inner border.

    Habitat: Deep, easily worked (preferably sandy) soil.

    Young: 1–3; possibly 2 litters a year.   Map opposite

Pocket Mice, Kangaroo Mice, and Kangaroo Rats: Heteromyidae

MEMBERS of this family are mostly *small* with *fur-lined cheek pouches* that open on either side of the mouth. Front feet are *weak* and hind feet and legs are strong and well developed. Tail is generally as long as or longer than head and body. Except for the genus *Liomys*, the upper incisors are grooved on front faces. All are adapted for arid or semi-arid conditions; they do not need drinking water. Burrow into ground for nest sites. Usually prefer pliable, *sandy soil.* All are nocturnal; may be seen dead along the highway or hopping across in front of headlights. Eyeshine dull amber. Known as fossils from Miocene.

Pocket mice include the smallest members of this family; head and body not more than 5 in. They vary from pale yellowish to dark gray, with paler belly, but *never* have striking color patterns on face or body. Tail never swollen along its middle. Possibly some hibernate or remain in den during severe weather. All store food, chiefly seeds.

Kangaroo mice are small silky-haired members of this group; head and body, 3 in. Tail *swollen* along its middle, smaller at base and tip, and *never crested* with long hairs at tip. Head is large for the animal.

Kangaroo rats are largest members of this family; head and body

up to 6½ in. They have extremely *long hind legs* and small front
legs and front feet. Belly always *white;* upperparts vary from pale
yellow to dark brownish. *Long tail* usually dark above and below,
with side stripes of white and with a crest of long hairs on terminal
⅕ or more. There are distinct *facial markings* of white and usually
black. On most of them, a definite *white band crosses thigh region*
and joins the tail. Variation is mostly in intensity of coloration,
not pattern.
Economic status: Members of this family, for the most part,
occupy uncultivated areas. They do no harm. By eating many
weed seeds, they may be beneficial.

MEXICAN POCKET MOUSE   *Liomys irroratus*   p. 148
  Recognition: Head and body 4–5 in.; tail 4–5 in.; wt. 1⅕–1¾ oz.
  This large pocket mouse barely enters the *Brownsville* area of
  Texas. It is dark gray above, white on belly, and has a pale
  yellow line along the side; hair on back and rump *stiff and spinelike.* Upper incisors not grooved on front faces. Skull (p. 248)
  has 20 teeth. There are 6 mammae.
  Similar species: (1) Hispid Pocket Mouse (p. 146) — tail shorter
  than head and body; upper incisors with grooves on front faces.
  (2) Merriam Pocket Mouse — smaller, yellowish; fur silky.
  Habitat: Dense thickets on low ridges.   Map opposite

WYOMING POCKET MOUSE   *Perognathus fasciatus*
  Recognition: Head and body 2⅘ in.; tail 2½ in.; wt. ¼–⅓ oz.
  Found on the plains, this is one of the *silky* pocket mice — the
  fur is soft. Color *olive-gray*, with pale *yellow on ears* and a yellow
  wash along sides. Skull has 20 teeth. There are 6 mammae.
  Similar species: (1) Plains and (2) Silky Pocket Mice — smaller;
  yellowish above or with yellow patches behind ears. (3) Hispid
  Pocket Mouse (p. 146) — larger; fur coarse.
  Habitat: Shortgrass prairies, sandy loam.
  Young: 4–6; gestation period about 4 weeks; 1 litter a year.
                                                      Map opposite
PLAINS POCKET MOUSE   *Perognathus flavescens*
  Recognition: Head and body 2¼–2¾ in.; tail 2–2⅗ in.; wt.
  ¼–⅓ oz. A small *pale yellowish* pocket mouse with *white belly;*
  no clear yellow patches behind ears. Skull has 20 teeth. There
  are 6 mammae.
  Similar species: (1) Wyoming Pocket Mouse — gray. (2) Merriam and (3) Silky Pocket Mice — clear yellow patches behind
  ears. (4) Bailey and (5) Hispid Pocket Mice (p. 146) — larger.
  Habitat: Open areas with sparse vegetation and sandy soil.
  Habits: Feeds mostly on small seeds; burrows usually beneath
  bushes; entrances plugged during day. Home range about ⅒
  acre. Breeds April–July.
  Young: 4–5; probably 2 litters a year.   Map opposite

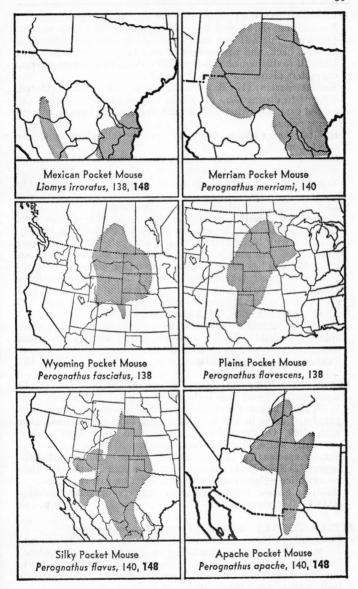

Mexican Pocket Mouse
Liomys irroratus, 138, **148**

Merriam Pocket Mouse
Perognathus merriami, 140

Wyoming Pocket Mouse
Perognathus fasciatus, 138

Plains Pocket Mouse
Perognathus flavescens, 138

Silky Pocket Mouse
Perognathus flavus, 140, **148**

Apache Pocket Mouse
Perognathus apache, 140, **148**

MERRIAM POCKET MOUSE *Perognathus merriami*

Recognition: Head and body $2\frac{1}{4}$–$2\frac{3}{4}$ in.; tail $1\frac{1}{2}$–2 in.; wt. $\frac{1}{4}$–$\frac{1}{3}$ oz. Fur soft and silky; rich *fulvous* sprinkled with dark hairs on back, and with yellow patches behind ears; belly *white.* Difficult to distinguish this from Silky Pocket Mouse on external characters alone. Skull has 20 teeth.

Similar species: (1) Silky Pocket Mouse — less richly colored, difficult to distinguish. (2) Plains Pocket Mouse — no patches behind ears. (3) Other pocket mice — distinctly larger and with coarse pelage.

Habitat: Open plains, sandy or gravelly soil, short or sparse vegetation.

Habits: Burrows usually at base of shrub or cactus; breeding season April–Nov.

Young: 3–6; 2 or more litters a year. Map p. 139

SILKY POCKET MOUSE *Perognathus flavus* p. 148

Recognition: Head and body 2–$2\frac{1}{2}$ in.; tail $1\frac{3}{4}$–$2\frac{1}{4}$ in.; wt. $\frac{1}{4}$–$\frac{1}{3}$ oz. Fur soft; upperparts *pale yellow,* faintly to heavily sprinkled with black hairs; a clear *yellow patch behind each ear;* belly *white.* Tail usually slightly *shorter than head and body,* not crested. Skull has 20 teeth. There are 6 mammae.

Similar species: (1) Merriam Pocket Mouse — more richly colored; difficult to distinguish. (2) Wyoming (olive-gray) and (3) Plains Pocket Mice — no yellow patches behind ears. (4) All other pocket mice — tail more than $2\frac{1}{2}$ in.

Habitat: Shortgrass prairies, sandy, occasionally rocky, soils.

Habits: Probably similar to those of the directly preceding species. Has lived 5 years in captivity.

Young: 2–6; possibly 2 litters a year. Map p. 139

APACHE POCKET MOUSE *Perognathus apache* p. 148

Recognition: Head and body $2\frac{2}{5}$–3 in.; tail $2\frac{2}{5}$–$2\frac{4}{5}$ in.; wt. $\frac{1}{4}$–$\frac{2}{5}$ oz. The soft fur of this inhabitant of some of our sparsely populated areas in the West is usually *buff,* slightly sprinkled with black. On the white sands, Otaro Co., New Mexico, they are nearly white. Belly is *white.* Skull has 20 teeth.

Similar species: (1) Arizona Pocket Mouse — similar; slightly larger. (2) Silky Pocket Mouse — tail less than $2\frac{1}{2}$ in. (3) Other pocket mice — larger and with long hairs toward tip of tail.

Habitat: Sparse brush, scattered junipers or pines; usually 5000–7200-ft. elevation. Map p. 139

LITTLE POCKET MOUSE *Perognathus longimembris*

Recognition: Head and body $2\frac{1}{5}$–$2\frac{4}{5}$ in.; tail 2–$3\frac{2}{5}$ in.; wt. $\frac{1}{4}$–$\frac{1}{3}$ oz. Fur *soft;* upperparts *buffy* to grayish buff; belly white. Difficult to distinguish from San Joaquin Pocket Mouse (below), but the ranges, for the most part, are distinct. Skull has 20 teeth. There are 6 mammae.

Similar species: (1) San Joaquin Pocket Mouse — confined to San Joaquin and Sacramento Valleys, California. (2) Arizona Pocket Mouse — larger; tail longer. (3) Great Basin Pocket Mouse — larger; dark olive-gray. (4) All other pocket mice — larger; long hairs toward tip of tail. (5) Dark Kangaroo Mouse (p. 147) — brownish; tail swollen in middle. (6) Pale Kangaroo Mouse (p. 151) — whitish; tail swollen in middle.
Habitat: Valleys and slopes; sandy soil covered with *desert pavement* of small pebbles; sagebrush, creosote bush, and cactus; occasionally scattered piñon pines and junipers.
Habits: Feeds primarily on small seeds; may range 350 yds. in 24 hrs.; has lived 7½ years in captivity.
Young: Born April–July; 3–7; 1 or 2 litters a year.
Map p. 142

ARIZONA POCKET MOUSE *Perognathus amplus*

Recognition: Head and body 2⅘–3 in.; tail 3–3⅘ in.; wt. 3/7–½ oz. Upperparts *pinkish buff*, sparsely sprinkled with black hairs on back; belly *white;* fur *soft and silky*. Tail *longer than head and body*. Skull has 20 teeth.
Similar species: (1) Apache and (2) Little Pocket Mice — smaller. (3) Silky Pocket Mouse — smaller; tail less than 2½ in. (4) Bailey, (5) Rock, and (6) Desert Pocket Mice — all larger and with long hairs toward tip of tail.
Habitat: Arid desert, scattered vegetation. Map p. 142

SAN JOAQUIN POCKET MOUSE *Perognathus inornatus*

Recognition: Head and body 2½–3⅕ in.; tail 2⅘–3 in. This soft-haired, buffy pocket mouse is confined to the *San Joaquin and Sacramento Valleys*, California. Only other pocket mouse of similar size and coloration with which this mouse might be confused is the Little Pocket Mouse (above), but ranges distinct for the most part. Skull has 20 teeth.
Similar species: (1) Little Pocket Mouse — difficult to distinguish; should be sent to a museum for identification. (2) White-eared Pocket Mouse — in pine zone. (3) California Pocket Mouse — olive-brown.
Habitat: Dry, open, grassy or weedy areas; fine-textured soil.
Map p. 142

GREAT BASIN POCKET MOUSE p. 148
Perognathus parvus

Recognition: Head and body 2½–3 in.; tail 3¼–4 in.; wt. ⅔–1 oz. Olive-gray, usually washed with fulvous on belly; fur soft; tail paler below than above, not particularly bushy on the end. Skull has 20 teeth. There are 6 mammae.
Similar species: (1) Little Pocket Mouse — smaller; buffy. (2) Longtail and (3) Desert Pocket Mice — tail with long hairs, distinctly bushy near tip. (4) Kangaroo Mice (pp. 147–51) — belly white, tail swollen in middle.

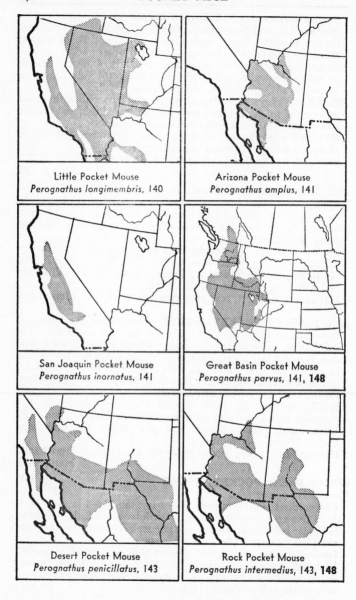

Little Pocket Mouse
Perognathus longimembris, 140

Arizona Pocket Mouse
Perognathus amplus, 141

San Joaquin Pocket Mouse
Perognathus inornatus, 141

Great Basin Pocket Mouse
Perognathus parvus, 141, **148**

Desert Pocket Mouse
Perognathus penicillatus, 143

Rock Pocket Mouse
Perognathus intermedius, 143, **148**

Habitat: Sagebrush, chaparral, piñon and yellow pines.
Habits: Inactive in winter. Solitary for most of life. Burrows beneath bushes, closed during day; stores seeds in den. Has lived 4½ years in captivity.
Young: Born late spring and early summer; 3–8, usually 4–5; probably 1 litter a year. Map opposite

WHITE-EARED POCKET MOUSE *Perognathus alticolus*
Recognition: Head and body 3–3⅖ in.; tail 3–3⅗ in. Hair soft; upperparts olivaceous buff; *ears* and underparts *white* or *whitish.* Skull has 20 teeth.
Similar species: (1) San Joaquin Pocket Mouse — ears not whitish; below pines. (2) California and (3) San Diego Pocket Mice — fur harsh; usually below pines.
Habitat: Scattered pines with undergrowth of grass or bracken ferns; 5400–6000-ft. elevation.
Range: Mt. Pinos and western part of San Bernardino Mts., California.

WALKER PASS POCKET MOUSE *Perognathus xanthonotus*
Recognition: Head and body 3⅖ in.; tail 3⅖ in. Skull has 20 teeth.
Similar species: Other pocket mice within its range — either have harsh fur or occur in low valleys.
Habitat: Chaparral, sagebrush, bunchgrass; 4600–5300-ft. elevation.
Range: Known only from eastern slope of Walker Pass, Kern Co., California.

DESERT POCKET MOUSE *Perognathus penicillatus*
Recognition: Head and body 3–3⅘ in.; tail 3½–4⅘ in.; wt. ½–⅘ oz. Pale *yellowish* brown to yellowish gray; *tail crested, longer than head and body;* hair slightly harsh, but *no rump spines.* Skull has 20 teeth.
Similar species: (1) Rock Pocket Mouse — rocky situations. (2) Bailey Pocket Mouse — larger; grayish. (3) Longtail Pocket Mouse — slate-gray. (4) San Diego, (5) Spiny, and (6) Nelson Pocket Mice — spinelike hairs on rump. (7) All other pocket mice — no crest on tail.
Habitat: Open, sandy, desert floors preferred; sparse vegetation.
Habits: Inactive in winter; home range less than 1 acre.
Young: Born May–Sept.; 2–5. Map opposite

ROCK POCKET MOUSE *Perognathus intermedius* p. 148
Recognition: Head and body 3–3⅘ in.; tail 3⅕–4 in.; wt. ⅖–⅘ oz. Usually *gray* sprinkled with fulvous; on some lava areas nearly *black;* tail *crested.* Some have indistinct spinelike hairs on rump. Skull (p. 248) has 20 teeth.

Similar species: (1) Desert Pocket Mouse — on sandy soils. (2) Bailey Pocket Mouse — larger. (3) All other pocket mice within its range — no crest on tail.

Habitat: Rocky slopes, old lava flows, sparse vegetation.

Young: Born May–July; 3–6. Map p. 142

NELSON POCKET MOUSE *Perognathus nelsoni*

Recognition: Head and body 3–3⅖ in.; tail 4–4⅗ in.; wt. ½–⅗ oz. Upperparts mixed fulvous and light brown; hair hispid, *spinelike* on rump; *tail crested*, longer than head and body. Similar to Rock Pocket Mouse (above) and may belong to same species. No other pocket mouse within its range has spinelike hairs on rump.

Habitat: Rocky areas with sparse vegetation; 2300–4800-ft. elevation. Map opposite

SAN DIEGO POCKET MOUSE *Perognathus fallax*

Recognition: Head and body 3⅕–3½ in.; tail 3½–4⅘ in. Upperparts dark *rich brown* flecked *with* deep *fulvous;* definite *spinelike hairs on rump;* belly white; a deep fulvous line along each side; tail crested. Skull has 20 teeth.

Similar species: (1) California Pocket Mouse — similar; difficult to distinguish; usually found in chaparral or live-oak belt, not on low desert. (2) Spiny Pocket Mouse — pale yellowish. (3) All other pocket mice within its range — no spinelike hairs on rump.

Habitat: Open, sandy areas grown to weeds. Map opposite

CALIFORNIA POCKET MOUSE p. 148
Perognathus californicus

Recognition: Head and body 3⅕–3⅗ in.; tail 4–5⅘ in. This is the common pocket mouse along the coast of the southern part of California. Color *olive-brown* flecked *with fulvous.* Tail *crested, longer than head and body.* Spinelike hairs on rump. Skull has 20 teeth.

Similar species: (1) San Diego Pocket Mouse — difficult to distinguish; usually found lower on desert. (2) Other pocket mice within its range — no rump spines.

Habitat: Slopes covered with chaparral or live-oaks.

Map opposite

SPINY POCKET MOUSE *Perognathus spinatus*

Recognition: Head and body 3–3⅗ in.; tail 3⅕–5 in. Upperparts *pale yellowish* mixed with light brown; *tail long and crested;* distinct *spinelike hairs on rump.* Skull has 20 teeth.

Similar species: (1) San Diego Pocket Mouse — dark brownish. (2) All other pocket mice within its range — no spines on rump.

Habitat: Rough-surfaced mesas and rocky slopes, sparse vegetation, hot desert. Map opposite

POCKET MICE   145

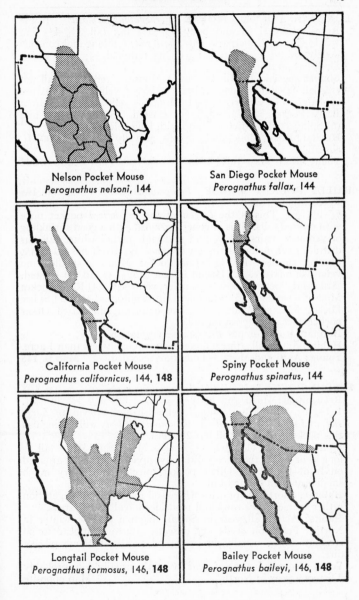

Nelson Pocket Mouse
Perognathus nelsoni, 144

San Diego Pocket Mouse
Perognathus fallax, 144

California Pocket Mouse
Perognathus californicus, 144, **148**

Spiny Pocket Mouse
Perognathus spinatus, 144

Longtail Pocket Mouse
Perognathus formosus, 146, **148**

Bailey Pocket Mouse
Perognathus baileyi, 146, **148**

LONGTAIL POCKET MOUSE *Perognathus formosus* p. 148

Recognition: Head and body $3\frac{1}{5}$–$3\frac{4}{5}$ in.; tail $3\frac{4}{5}$–$4\frac{4}{5}$ in.; wt. $\frac{1}{2}$–$\frac{5}{6}$ oz. Upperparts *gray; hair soft; tail* long and conspicuously *crested with long hairs* on its terminal $\frac{1}{3}$; belly white. Skull has 20 teeth.

Similar species: (1) Little Pocket Mouse — yellowish; tail not crested. (2) Bailey Pocket Mouse — larger; yellowish admixture of hairs. (3) Desert Pocket Mouse — yellowish. (4) Great Basin Pocket Mouse — tail not crested. (5) San Diego and (6) Spiny Pocket Mice — rump with long spinelike hairs.

Habitat: Rocky slopes and canyons, gravelly soil; up to 8000-ft. elevation.

Young: Born May–July; 4–6. Map p. 145

BAILEY POCKET MOUSE *Perognathus baileyi* p. 148

Recognition: Head and body $3\frac{3}{5}$–$4\frac{1}{5}$ in.; tail $4\frac{2}{5}$–5 in.; wt. $\frac{5}{6}$–$1\frac{1}{3}$ oz. This is the *largest* of the *soft-haired* pocket mice with crested tails. It is in general grayish with a good sprinkling of yellowish hairs. Belly and underside of tail white; tail has distinct *crest* of long hairs on *terminal* $\frac{1}{3}$. Skull has 20 teeth.

Similar species: (1) Longtail Pocket Mouse — smaller; no yellowish mixture. (2) Hispid Pocket Mouse — tail not crested. (3) Desert Pocket Mouse — smaller; yellowish. (4) Rock Pocket Mouse — smaller. (5) San Diego, (6) California, and (7) Spiny Pocket Mice — smaller; spinelike hairs on rump. (8) Other pocket mice — no crest on tail.

Habitat: Rocky slopes with sparse vegetation.

Habits: Active all winter; home range probably less than 1 acre.

Young: April and May; 3–4 embryos recorded. Map p. 145

HISPID POCKET MOUSE *Perognathus hispidus* p. 148

Recognition: Head and body $4\frac{1}{2}$–5 in.; tail $3\frac{1}{2}$–$4\frac{1}{2}$ in.; wt. 1–$1\frac{2}{3}$ oz. *Harsh* hair, mixed yellowish and brownish. *Large size, and noncrested tail shorter than head and body* will distinguish this pocket mouse. Skull has 20 teeth.

Similar species: (1) Mexican Pocket Mouse (p. 138) — tail as long as or longer than head and body; upper incisors not grooved on front faces. (2) Other pocket mice — either very much smaller or with crested tail.

Habitat: Shortgrass prairies where soil is friable and vegetation rather sparse; fence rows and roadsides in cultivated areas.

Habits: Active all year in South, inactive part of winter in North. Feeds on seeds and insects. Burrows appear to go straight down, usually in open and mostly without pile of dirt.

Young: Born any time of year in South; usually 2–6; probably 2 litters a year in North. Map opposite

DARK KANGAROO MOUSE *Microdipodops megacephalus*
   Recognition: Head and body 2⅖–3 in.; tail 2⅔–4 in.; wt. ⅓–⅔
oz. This *small brownish or blackish* kangaroo mouse usually has
bases of hairs lead color and tip of tail blackish. Tail *swollen* in
middle. Skull has 20 teeth.
   Similar species: (1) Pale Kangaroo Mouse — whitish or light
buffy upperparts. (2) Great Basin Pocket Mouse (p. 141) —
belly washed with fulvous; tail not swollen in middle. (3) Little
Pocket Mouse (p. 140) — yellowish.
   Habitat: Fine sandy soil with sagebrush and rabbitbrush.
   Habits: Nocturnal; feeds mostly on seeds, but takes some insects; closes openings to burrows during day.
   Young: Born May to early July; 1–7 embryos reported.

Map p. 150

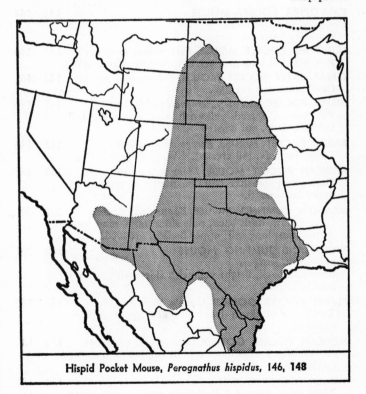

Hispid Pocket Mouse, *Perognathus hispidus*, 146, **148**

POCKET MICE, JUMPING MICE, POCKET GOPHERS
(Fur-lined cheek pouches or with long hind legs and tails)

	Map	Text
SILKY POCKET MOUSE, *Perognathus flavus*	139	140
Yellowish; soft fur; tail not crested; small size. W Central.		
APACHE POCKET MOUSE, *Perognathus apache*	139	140
Buffy; tail more than 2½ in. SW.		
ROCK POCKET MOUSE, *Perognathus intermedius*	142	143
Gray to black, sprinkled with fulvous; tail crested. SW.		
CALIFORNIA POCKET MOUSE	145	144
Perognathus californicus		
Spinelike hairs on rump. SW.		
LONGTAIL POCKET MOUSE, *Perognathus formosus*	145	146
Soft fur; tail long and crested; medium-sized. SW.		
GREAT BASIN POCKET MOUSE, *Perognathus parvus*	142	141
Olive-gray; soft fur. W.		
HISPID POCKET MOUSE, *Perognathus hispidus*	147	146
Fur coarse, mixed yellowish and brownish; tail medium-sized, not crested. Central.		
BAILEY POCKET MOUSE, *Perognathus baileyi*	145	146
Large; fur soft; tail crested. SW.		
MEXICAN POCKET MOUSE, *Liomys irroratus*	139	138
Dark gray; spinelike hairs on rump; no grooves on upper incisors. S.		
MEADOW JUMPING MOUSE, *Zapus hudsonius*	207	206
Olive-yellow, dark back, pale sides; large hind feet; no pouches; long tail; upper incisors grooved. N.		
WOODLAND JUMPING MOUSE	208	207
Napaeozapus insignis		
Brownish back, bright yellowish sides; white tip on long tail. NE.		
PLAINS POCKET GOPHER, *Geomys bursarius*	136	135
Two grooves down front of each upper incisor. Central.		
MEXICAN POCKET GOPHER, *Cratogeomys castanops*	136	137
One distinct groove down middle front of each upper incisor. SW.		
VALLEY POCKET GOPHER, *Thomomys bottae*	132	131
Three color phases; 1 indistinct groove near inner border of each incisor. SW.		

APACHE POCKET MOUSE

ROCK POCKET MOUSE

CALIFORNIA POCKET MOUSE

KY
CKET
USE

NGTAIL
CKET
USE

HISPID POCKET MOUSE

LEY POCKET MOUSE

GREAT BASIN POCKET MOUSE

ADOW
MPING
USE

WOODLAND

JUMPING MOUSE

MEXICAN POCKET MOUSE

PLAINS POCKET GOPHER

MEXICAN POCKET GOPHER

Pale phase   Brown phase   Dark phase   VALLEY POCKET GOPHER

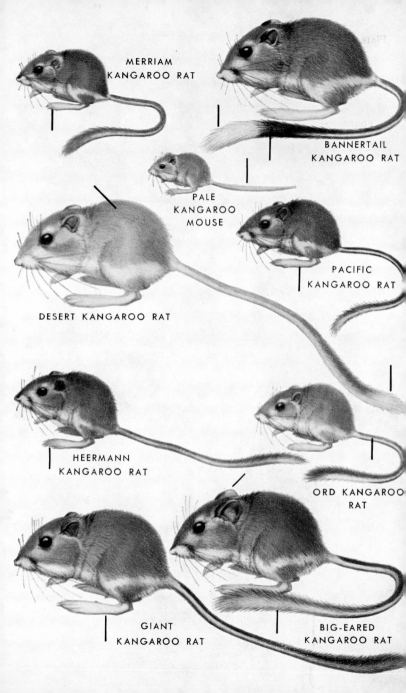

MERRIAM
KANGAROO RAT

BANNERTAIL
KANGAROO RAT

PALE
KANGAROO
MOUSE

PACIFIC
KANGAROO RAT

DESERT KANGAROO RAT

HEERMANN
KANGAROO RAT

ORD KANGAROO
RAT

GIANT
KANGAROO RAT

BIG-EARED
KANGAROO RAT

Plate 14   149

KANGAROO RATS AND MICE

(Fur-lined cheek pouches; deserts)

	Map	*Text*
MERRIAM KANGAROO RAT, *Dipodomys merriami* Four toes on hind foot; small size. SW.	155	156
BANNERTAIL KANGAROO RAT, *Dipodomys spectabilis* White tip on tail. SW.	150	151
PALE KANGAROO MOUSE, *Microdipodops pallidus* Tail swollen in middle; not crested. SW.	150	151
DESERT KANGAROO RAT, *Dipodomys deserti* Pale yellowish; white-tipped tail; large size. SW.	155	156
PACIFIC KANGAROO RAT, *Dipodomys agilis* Five toes on hind foot. SW.	155	154
HEERMANN KANGAROO RAT, *Dipodomys heermanni* Normally 4 toes on hind foot; valleys and foothills. W.	150	151
ORD KANGAROO RAT, *Dipodomys ordi* Dark tail stripes broader than white ones. W.	153	153
GIANT KANGAROO RAT, *Dipodomys ingens* Five toes on hind foot; large size. SW.	150	152
BIG-EARED KANGAROO RAT, *Dipodomys elephantinus* Large ears; end of tail heavily crested. SW.		154

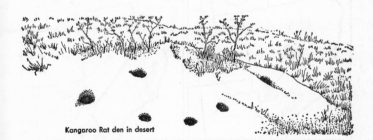

Kangaroo Rat den in desert

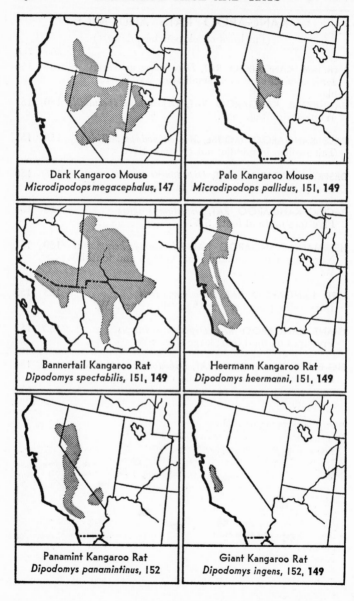

Dark Kangaroo Mouse
Microdipodops megacephalus, 147

Pale Kangaroo Mouse
Microdipodops pallidus, 151, **149**

Bannertail Kangaroo Rat
Dipodomys spectabilis, 151, **149**

Heermann Kangaroo Rat
Dipodomys heermanni, 151, **149**

Panamint Kangaroo Rat
Dipodomys panamintinus, 152

Giant Kangaroo Rat
Dipodomys ingens, 152, **149**

PALE KANGAROO MOUSE   *Microdipodops pallidus*   p. 149
  Recognition: Head and body 3 in.; tail 3–4 in.; wt. ⅓–⅔ oz.
  Upperparts *whitish* or *pale buff;* hairs of belly and underside of
  tail *white to bases;* tail *swollen* in middle, no black tip. Skull
  (p. 248) has 20 teeth.
  Similar species: (1) Dark Kangaroo Mouse — brownish or
  blackish; tail with blackish tip. (2) Great Basin Pocket Mouse
  (p. 141) — olive-gray. (3) Little Pocket Mouse (p. 140) —
  yellowish.
  Habitat: Fine sand and scattered brush.
  Habits: Probably similar to those of Dark Kangaroo Mouse
  (above).   Map opposite

BANNERTAIL KANGAROO RAT   p. 149
Dipodomys spectabilis
  Recognition: Head and body 5–6 in.; tail 7–9 in.; wt. 4–6⅕ oz.
  Most spectacularly marked of any of the kangaroo rats. A *large,
  4-toed* species with *prominent white tip on tail.* Narrow white
  side stripes on tail end about ⅔ distance to tip; there is then a
  black band followed by the white tip. Skull has 20 teeth. There
  are 6 mammae.
  Similar species: (1) Ord and (2) Merriam Kangaroo Rats —
  smaller; no white tip on tail.
  Habitat: Arid or semi-arid grassland with scattered brush, mesquite, or junipers.
  Habits: Active throughout year. Nocturnal. Builds mounds of
  mixed earth and plant debris up to 10 ft. across and 3 ft. high;
  up to 12 burrow openings in mound. Stores seeds in den; more
  than 12 lb. removed from 1 den. Home range usually not more
  than 600 ft. across; may move nearly a mile. Populations 1–2
  per acre. Has lived longer than 2 years in wild.
  Young: Born Jan.–Aug.; 1–4; gestation period, 27± days; 1–2,
  sometimes 3 litters a year.   Map opposite

HEERMANN KANGAROO RAT   p. 149
Dipodomys heermanni
  Recognition: Head and body 4–5 in.; tail 6½–8½ in.; wt. 1¾–
  3⅓ oz. A medium-sized kangaroo rat; either 4 or 5 toes on each
  hind foot; normally 4. Tip of tail white or dusky. The species is
  difficult to characterize on external characters; skull must be
  examined for certain identification in some parts of its range.
  Skull has 20 teeth.
  Similar species: (1) Giant Kangaroo Rat — larger; head and
  body over 5 in.; 5 toes. (2) Santa Cruz Kangaroo Rat — 5 toes
  on hind foot; a white band across outer flank. (3) Big-eared
  Kangaroo Rat — tail heavily crested. (4) Fresno Kangaroo
  Rat — tail not longer than 6 in.
  Habitat: Dry grassy plains and partly open gravelly ground on
  slopes with sparse chaparral.

Habits: Active throughout year. Nocturnal, prefers moonless nights. Stores seeds, but in small amounts; eats much green vegetation. Mounds at den entrances, long and narrow; many burrow entrances without mounds; 1–6 entrances to each burrow system; burrows 6–24 in. deep 10–40 ft. long. Home range usually less than 400 ft. across; some move ½ mi. or more. Populations 1–7 per acre. Breeding season Feb.–Oct., height in April.
Young: 2–5; 1–3 litters a year. Naked. Females breed 1st year. Map p. 150

PANAMINT KANGAROO RAT *Dipodomys panamintinus*
Recognition: Head and body 5 in.; tail 6⅖–7⅗ in.; wt. 2¼–3⅓ oz. There are *5 toes* on each hind foot. Dark stripe on underside of tail tapers to point near end. Skull has 20 teeth.
Similar species: (1) Great Basin Kangaroo Rat — chiefly in sagebrush and greasewood. (2) Pacific Kangaroo Rat — dark stripe on underside of tail continues to tip. (3) Ord Kangaroo Rat — smaller; tail not more than 6 in. (4) Merriam Kangaroo Rat — smaller; 4 toes on hind foot. (5) Desert Kangaroo Rat — larger, pale; no black markings; 4 toes on hind foot.
Habitat: Sandy or gravelly soil, tree yuccas, piñon pines, scattered sagebrush. Map p. 150

STEPHENS KANGAROO RAT *Dipodomys stephensi*
Recognition: Head and body 5½ in.; tail 6½–7⅕ in.; wt. 2⅔ oz. This *5-toed* kangaroo rat is found only in the *San Jacinto Valley*, California. Skull has 20 teeth.
Similar species: (1) Pacific Kangaroo Rat — difficult to distinguish without skull. (2) Merriam Kangaroo Rat — smaller; 4 toes on hind foot.
Habitat: Dry, open, or sparsely brushy areas; sandy or gravelly soil.
Range: San Jacinto Valley, w. Riverside and s. San Bernardino Cos., California.

GIANT KANGAROO RAT *Dipodomys ingens* p. 149
Recognition: Head and body 5⅗–6 in.; tail 7–8 in.; wt. 4½–6⅓ oz. This is the *largest* of the kangaroo rats. It has *5 toes on each hind foot*. Skull has 20 teeth. There are 6 mammae.
Similar species: (1) Heermann, (2) Fresno (4-toed), (3) Pacific, and (4) Santa Cruz Kangaroo Rats — all with head and body less than 5½ in.
Habitat: Fine sandy loam with sparse vegetation.
Habits: Nocturnal. Eats mostly green food when available, also seeds. Burrows in groups of 2–4 and widely spaced. May display territorial behavior. Breeding season Jan.–May.
Young: Usually 3–4, occasionally 6. Map p. 150

ORD KANGAROO RAT *Dipodomys ordi* p. 149

Recognition: Head and body 4–4½ in.; tail 5–6 in.; wt. 1½–2½ oz. This is the most widely distributed of the kangaroo rats. May have either 4 or 5 toes on each hind foot. *Dark tail stripes broader* than white ones; ventral stripe *tapers to a point* near tip of tail. Lower incisors rounded, not flat across front. Skull has 20 teeth.

Similar species: (1) Panamint Kangaroo Rat — tail more than 6 in. (2) Merriam Kangaroo Rat — always 4 toes; light tail stripes broader than dark ones. (3) Great Basin Kangaroo Rat — lower incisors flat and chisel-like. (4) Texas, (5) Bannertail, and (6) Desert Kangaroo Rats — white tip on tail.

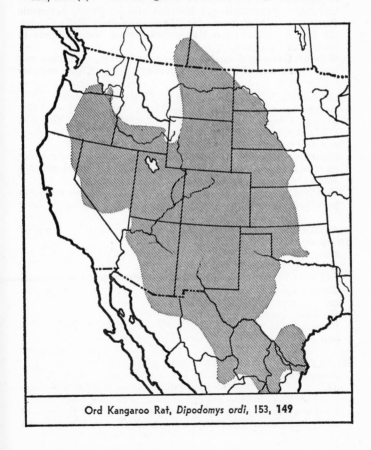

Ord Kangaroo Rat, *Dipodomys ordi*, 153, **149**

Habitat: Sandy soils preferred, but it is sometimes found on rather hard soils.
Habits: Active throughout year; nocturnal. Will drink water when available; stores seeds.
Young: Born May–June; 2–5; may be 2 litters a year.
Map p. 153

PACIFIC KANGAROO RAT *Dipodomys agilis* p. 149
Recognition: Head and body $4\frac{2}{5}$–5 in.; tail $6\frac{1}{5}$–8 in.; wt. $1\frac{3}{5}$–$2\frac{7}{10}$ oz. This is the common kangaroo rat of the Pacific Coast of s. California. Dark ventral stripe continues to tip of tail; *5 toes* on each hind foot. Skull has 20 teeth.
Similar species: (1) Stephens Kangaroo Rat — difficult to distinguish without skull. (2) Merriam and (3) Fresno Kangaroo Rats — smaller; 4 toes. (4) Giant Kangaroo Rat — larger. (5) Panamint Kangaroo Rat — dark ventral stripe tapers to point near tip of tail.
Habitat: Gravelly or sandy soil, slopes or washes, open chaparral; from near sea level to 7500-ft. elevation. Map opposite

SANTA CRUZ KANGAROO RAT *Dipodomys venustus*
Recognition: Head and body $4\frac{4}{5}$–$5\frac{1}{5}$ in.; tail 7–8 in.; wt. $2\frac{7}{10}$–$3\frac{1}{5}$ oz. Along a narrow strip of the Pacific Coast of California, this *5-toed*, *richly colored* kangaroo rat may be found. Has *large ears* and a white band across flank. Skull has 20 teeth.
Similar species: (1) Heermann Kangaroo Rat — usually 4 toes on hind foot; no white band across flank. (2) Giant Kangaroo Rat — head and body longer than $5\frac{1}{2}$ in.
Habitat: Slopes with chaparral, oaks, pines; also flat areas; up to 5900-ft. elevation. Map opposite

BIG-EARED KANGAROO RAT p. 149
Dipodomys elephantinus
Recognition: Head and body 5 in.; tail 7–8 in.; wt. $2\frac{4}{5}$–$3\frac{1}{5}$ oz. A handsome, *big-eared* kangaroo rat; 5 toes on each hind foot; end of tail heavily crested with long hairs. Skull has 20 teeth.
Similar species: Heermann Kangaroo Rat — tail not heavily crested, may have only 4 toes.
Habitat: Chaparral-covered slopes.
Range: Southern part of Gabilan Range, vicinity of Pinnacles, San Benito and Monterey Cos., California.

GREAT BASIN KANGAROO RAT *Dipodomys microps*
Recognition: Head and body 4–5 in.; tail $5\frac{3}{5}$–$7\frac{1}{3}$ in.; wt. $2\frac{1}{2}$–$3\frac{1}{5}$ oz. Medium-sized; 5 toes; insides of cheek pouches blackish in some; lower incisors flat across front. Skull has 20 teeth.
Similar species: (1) Panamint Kangaroo Rat — chiefly in yucca and piñon pines. (2) Merriam Kangaroo Rat — small; 4 toes.

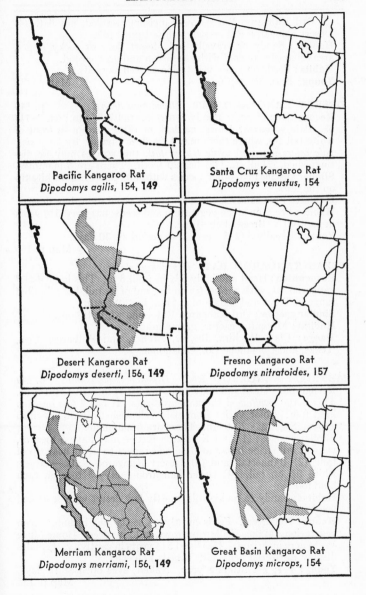

Pacific Kangaroo Rat
Dipodomys agilis, 154, **149**

Santa Cruz Kangaroo Rat
Dipodomys venustus, 154

Desert Kangaroo Rat
Dipodomys deserti, 156, **149**

Fresno Kangaroo Rat
Dipodomys nitratoides, 157

Merriam Kangaroo Rat
Dipodomys merriami, 156, **149**

Great Basin Kangaroo Rat
Dipodomys microps, 154

(3) Ord Kangaroo Rat — lower incisors rounded, not flat. (4) Desert Kangaroo Rat — pale; white-tipped tail.
Habitat: Sandy or gravelly soil, desert floor or rocky slopes, areas sparsely covered with sagebrush and greasewood.
Habits: Feeds on green vegetation as well as seeds.
Young: Born May–June; 1–4.   Map p. 155

DESERT KANGAROO RAT *Dipodomys deserti*   p. 149
Recognition: Head and body 5–6½ in.; tail 7–8½ in.; wt. 3–5⅙ oz. Pale *yellowish;* 4 toes; *no* dark markings except in front of white tail tip, where there may be a dusky band. By *large size, pale coloration,* and *white tip on tail,* this species may be distinguished. Skull (p. 248) has 20 teeth. There are 6 mammae.
Similar species: No other species within its range has a white tip on the tail.
Habitat: Fine sandy areas with sparse vegetation, low deserts.
Habits: Feeds on green vegetation and seeds; has lived 5½ years in captivity. Breeds Feb.–June.
Young: Usually 3 (2–5); gestation period 29–30 days.
                                                                 Map p. 155

TEXAS KANGAROO RAT *Dipodomys elator*
Recognition: Head and body 5¾ in.; tail 8 in. This large *4-toed* kangaroo rat, with a *white tip* on the end of its tail, has a limited range in Texas and Oklahoma. Skull has 20 teeth.
Similar species: Ord Kangaroo Rat — no white tip on tail.
Habitat: Mesquite, cactus, grama grass.
Range: Clay, Wichita, Baylor, Archer, and Wilbarger Cos., Texas, and Comanche Co., Oklahoma.

MERRIAM KANGAROO RAT *Dipodomys merriami*   p. 149
Recognition: Head and body 4 in.; tail 5–6⅔ in.; wt. 1⅙–1¾ oz. This is the *smallest* of the kangaroo rats. It has *4 toes* on each hind foot. Color varies from pale yellowish to dark brownish above. Skull has 20 teeth. There are 6 mammae.
Similar species: (1) Ord Kangaroo Rat — may have 5 toes, or, ventral tail stripe broad at base and tapers to point near tip of tail. (2) Bannertail and (3) Desert Kangaroo Rats — larger; white tip on tail. (4) Other kangaroo rats — 5 toes on each hind foot.
Habitat: Sandy to rocky soils, mostly low desert with scattered vegetation.
Habits: Nocturnal. Feeds mostly on seeds, but includes green vegetation. Makes shallow burrows, 6–13 in. deep. Home range ⅓–½ acre in Arizona. Has lived 5½ years in captivity. Females display territorial behavior. Breeds Feb.–Oct.
Young: 1–4; 1–2 litters a year. Naked; eyes open at 13 days.
                                                                 Map p. 155

FRESNO KANGAROO RAT *Dipodomys nitratoides*
  Recognition: Head and body 3⅜–4 in.; tail 4⅘–6 in.; wt. 1–1¾ oz. By its *small size* and *4 toes* on each hind foot, this inhabitant of the *San Joaquin Valley*, California, may be distinguished from other kangaroo rats. Skull has 20 teeth.
  Similar species: (1) Heermann Kangaroo Rat — larger; tail longer than 6 in. (2) Other kangaroo rats — 5 toes.
  Habitat: Arid, often alkaline, plains with sparse growths of grass and low brush. Map p. 155

Beaver: Castoridae

THERE is but one living genus (*Castor*) in this family. The Beaver is the largest rodent here considered. Fossils date back to Lower Oligocene.

BEAVER *Castor canadensis* p. 196
  Recognition: Head and body 25–30 in.; tail 9–10 in.; wt. 30–60 lb. A stick-and-mud *dam across a stream* or a large *conical house* of similar material at the edge of a lake and stumps of small trees in the vicinity showing tooth marks will reveal the presence of the Beaver. A loud report, as the Beaver dives below the surface of the water, will also indicate its presence. Rich brown in color; tail naked, scaly, *shaped like a paddle* (flat, about 6 in. wide). Huge front teeth chestnut-colored on front faces; hind feet webbed, 2nd claw double. Skull (p. 249) has 20 teeth. There are 4 mammae.
  Similar species: (1) River Otter (p. 62) — tail covered with fur. (2) Muskrat (p. 203) — smaller; tail slender and flattened from side to side. (3) Nutria (p. 210) — tail round, haired.
  Habitat: Streams and lakes with trees or alders on banks.
  Habits: Chiefly nocturnal, occasionally seen by day; appears shortly after sundown. Preferred food is aspen, poplar, birch, maple, willow, and alder; feeds on bark and small twigs; stores branches and small sections of logs underwater near lodge. Family groups of parents, yearlings, and kits may occupy a lodge; 2-year-olds are driven out or leave parental home. May burrow in bank for den along swift streams. Colony defends territory against other colonies; all may share in repairing dam. Has moved 150 mi. or more from birth place, usually under 6 mi. Lives 11 years in wild, 19 years in captivity. Females breed at 2½ years.
  Young: Born April–July; usually 2–4, occasionally 8; gestation period about 128 days; 1 litter a year. Kits furred and with eyes open.
  Economic status: An important fur animal and water conservationist; timber destroyed is mostly low-grade; occasionally

floods roads or fields; meat edible. Exterminated in much of
former range, now being reintroduced widely. May be seen in
most of the northern parks — Algonquin Provincial and Jasper
Natl. Parks in Canada; Glacier, Yellowstone, Grand Teton,
Mt. Rainier, Olympic, and Rocky Mt. Natl. Parks in U.S.

Map below

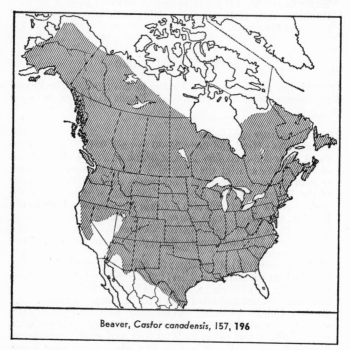

Beaver, *Castor canadensis*, 157, **196**

Mice, Rats, Lemmings, and Voles: Cricetidae

THIS family includes small to medium-sized rodents (head and
body 2–10 in.; tail ⅖–8 in., except Muskrat, which may have head
and body 14 in.). Most of them have 4 toes on the front foot, some
have 5, and all have 5 toes on the hind foot. Tails rarely bushy,
mostly covered with short hair. Mice and rats have large ears and
eyes and long tails; lemmings and voles have short tails, small
ears and eyes, and usually long fur on body. They live mostly on
and in the ground, some in trees (in part), some in rocky situations,
and some are partially aquatic. A representative of this family

will be found wherever one is in N. America. Fossils date back to Oligocene, possibly Upper Eocene time. All have 2 gnawing teeth and 6 cheek teeth in upper and lower jaws (16 teeth).

Harvest Mice

EXTERNALLY, these small brown mice resemble House Mice. One certain way to distinguish them from all other small brownish mice is to examine the upper incisors. If each of these has a distinct *groove* down the front, lengthwise, it is probably a harvest mouse. Other mice with grooved teeth have external cheek pouches, or extremely long scaly tails, or tails less than 1 in. long. Skull has 16 teeth. There are 6 mammae.
Economic status: In most of range very little competition with man; probably neutral.

EASTERN HARVEST MOUSE p. 164
Reithrodontomys humulis

Recognition: Head and body 2⅗–3 in.; tail 1⅘–2½ in.; wt. ⅓–½ oz. This *rich-brown* mouse, with belly and underside of tail slightly paler than back, is the only kind of harvest mouse over most of its range.
Similar species: (1) Fulvous Harvest Mouse — longer tail, white belly. (2) Pygmy Mouse (p. 172) — smaller; upper incisors not grooved.
Habitat: Old fields, marshes, wet meadows.
Young: Born May–Nov.; 2–5. Map below

PLAINS HARVEST MOUSE *Reithrodontomys montanus*

Recognition: Head and body 2⅕–3 in.; tail 2–2⅗ in.; wt. ⅕–⅓ oz. This is a *pale grayish* mouse, faintly *washed with fulvous*

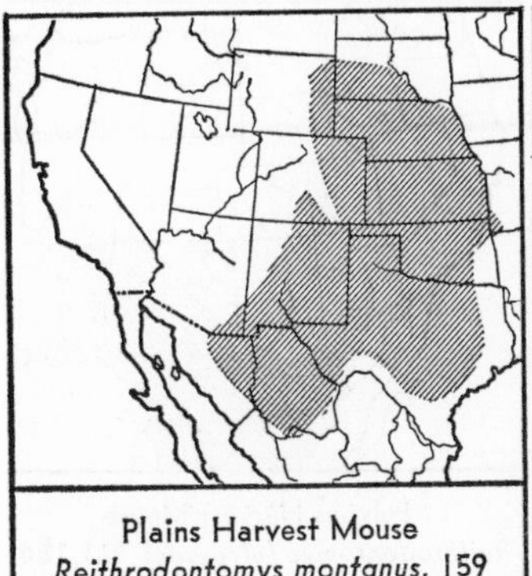

Plains Harvest Mouse
Reithrodontomys montanus, 159

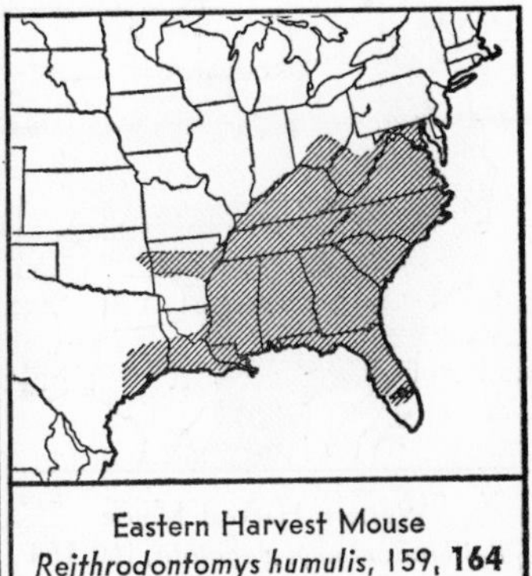

Eastern Harvest Mouse
Reithrodontomys humulis, 159, **164**

and often with an indistinct dark area down middle of back. Belly, feet, and underside of tail white.

Similar species: (1) Western Harvest Mouse — may be difficult to distinguish; tail usually more than 2½ in. (2) Fulvous Harvest Mouse — tail longer than 3 in. (3) Pygmy Mouse (p. 172) — shorter tail, upper incisors not grooved.

Habitat: Chiefly uplands; well-drained soil, shortgrass and other low vegetation, often sparse.

Habits: Breeds throughout year in South.

Young: 2–5; gestation period 21 days. Weaned at 2 weeks.

Map p. 159

WESTERN HARVEST MOUSE   p. 164
Reithrodontomys megalotis

Recognition: Head and body 2⅖–3 in.; tail 2⅓–3⅕ in.; wt. ⅛–⅜ oz. This wide-ranging harvest mouse is found from the Great Lakes to the Pacific Coast. Color ranges from *pale gray*, slightly washed with fulvous, to *brown*. Belly and underside of tail range from white to deep gray. Occurs on Santa Catalina and Santa Cruz Is., California. Skull (p. 245) has 16 teeth.

Similar species: (1) Plains Harvest Mouse — may be difficult to distinguish; tail usually less than 2½ in. (2) Salt Marsh Harvest Mouse — belly deep fulvous. (3) Fulvous Harvest Mouse — bright fulvous sides; tail usually more than 3⅓ in. (4) Pygmy Mouse (p. 172) — shorter tail, upper incisors not grooved.

Habitat: Grassland, open desert, weed patches; usually dense vegetation and near water.

Habits: Active throughout year. Feeds mostly on seeds, but eats some insects. Nests usually on surface of ground or above-ground in vines, tall vegetation, woodpecker hole in fence post

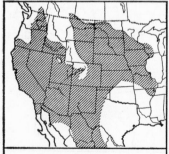

Western Harvest Mouse
Reithrodontomys megalotis, 160, **164**

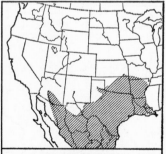

Fulvous Harvest Mouse
Reithrodontomys fulvescens, 161, **164**

or small tree. Breeds every month of year in some part of its range; usually 2 months when not breeding (Jan. and March in California).

Young: Usually 2–4 (1–9); gestation period 23–24 days. Naked, blind. Females breed at 4½ months. Map opposite

SALT MARSH HARVEST MOUSE p. 164

Reithrodontomys raviventris

Recognition: Head and body 2⅗–3⅕ in.; tail 2⅕–3⅖ in. Body *rich brown* washed with deep *fulvous*, especially on belly; tail about same color all around; found only in *salt marshes* in San Francisco Bay area.

Similar species: Western Harvest Mouse — belly white or gray, not rusty.

Habitat: Salt marshes.

Habits: Appropriates old nest of song sparrow above high-water level.

Range: Bayside marshlands around San Francisco Bay, including lower part of the Sacramento River, California.

FULVOUS HARVEST MOUSE p. 164

Reithrodontomys fulvescens

Recognition: Head and body 2⅘–3⅕ in.; tail 3⅓–4 in.; wt. ½–1 oz. This is the most strikingly colored as well as the *largest* of the harvest mice here considered. *Grayish brown*, with *bright fulvous along sides* and with a *white belly*. Tail paler below than above.

Similar species: (1) Eastern Harvest Mouse — smaller; dark brown; gray belly. (2) Plains Harvest Mouse — tail less than 3 in. (3) Western Harvest Mouse — sides not bright fulvous; tail usually 3 in. or less. (4) Pygmy Mouse (p. 172) — shorter tail, upper incisors not grooved.

Habitat: Grasslands with scattered brush and mesquite; weedy fields and fence rows.

Habits: Nests in underground burrow, converted bird nest, or nest of own making in bushes or tall grass. Breeding season probably Feb.–Oct.

Young: 2–5; probably more than 1 litter a year. Naked, blind. Map opposite

White-footed and Pygmy Mice

THESE medium-sized mice all have *white feet*, usually white bellies, and some shade of brown or fulvous backs. Tails relatively *long*, as long as head and body in many. They are nocturnal, live in woods, prairies, rocks, and occasionally around buildings. Most are ground dwellers, but some nest in trees. Gestation period is 21–27 days. Young are born naked and blind. Skull has 16 teeth.

Similar species: (1) Grasshopper Mice (p. 172) — short tail with white tip. (2) Harvest Mice (above) — grooves down front of upper incisor teeth. (3) Rice Rat (p. 178) — fur of belly woolly; tail long and scantily haired, with scales showing through. (4) House Mouse (p. 205) — belly not white, or tail is naked and longer.

Economic status: Neutral for the most part; sometimes enter dwellings and do some damage; easily eliminated with a few snap traps baited with rolled oats.

CACTUS MOUSE *Peromyscus eremicus* p. 165

Recognition: Head and body 3⅕–3⅗ in.; tail 3⅘–5⅖ in.; wt. ⅗–1⅖ oz. Body *pale gray*, faintly washed with fulvous; belly whitish; tail long, thinly haired, and faintly bicolored. There are 4 mammae.

Similar species: (1) Merriam Mouse — slightly larger; difficult to distinguish. (2) White-ankled Mouse — head and body usually smaller; ankles white. (3) Canyon Mouse — tail with slight tuft of long hairs at tip. (4) Deer Mouse — tail well haired and distinctly bicolored. (5) White-footed Mouse — tail relatively shorter. (6) Brush Mouse — tail with long hairs toward tip. (7) Piñon Mouse (p. 170) — huge ears; foothills. (8) Rock Mouse (p. 170) — huge ears; tail well haired.

Habitat: Low deserts with sandy soil and scattered vegetation; rocky outcrops; may go as high as piñon pine zone.

Habits: Normally lives in burrows in ground or among rocks; climbs trees for food; feeds on seeds, insects, and possibly some green vegetation.

Young: 1–4; may be 3–4 litters a year. Map opposite

MERRIAM MOUSE *Peromyscus merriami*

Recognition: Head and body 3⅘–4 in.; tail 4–4⅘ in. Similar to Cactus Mouse; ranges overlap very little.

Similar species: (1) Cactus Mouse — slightly smaller; difficult to distinguish. (2) Deer Mouse — tail well haired and distinctly bicolored. (3) White-footed Mouse — tail relatively shorter. (4) Brush Mouse — tail with long hairs toward tip.

Habitat: Mesquite and scattered brush, low desert.

Range: Pinal, Pima, and Santa Cruz Cos., Arizona.

CALIFORNIA MOUSE *Peromyscus californicus* p. 165

Recognition: Head and body 3⅘–4⅗ in.; tail 5–5⅘ in.; wt. 1½–1¾ oz. This is the *largest* mouse *of this genus* here considered. *Dark brown*, with top of *tail blackish;* feet and belly whitish; ears large. Size alone will serve to distinguish this species. There are 4 mammae.

Similar species: All other mice — smaller and with tail usually under 5 in.

Habitat: Slopes grown with live-oaks and dense chaparral.

Habits: Stores acorns in nests that are often in houses of Dusky-footed Woodrat; also uses buildings for nesting sites. Nest of twigs and sticks, lined with fine grasses. Breeds throughout year, mostly spring, summer, and fall.
Young: Usually 2 (1–3); may be several litters a year.

Map below

CANYON MOUSE *Peromyscus crinitus* p. 165
Recognition: Head and body 3–3⅖ in.; tail 3½–4⅓ in. Body *buffy gray to buff;* fur long and lax; the long *well-haired tail* has a slight *tuft* on end; belly and underside of tail whitish. There are 4 mammae.
Similar species: (1) Cactus Mouse — tail not tufted. (2) Deer Mouse — where they occur together, tail less than 3½ in. (3) Brush Mouse — brown. (4) Piñon and (5) Rock Mice —

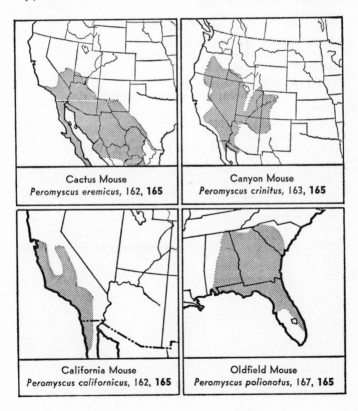

Cactus Mouse
Peromyscus eremicus, 162, **165**

Canyon Mouse
Peromyscus crinitus, 163, **165**

California Mouse
Peromyscus californicus, 162, **165**

Oldfield Mouse
Peromyscus polionotus, 167, **165**

SMALL MICE

	Map	*Text*
EASTERN HARVEST MOUSE, *Reithrodontomys humulis* Color rich brown; grooves down front of upper incisors. SE.	159	159
WESTERN HARVEST MOUSE *Reithrodontomys megalotis* Color gray, washed with fulvous, to brown; grooves on upper incisors. W, Central.	160	160
SALT MARSH HARVEST MOUSE *Reithrodontomys raviventris* Belly fulvous; salt marshes. W.		161
FULVOUS HARVEST MOUSE *Reithrodontomys fulvescens* Sides fulvous; tail long; upper incisors grooved. S.	160	161
HOUSE MOUSE, *Mus musculus* Grayish brown with gray or buffy belly; tail scaly; incisors smooth. N, S, E, W.		205
PYGMY MOUSE, *Baiomys taylori* Dark grayish brown; incisors smooth; small size. S.	171	172
NORTHERN GRASSHOPPER MOUSE *Onychomys leucogaster* *Two color phases;* tail short with white tip. W.	173	173

Harvest Mouse
and nest

EASTERN HARVEST MOUSE

WESTERN HARVEST MOUSE

SALT MARSH HARVEST MOUSE

FULVOUS HARVEST MOUSE

HOUSE MOUSE

PYGMY MOUSE

Cinnamon phase   Gray phase

NORTHERN GRASSHOPPER MOUSE

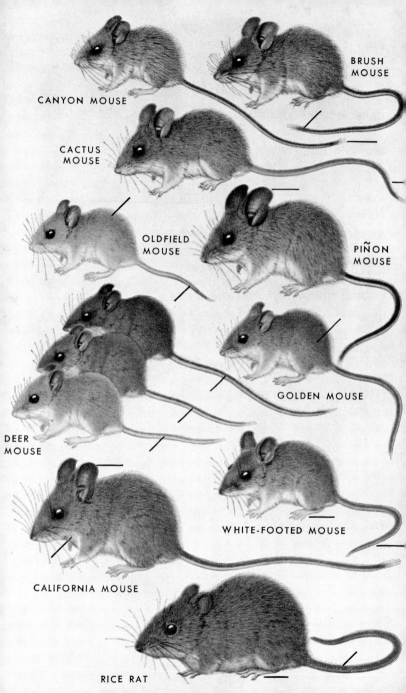

CANYON MOUSE

BRUSH MOUSE

CACTUS MOUSE

OLDFIELD MOUSE

PIÑON MOUSE

DEER MOUSE

GOLDEN MOUSE

CALIFORNIA MOUSE

WHITE-FOOTED MOUSE

RICE RAT

Plate 16   165

MICE WITH LONG TAILS
(Usually with white bellies and feet)

	Map	*Text*

CANYON MOUSE, *Peromyscus crinitus*   163   163
  Buffy gray to buff; tuft on end of long tail. W.

BRUSH MOUSE, *Peromyscus boylei*   169   169
  Tail well haired. SW, S Central.

CACTUS MOUSE, *Peromyscus eremicus*   163   162
  Pale gray faintly washed with fulvous; long tail
  slightly haired; desert. SW.

OLDFIELD MOUSE, *Peromyscus polionotus*   163   167
  Whitish to pale cinnamon; tail short and bicolored;
  small size. SE.

PIÑON MOUSE, *Peromyscus truei*   171   170
  Large ears; tail bicolored. SW.

DEER MOUSE, *Peromyscus maniculatus*   166   167
  Variations in color; tail bicolored. N, S, E, W.

GOLDEN MOUSE, *Peromyscus nuttalli*   171   172
  Rich golden cinnamon; nests in trees and vines. SE.

WHITE-FOOTED MOUSE, *Peromyscus leucopus*   166   168
  Tail usually shorter than head and body. N, S, E, W.

CALIFORNIA MOUSE, *Peromyscus californicus*   163   162
  Dark brown; top of tail blackish; big ears; large
  size. SW.

RICE RAT, *Oryzomys palustris*   179   178
  Body grayish brown, sometimes washed with ful-
  vous; feet whitish; tail scaly; near water. SE.

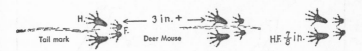

H.   ←—— 3 in. + ——→   H.F. 7/8 in.
Tail mark   F.   Deer Mouse

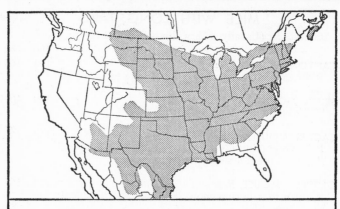

White-footed Mouse, *Peromyscus leucopus*, 168, **165**

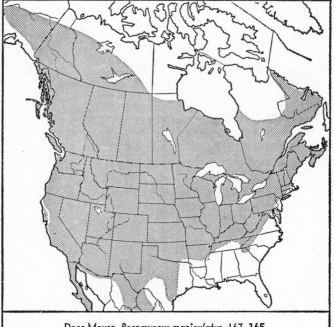

Deer Mouse, *Peromyscus maniculatus*, 167, **165**

ears huge, nearly 1 in. high; head and body longer than 3½ in. (6) California Mouse — tail 5 in. or longer.
Habitat: Rocky canyons and slopes and old lava-covered areas; arid conditions.
Habits: Nests among the rocks or in burrow beneath them.
Young: Born spring and probably summer; 3–5. Map p. 163

DEER MOUSE *Peromyscus maniculatus* p. 165
Recognition: Head and body 2⅘–4 in.; tail 2–5 in.; wt. ⅔–1¼ oz. The most widely distributed and most variable of members of this genus. Color ranges from pale grayish buff to deep reddish brown. Tail always *sharply bicolored*, white below, dark above. Often difficult to distinguish from similar species. Skull (p. 245) has 16 teeth. There are 6 mammae.
Similar species: (1) White-footed Mouse — in South, tail not distinctly bicolored; in northeastern forests, tail less than 3⅗ in., difficult to distinguish. (2) Cactus and (3) Merriam Mice — tail not sharply bicolored, scantily haired. (4) Canyon Mouse — tail longer than head and body; fur long and lax. (5) Cotton Mouse — head and body larger; dark brown. (6) Brush and (7) White-ankled Mice — tail as long as, or longer than, head and body. (8) Piñon and (9) Rock Mice — huge ears, nearly 1 in. high. (10) Golden Mouse — head and body uniform cinnamon. (11) California Mouse — larger.
Habitat: Nearly every dry-land habitat within its range is occupied somewhere by this species; forests in some areas, grassland in others, a mixture in still others.
Habits: Nests in burrow in ground, in trees, stumps, and buildings. Feeds on seeds, nuts, acorns, insects; stores food. Home range ½–3 acres or more. Summer population of 10–15 per acre is high; some congregate in winter. Rarely lives more than 2 years in wild, 5–8 years in captivity. Females may display territorial behavior in breeding season. Breeding season normally Feb.–Nov.; varies with latitude.
Young: Usually 3–5 (1–8); 2–4 litters a year. Breed at 5–6 weeks. Map opposite

SITKA MOUSE *Peromyscus sitkensis*
Recognition: Head and body 4⅓–4⅗ in.; tail 3⅘–4½ in.; wt. 1⅕–1⅗ oz. This large white-footed mouse is found only on islands. There are 6 mammae.
Habits: Feeds largely on spruce seeds and small invertebrate animals.
Young: Average of 6 per litter; probably 2 litters a year.
Range: Kunghit, Frederick, and Hippa Is., B.C.; Baranof, Chichagof, and Forrester Is., Alaska.

OLDFIELD MOUSE *Peromyscus polionotus* p. 165
Recognition: Head and body 3⅖–3⅘ in.; tail 1⅗–2⅖ in.

Upperparts *whitish* to *pale cinnamon;* belly and feet white. There are 6 mammae.

Similar species: (1) White-footed, (2) Cotton, and (3) Florida Mice — dark brown or with tail more than 2⅖ in. (4) Golden Mouse — bright cinnamon over head and body; tail 3 in. or longer.

Habitat: Sand beaches and fallow sandy fields.

Habits: Feeds on seeds and berries. Makes own burrows with mounds of earth at entrances; burrow openings usually closed during day. Home range up to 900 ft. in greatest diam. Populations up to 6 per acre, usually fewer. Has lived 5 years and 3 months in captivity. Females may display territorial behavior during breeding season. Breeds all year, mostly in winter.

Young: Average of 4 per litter; probably 2 or more litters a year.

Map p. 163

WHITE-FOOTED MOUSE *Peromyscus leucopus* p. 165

Recognition: Head and body 3⅗–4⅕ in.; tail 2⅖–4 in.; wt. ½–1⅒ oz. Upperparts pale to rich reddish brown; belly and feet white; tail usually *shorter than head and body.* In parts of its range it is difficult to distinguish from other species. There are 6 mammae.

Similar species: (1) Deer Mouse — tail always sharply bicolored; in northeastern forests tail more than 3⅗ in.; difficult to distinguish. (2) Cotton Mouse — slightly larger; difficult to distinguish. (3) Brush Mouse — tail longer than head and body. (4) Cactus and (5) White-ankled Mice — hairs distinctly longer on terminal 1 in. of tail. (6) Oldfield Mouse — tail less than 2⅖ in. (7) Piñon and (8) Rock Mice — ears nearly 1 in. high. (9) Merriam Mouse — tail scantily haired. (10) Golden Mouse — head and body rich cinnamon.

Habitat: Wooded or brushy areas preferred; sometimes open areas.

Habits: Feeds on seeds, nuts, insects; stores seeds and nuts. Nests any place that affords shelter, belowground, in old bird or squirrel nests, buildings, stumps, and logs. Home range, ½–1½ acres. Populations of 4–12 per acre. Lives 5 years or more in captivity, 2–3 years in wild. Females display territorial behavior during breeding season. Breeding season in North, March–June and Sept.–Nov.; in South probably all year.

Young: 2–6; 2–4 litters a year. Females breed at 10–11 weeks.

Map p. 166

COTTON MOUSE *Peromyscus gossypinus*

Recognition: Head and body 3⅗–4⅗ in.; tail 2⅘–3⅗ in.; wt. 1–1⅘ oz. Upperparts *dark brown* with a slight fulvous mixture, whitish below; tail may or may not be bicolored. There are 6 mammae.

Similar species: (1) White-footed Mouse — slightly smaller;

difficult to distinguish. (2) Deer Mouse — smaller. (3) Oldfield Mouse — pale; tail less than 2½ in. (4) Golden Mouse — bright cinnamon. (5) Florida Mouse — larger; sandy ridges.

Habitat: Wooded areas, along streams or bordering fields, swampland.

Habits: Climbs trees. Feeds on seeds and possibly on insects. Nests in trees, under logs, in buildings. Breeds Aug.–May.

Young: Usually 3–4 (1–7); 4 or more litters a year.

Map below

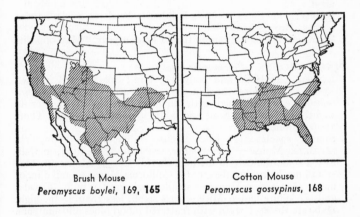

Brush Mouse
Peromyscus boylei, 169, **165**

Cotton Mouse
Peromyscus gossypinus, 168

BRUSH MOUSE *Peromyscus boylei*   p. 165

Recognition: Head and body 3⅗–4⅕ in.; tail 3⅗–4⅖ in.; wt. ¾–1¼ oz. Color ranges from *grayish brown* to fairly *dark brown* washed with *fulvous* on the sides; *well-haired tail* about as long as head and body, often slightly longer. There are 6 mammae.

Similar species: (1) White-ankled Mouse — head and body slightly smaller; ankles white. (2) Piñon and (3) Rock Mice — ears nearly 1 in. high; in California some may be difficult to distinguish. (4) Cactus and (5) Merriam Mice — tail scantily haired. (6) California Mouse — large; tail 5 in. or more. (7) Canyon Mouse — pale gray or buffy. (8) Deer and (9) White-footed Mice — tail shorter than head and body. (10) Golden Mouse — bright cinnamon.

Habitat: Chaparral areas of arid and semi-arid regions; rocky situations.

Habits: Good climber. Feeds on pine nuts, acorns, seeds, berries. Nests under rocks, in crevices, and under debris. Breeds throughout most of year, height of season spring and summer.

Young: 2–6; probably 4 or more litters a year.   Map above

WHITE-ANKLED MOUSE *Peromyscus pectoralis*

Recognition: Head and body $3\frac{3}{5}$ in.; tail $3\frac{4}{5}$–$4\frac{2}{5}$ in.; wt. $\frac{3}{4}$–$1\frac{2}{5}$ oz. Body *pale grayish;* tail *longer* than head and body; ankles white. There are 6 mammae.

Similar species: (1) Brush Mouse — head and body slightly smaller, ankles dusky. (2) Cactus Mouse — head and body usually larger, ankles dusky. (3) Deer and (4) White-footed Mice — tail shorter than head and body.

Habitat: Rocky areas with scattered oaks and junipers; chaparral.

Habits: Sometimes occupies buildings. Feeds on seeds, berries, acorns. Breeds April–Oct.

Young: 3–7; probably more than 1 litter a year. Map opposite

PIÑON MOUSE *Peromyscus truei* p. 165

Recognition: Head and body $3\frac{3}{5}$–4 in.; tail $3\frac{2}{5}$–$4\frac{4}{5}$ in.; wt. $\frac{2}{3}$–$1\frac{1}{10}$ oz. A *large-eared* mouse, ears nearly 1 in. high; *grayish brown,* heavily washed with fulvous; tail slightly shorter to slightly longer than head and body, *distinctly bicolored.* There are 6 mammae.

Similar species: (1) Rock Mouse — difficult to distinguish. (2) Brush Mouse — ears smaller, less than $\frac{3}{4}$ in. high; in California some difficult to distinguish. (3) Cactus Mouse (p. 162) — tail not hairy; low desert. (4) California Mouse — tail 5 in. or more. (5) Canyon Mouse — smaller; pale gray or buff. (6) Deer and (7) White-footed Mice — ears small, less than $\frac{1}{2}$ in. high.

Habitat: Rocky terrain with scattered piñon pines and junipers.

Habits: A good climber. Feeds chiefly on seeds and nuts. May nest in trees and among rocks. Breeds principally in spring and summer.

Young: 3–6; probably more than 1 litter a year. Map opposite

ROCK MOUSE *Peromyscus difficilis*

Recognition: Head and body $3\frac{3}{5}$–4 in.; tail $3\frac{3}{5}$–$4\frac{2}{5}$ in.; wt. $\frac{5}{6}$–$1\frac{1}{7}$ oz. The Rock Mouse is similar to the Piñon Mouse, is intermediate between it and the Brush Mouse (above), and is difficult to distinguish even in a museum. See Piñon Mouse for characters and similar species. There are 6 mammae.

Formerly known as *P. nasutus.*

Habitat: Rock outcrops, cliffs, canyon walls.

Young: Born early spring to Oct.; usually 3–4 (1–6).

Map opposite

FLORIDA MOUSE (Gopher Mouse) *Peromyscus floridanus*

Recognition: Head and body $4\frac{2}{5}$–5 in.; tail $3\frac{1}{5}$–$3\frac{4}{5}$ in. A *large* mouse with nearly naked ears and large hind feet. There are 6 mammae.

Similar species: (1) Cotton Mouse — smaller; in woods. (2)

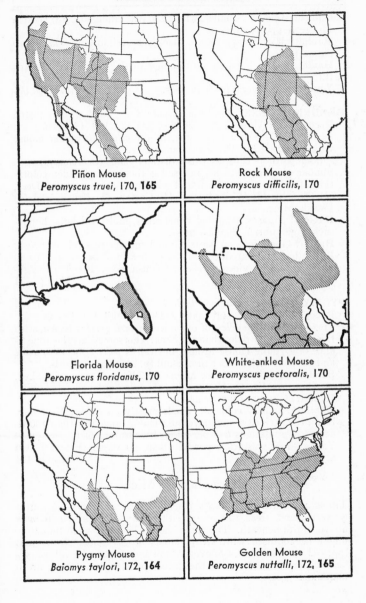

Piñon Mouse
Peromyscus truei, 170, **165**

Rock Mouse
Peromyscus difficilis, 170

Florida Mouse
Peromyscus floridanus, 170

White-ankled Mouse
Peromyscus pectoralis, 170

Pygmy Mouse
Baiomys taylori, 172, **164**

Golden Mouse
Peromyscus nuttalli, 172, **165**

Oldfield Mouse — smaller; whitish to pale cinnamon. (3) Golden Mouse — bright cinnamon.
Habitat: High sandy ridges, blackjack and turkey oaks, scrub palmetto.
Habits: Shares burrows with gopher turtle; in captivity breeds throughout year.
Young: 1–3; several litters a year. Map p. 171

GOLDEN MOUSE *Peromyscus nuttalli* p. 165
Recognition: Head and body 3 2/5–3 4/5 in.; tail 3–3 3/5 in.; wt. 2/3–6/7 oz. This is a handsome, bright *golden-cinnamon* mouse with a *white belly*. There are 6 mammae.
Some authors consider this a distinct genus (*Ochrotomys*).
Similar species: No other mouse has the striking golden coloration of this one. Others found within its range are: (1) Deer, (2) Oldfield, (3) White-footed, (4) Cotton, (5) Brush, and (6) Florida Mice.
Habitat: Forests, edges of canebrakes, moist thickets, honeysuckle, greenbrier, Spanish moss.
Habits: Gregarious on occasion; at home in trees, vines, brush. Builds leaf and shredded-bark nest (6–8 in. diam. and 5–10 ft. aboveground) in vines, thickets, Spanish moss. Breeds throughout spring and summer. Map p. 171

PYGMY MOUSE *Baiomys taylori* p. 164
Recognition: Head and body 2–2 1/2 in.; tail 1 2/5–1 4/5 in.; wt. 1/4–1/3 oz. This, *smallest* of our mice, is *dark grayish brown*, with the belly slightly paler than the back. Has somewhat the appearance of a young House Mouse, but tail is *paler below than above* and covered with short hairs. Skull (p. 245) has 16 teeth.
Similar species: (1) House Mouse (p. 205) — larger; tail naked. (2) Harvest Mice (p. 159) — upper incisors grooved.
Habitat: Grassy or weedy areas.
Habits: Partially colonial. Feeds mostly on seeds. Nest may be on the surface or underground. Home range less than 100 ft. across. Populations 6–8 per acre. Breeds Jan.–Oct.
Young: 1–5; gestation period about 20 days; several litters a year. Map p. 171

Grasshopper Mice

THESE mice are inhabitants chiefly of the *prairies* and southwestern *desert* areas. They are either *gray* or *pinkish cinnamon* above, white beneath. The fur is short. The only mice that they might be confused with are members of the genus *Peromyscus* (pp. 162 ff). The *short, white-tipped* tail and stout body will usually be sufficient to distinguish the grasshopper mouse. There are 6 mammae.

Habitat: Open country; grass, sagebrush, greasewood, sandy or gravelly soil.

Habits: Carnivorous; eat insects, scorpions, other mice, lizards; also eat some seeds. Live mostly in burrows of other animals — ground squirrels, prairie dogs, pocket gophers. Voice, a shrill whistle, apparently a call note.

Young: Born Feb.–Sept.; usually 4–5 (2–7); gestation period 32–47 days; 2–3 litters a year. Naked, blind.

Economic status: Beneficial or neutral; destroy many insects and do little harm.

NORTHERN GRASSHOPPER MOUSE   p. 164
Onychomys leucogaster

Recognition: Head and body 4–5 in.; tail 1–2⅜ in.; wt. ⅝–1⅜ oz. This is a stocky, heavy-bodied, *gray* or *pinkish-cinnamon* mouse with a relatively *short, white-tipped tail.* Skull (p. 245) has 16 teeth.

Similar species: Southern Grasshopper Mouse — smaller; tail usually more than ½ length of head and body; low valleys.

Map below

SOUTHERN GRASSHOPPER MOUSE   *Onychomys torridus*

Recognition: Head and body 3½–4 in.; tail 1⅜–2 in.; wt. ¾–⅝ oz. Body *grayish* or *pinkish cinnamon;* belly *white;* tip of tail *white.* Skull has 16 teeth.

Similar species: Northern Grasshopper Mouse — larger; usually above valley floors where the two overlap.   Map below

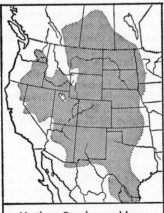

Northern Grasshopper Mouse
Onychomys leucogaster, 173, **164**

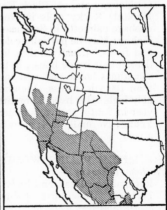

Southern Grasshopper Mouse
Onychomys torridus, 173

Woodrats

THE woodrats, also known as "packrats" or "traderats," are about the size of ordinary house rats, but are easily distinguished from the latter by the *hairy*, not scaly, tail, and soft, fine fur covering the body. Further, their ears are *larger* and usually they have *white* feet and bellies. In the mts. they are commonly found along rock cliffs, where their small piles of sticks and rubbish on rock ledges indicate their presence. On the plains they build stick and cactus houses (2–4 ft. in diam. at base and nearly as high) in clumps of cactus, yucca, or brush. On the West Coast their nests (houses) may be in live-oak trees. They are nocturnal; seldom seen by day. Skull has 16 teeth. There are 4 mammae.

Similar species: (1) Norway and (2) Black Rats (pp. 204, 205) — tails scaly, not covered with hair. (3) Cotton Rats (p. 179) — fur coarse; blackish brown mixed with buff or whitish; ears small.

Economic status: Neutral, live mostly in wild areas; may cause some damage to cabins when unattended.

EASTERN WOODRAT *Neotoma floridana*   p. 181
  Recognition: Head and body 8–9 in.; tail 6–8 in.; wt. 7–13½ oz. This is a large, *grayish-brown* woodrat with *white or grayish belly* and with the tail, which is *shorter* than head and body, *white or gray beneath, brown above*.
  Similar species: (1) Southern Plains Woodrat — steel-gray, not washed with brown. (2) Bushytail Woodrat — tail squirrel-like. (3) Norway and (4) Black Rats (pp. 204, 205) — tail scaly.
  Habitat: Rocky cliffs in Northeast; hammocks, swamps, and cabbage palmetto in Southeast; yuccas and cacti in West.
  Habits: May be partially colonial. Feeds chiefly on seeds, nuts, and fruits. Usually builds houses of sticks, rocks, bones, and debris; nest inside house, in burrow beneath, or in rock crevice; sometimes house and nest in a tree. Home range rarely more than 100 yds. across. Populations of 2–3 adults per acre probably high. Has lived 33 months in the wild. Breeds throughout year in South, spring, summer, and fall in North.
  Young: Normally 2–4; gestation period 30–37 days; 2–3 litters a year.   Map p. 177

SOUTHERN PLAINS WOODRAT   p. 181
Neotoma micropus
  Recognition: Head and body 7½–8½ in.; tail 5½–6½ in.; wt. 7–11 oz. Upperparts *steel-gray;* belly gray; hairs of *throat, breast*, and feet *white to bases;* tail blackish above, gray below.
  Similar species: (1) Whitethroat Woodrat — back mixed with fulvous. (2) Desert Woodrat — smaller; throat hairs not white at bases; back has fulvous mixture. (3) Mexican and (4) Stephens

Woodrats — throat hairs slate at bases. (5) Eastern Woodrat — upperparts grayish brown.
Habitat: Semi-arid brushland; cacti, mesquite, thornbush; low valleys and plains.
Habits: Feeds on cactus, seeds, acorns. Houses made of cactus, brush, and rubbish are 3–5 ft. high and usually placed among cactus or thorny vegetation. Breeds in early spring.
Young: 2–4; gestation period about 33 days; probably 1 litter a year. Map p. 177

WHITETHROAT WOODRAT *Neotoma albigula* p. 181
Recognition: Head and body 7½–8½ in.; tail 5½–7⅓ in.; wt. 4⅘–10 oz. Body *gray* washed with *fulvous* above; belly *white or grayish;* hairs of throat *white to their bases;* feet *white;* tail whitish below, brown above. Skull (p. 245) has 16 teeth.
Similar species: (1) Southern Plains Woodrat — steel-gray above. (2) Desert, (3) Stephens, and (4) Mexican Woodrats — hairs of throat slate at bases. (5) Dusky-footed Woodrat — tail blackish above; hind feet dusky near ankles. (6) Bushytail Woodrat — tail squirrel-like; high mts.
Habitat: Brushland and rocky cliffs with shallow caves.
Habits: Feeds on cactus, mesquite beans, and various seeds; may store some food in house. Houses 2–3 ft. high, built usually among cactus, brush, or in caves in cliffs. Home range probably under 100 ft. across in most instances. Populations of 10–20 adults per acre. Breeds Jan.–Aug.
Young: Usually 2 (1–3); probably more than 1 litter a year. Map p. 177

DESERT WOODRAT *Neotoma lepida* p. 181
Recognition: Head and body 5⅘–7 in.; tail 4⅓–6⅖ in.; wt. 3⅓–6 oz. Body pale to dark *gray* variously *washed with fulvous;* belly *grayish to fulvous;* bases of hairs everywhere *slate color.*
Similar species: (1) Mexican Woodrat — tail white, not gray, below; difficult to distinguish without skull. (2) Stephens Woodrat — hind foot with dusky patch on top, below ankle; tail slightly bushy. (3) Southern Plains and (4) Whitethroat Woodrats — hairs of throat white to bases. (5) Dusky-footed Woodrat — larger; hind feet dusky above. (6) Bushytail Woodrat — tail squirrel-like.
Habitat: Desert floors or rocky slopes with scattered cactus, yucca, or other low vegetation.
Habits: Feeds mostly on seeds, fruits, acorns, cactus. Houses of rubbish usually on ground or along cliffs, occasionally in trees. Has lived 5 years 7 months in captivity.
Young: Usually 2–3 (1–5); gestation period 30–36 days; 4 or more litters a year. Partially pigmented at birth; eyes open at 13 days; sexually mature at 60 days. Map p. 177

STEPHENS WOODRAT *Neotoma stephensi*

Recognition: Head and body 6–8⅖ in.; tail 4⅕–5⅗ in. Body grayish buff, darker on top; belly washed with buff; *dusky wedge* on *top of hind foot*, ¼–⅓ distance below ankle; tail *slightly bushy* on end, whitish below, blackish above.

Similar species: (1) Desert, (2) Whitethroat, and (3) Mexican Woodrats — top of hind foot white to ankle; tail not slightly bushy. (4) Bushytail Woodrat — tail squirrel-like, not blackish above, where ranges meet. (5) Southern Plains Woodrat — upperparts steel-gray. Map opposite

MEXICAN WOODRAT *Neotoma mexicana* p. 181

Recognition: Head and body 6½–7¾ in.; tail 6–6½ in. Normally *gray* with a *fulvous wash,* nearly black in some lava areas; belly grayish white; tail distinctly bicolored, *white below, blackish above.*

Similar species: (1) Desert Woodrat — hardly distinguishable without skull; tail less sharply bicolored. (2) Stephens Woodrat — tail slightly bushy; hind foot dusky on top below ankle, may be difficult to distinguish. (3) Southern Plains and (4) Whitethroat Woodrats — hairs of throat white to bases; valleys and plains. (5) Bushytail Woodrat — tail squirrel-like.

Habitat: Rocks and cliffs, mts.

Habits: Feeds on acorns, nuts, seeds, fruits, mushrooms, and cactus plants when available; may store some food. Does not normally build houses like most other woodrats, but deposits sticks and rubbish among crevices in rocks and cliffs, under logs or tree roots, and in deserted buildings.

Young: Born in spring and summer; 2–4. Map opposite

DUSKY-FOOTED WOODRAT *Neotoma fuscipes* p. 181

Recognition: Head and body 7⅗–9 in.; tail 6⅘–8⅔ in.; wt. 8–13¾ oz. Body *grayish brown above, grayish to whitish below;* tail may be slightly paler below than above; hind feet sprinkled on top with *dusky* hairs; a large rat.

Similar species: (1) Whitethroat Woodrat — usually smaller; hind feet white above. (2) Desert Woodrat — smaller; hind feet white. (3) Bushytail Woodrat — tail squirrel-like; hind feet white.

Habitat: Heavy chaparral, streamside thickets, deciduous or mixed woods.

Habits: Feeds on variety of seeds, nuts, acorns, fruits, green vegetation, and fungi; stores food in house near nest. Builds large stick houses on ground or in trees. Shows ownership of house (territorial). Has lived 4 years in wild.

Young: Most born May and June, but few from Jan. to Oct.; 1–3 per litter. Map p. 178

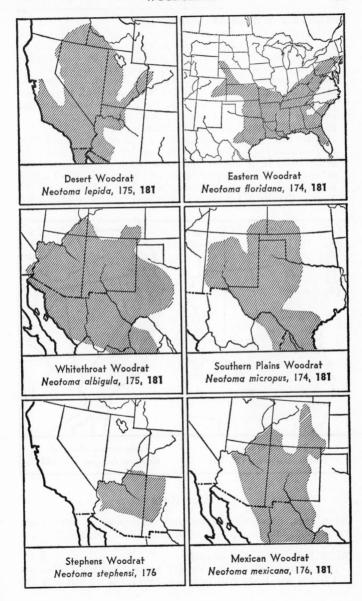

Desert Woodrat
Neotoma lepida, 175, **181**

Eastern Woodrat
Neotoma floridana, 174, **181**

Whitethroat Woodrat
Neotoma albigula, 175, **181**

Southern Plains Woodrat
Neotoma micropus, 174, **181**

Stephens Woodrat
Neotoma stephensi, 176

Mexican Woodrat
Neotoma mexicana, 176, **181**,

BUSHYTAIL WOODRAT *Neotoma cinerea* p. 181

Recognition: Head and body 7–9⅔ in.; tail 5⅕–7⅖ in.; wt. 7½–20⅖ oz. Body varies from *pale gray* washed with fulvous to *nearly black* above; hind feet white. May be distinguished from all other woodrats by its *long, bushy, squirrel-like tail.*

Similar species: (1) Whitethroat, (2) Desert, (3) Mexican, (4) Eastern, and (5) Dusky-footed Woodrats — all have short-haired tails that taper toward tip. (6) Stephens Woodrat — tail not squirrel-like, blackish above where ranges meet.

Habitat: High mts.; rimrock, rockslides, pines.

Habits: Climbs about cliffs easily. Feeds on green vegetation, twigs, shoots; may store some food as dry hay. Does not normally build large houses, but accumulates sticks, bones, and other material in rock crevices or under logs. Usually 1 family to a rockslide. Breeding season, May–Sept.

Young: Usually 2–4 (1–5); 1 litter a year. Map below

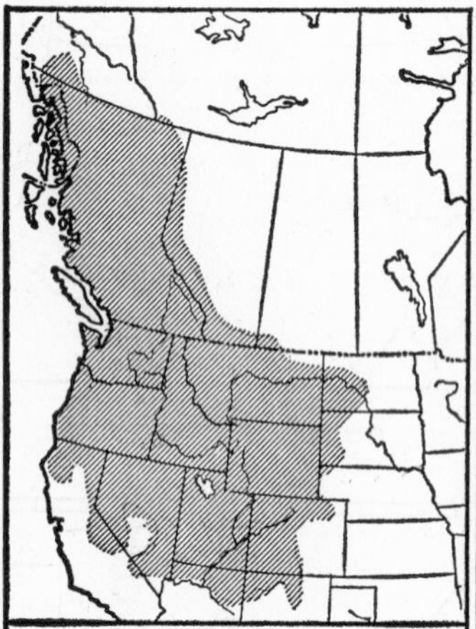

Bushytail Woodrat
Neotoma cinerea, 178, **181**

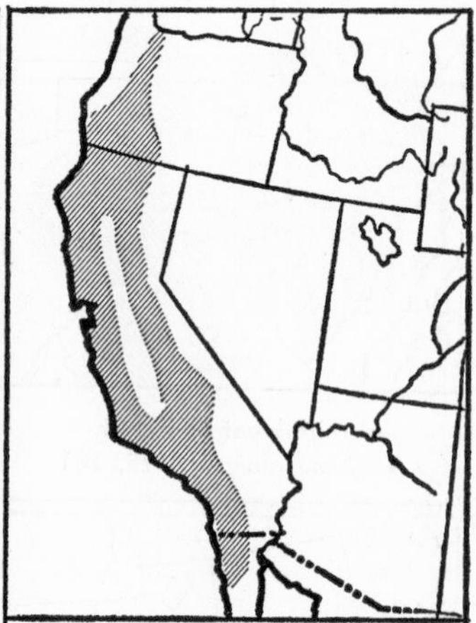

Dusky-footed Woodrat
Neotoma fuscipes, 176, **181**

Rice Rats

RICE RATS, primarily tropical and subtropical in distribution, range south into S. America. One species is found in U.S.

RICE RAT *Oryzomys palustris* p. 165

Recognition: Head and body 4¾–5⅕ in.; tail 4⅓–7⅕ in.; wt. 1⅗–2⅘ oz. Body *grayish brown*, sometimes washed with ful-

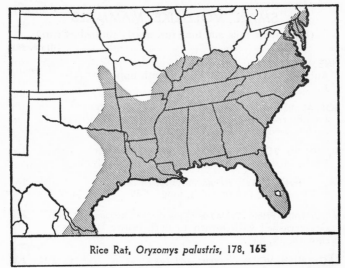

Rice Rat, *Oryzomys palustris*, 178, **165**

vous; *gray or fulvous* belly; *long, scaly tail* slightly paler below
than above; feet *whitish;* fur short and soft. Skull (p. 245) has
16 teeth. There are 8 mammae.

Similar species: (1) Hispid Cotton Rat (below) — fur long and
coarse; tail black above. (2) Norway and (3) Black Rats (pp.
204, 205) — tail not paler below. (4) All Mice — smaller.

Habitat: Marshy areas, grasses, sedges.

Habits: Chiefly nocturnal; semi-aquatic; makes surface runways. Feeds on green vegetation and seeds. Nests under debris
above high-water level. Breeds throughout year.

Young: Usually 3–4 (1–7); gestation period about 25 days;
several litters a year. Nearly naked, blind. Sexually mature at
50 days.

Economic status: Rarely interferes with man's activities; **can**
do damage in a rice field.   Map above

Cotton Rats

COTTON RATS are medium-sized, with grayish-brown to blackish-
brown coarse fur *heavily mixed* with pale buff. Finely haired tail,
blackish above, pale below, shorter than head and body. Feet
gray; ears nearly concealed by long fur. Young cotton rats are
similar in appearance to some voles.

Similar species: Woodrats (p. 174) — grayish; ears large.

Habitat: Tall grass, sedges, and weeds — moist areas.

Economic status: May do damage to alfalfa and other green **crops.**

SMALL VOLE-LIKE MAMMALS
(With short tails and long fur, nearly concealing ears)

	Map	*Text*

PINE VOLE, *Pitymys pinetorum* — 200 201
Auburn; soft fur; short tail; smooth upper incisors. E.

BOREAL REDBACK VOLE, *Clethrionomys gapperi* — 188 189
Usually reddish down middle of back; upper incisors not grooved. N, SE, SW.

SOUTHERN BOG LEMMING, *Synaptomys cooperi* — 184 184
Upper incisors grooved in front; short tail. NE.

TREE PHENACOMYS, *Phenacomys longicaudus* — 195 187
Body reddish; tail blackish, long. NW.

MOUNTAIN PHENACOMYS, *Phenacomys intermedius* — 188 187
Gray washed with brown to dark brown; incisors smooth. N, SW.

SAGEBRUSH VOLE, *Lagurus curtatus* — 200 202
Pale ash-gray; sagebrush. NW.

HISPID COTTON RAT, *Sigmodon hispidus* — 182 182
Coarse fur, mixed buff and black above, whitish below; large size. S.

PRAIRIE VOLE, *Microtus ochrogaster* — 199 201
Grayish to dark brown, with mixture of fulvous; short tail; smooth incisors; prairies. Central.

TOWNSEND VOLE, *Microtus townsendi* — 195 193
Blackish tail; dusky feet; large size. NW.

YELLOWNOSE VOLE, *Microtus chrotorrhinus* — 199 198
Yellow on nose. NE.

MEADOW VOLE, *Microtus pennsylvanicus* — 192 191
Grayish brown; long tail; upper incisors not grooved. N, SE, SW.

BROWN LEMMING, *Lemmus trimucronatus* — 185 186
Body reddish-brown, never white; tail short. NW, N Central.

GREENLAND COLLARED LEMMING — 185 184
Dicrostonyx groenlandicus
Dark stripe down back in summer; white in winter Arctic, Subarctic.

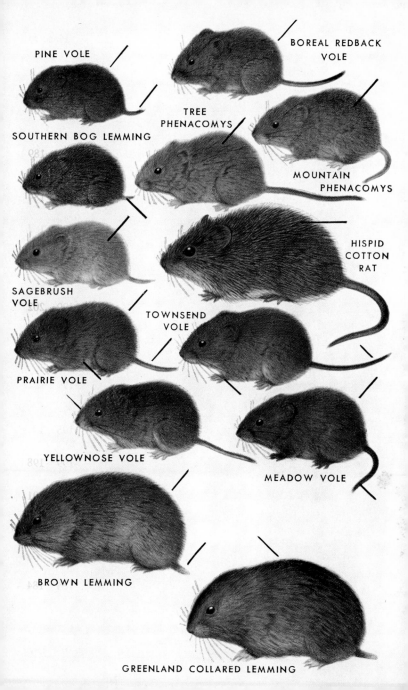

PINE VOLE

BOREAL REDBACK VOLE

TREE PHENACOMYS

SOUTHERN BOG LEMMING

MOUNTAIN PHENACOMYS

SAGEBRUSH VOLE

HISPID COTTON RAT

TOWNSEND VOLE

PRAIRIE VOLE

YELLOWNOSE VOLE

MEADOW VOLE

BROWN LEMMING

GREENLAND COLLARED LEMMING

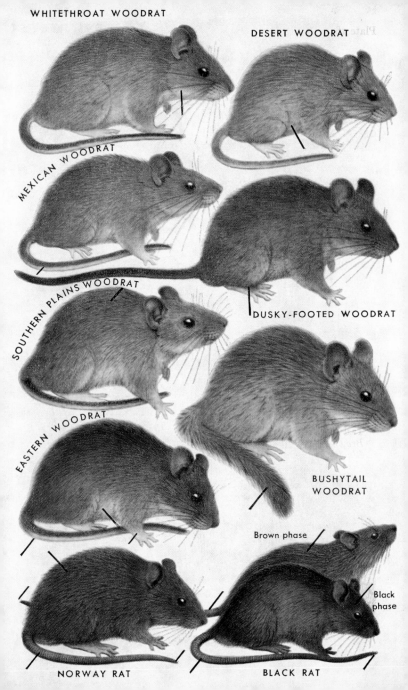

WHITETHROAT WOODRAT

DESERT WOODRAT

MEXICAN WOODRAT

SOUTHERN PLAINS WOODRAT

DUSKY-FOOTED WOODRAT

EASTERN WOODRAT

BUSHYTAIL WOODRAT

Brown phase

Black phase

NORWAY RAT

BLACK RAT

Plate 18   181

WOODRATS AND OTHERS

	Map	Text

WHITETHROAT WOODRAT, *Neotoma albigula*   177   175
   Gray washed with fulvous; hairs of throat white to skin; tail haired. SW.

DESERT WOODRAT, *Neotoma lepida*   177   175
   Gray washed with fulvous; hairs of belly slaty near skin; desert. SW.

MEXICAN WOODRAT, *Neotoma mexicana*   177   176
   Belly grayish white; tail white below; rocky areas. SW.

DUSKY-FOOTED WOODRAT, *Neotoma fuscipes*   178   176
   Body grayish brown; hind feet dusky; large size. W.

SOUTHERN PLAINS WOODRAT, *Neotoma micropus*   177   174
   Gray, no fulvous; tail haired. S Central.

BUSHYTAIL WOODRAT, *Neotoma cinerea*   178   178
   Tail squirrel-like, bushy. W.

EASTERN WOODRAT, *Neotoma floridana*   177   174
   Feet and belly whitish; tail haired. Central, NE, SE.

NORWAY RAT, *Rattus norvegicus*   204
   Grayish brown; tail scaly, long, but shorter than head and body. N, S, E, W.

BLACK RAT, *Rattus rattus*   205
   Tail longer than head and body; scaly. S.
   Brown phase: Body brown.
   Black phase: Body black.

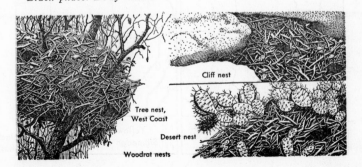

Cliff nest

Tree nest,
West Coast

Desert nest

Woodrat nests

HISPID COTTON RAT   *Sigmodon hispidus*   p. 180

Recognition: Head and body 5–8 in.; tail 3⅓–6 in.; wt. 4–7 oz. Long coarse body fur mixed buff and black above, *whitish below;* pale in West, dark in East. Skull (p. 245) has 16 teeth. There are 8–10 mammae.

Similar species: (1) Least Cotton Rat — buff belly; in mts. (2) Yellownose Cotton Rat — yellowish around nose. (3) Rice Rat (above) — tail scaly, as long as head and body.

Habits: Makes surface runways along which may be found small piles of cut grass stems. Feeds chiefly on green vegetation, also eats eggs of ground-nesting birds. Nests either on surface or in burrow. Home range 100–200 ft. across. Populations 10–12 per acre, fluctuate from year to year. Rarely lives more than 1 year in wild. Has extended range northward in recent years. Breeds all year.

Young: Usually 5–6 (2–12); gestation period about 27 days; as many as 9 litters a year. Leave nest at 4–7 days. Sexually mature in 40 days.   Map below

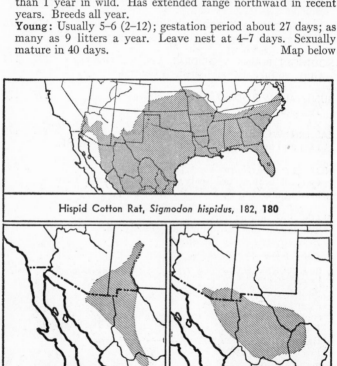

Hispid Cotton Rat, *Sigmodon hispidus,* 182, **180**

Least Cotton Rat
Sigmodon minimus, 183

Yellownose Cotton Rat
Sigmodon ochrognathus, 183

LEAST COTTON RAT *Sigmodon minimus*

Recognition: Head and body 5–6 in.; tail 3⅘–4⅕ in. This rat may be distinguished by the mixture of black and pale buff hairs of upperparts, and the *buff belly*. Skull has 16 teeth.

Similar species: (1) Hispid Cotton Rat — whitish belly; in valleys. (2) Yellownose Cotton Rat — gray belly.

Map opposite

YELLOWNOSE COTTON RAT *Sigmodon ochrognathus*

Recognition: Head and body 5–6 in.; tail 4–4⅗ in.; wt. 2–4 oz. This is a *foothills* or *mt.* form. Upperparts mixed buffy and blackish, washed with *fulvous* on *nose*, face, and rump; *belly gray*. Skull has 16 teeth.

Similar species: (1) Hispid Cotton Rat — no buff on nose. (2) Least Cotton Rat — buff belly.

Habitat: Dense vegetation; foothills and mts. Map opposite

Lemmings

THESE are small, vole-like mammals found mostly in the Far North. Their fur is long and soft and nearly conceals the small thin ears. The tail is usually less than 1 in. long. Relationships of lemmings are uncertain. The 3 genera are grouped here for convenience.

Economic status: Important food for foxes, especially those on tundra. Their abundance means money to the Eskimo fur trapper.

HUDSON BAY COLLARED LEMMING
Dicrostonyx hudsonius

Recognition: Head and body 4¾–5⅖ in.; tail ¾–⁹⁄₁₀ in.; wt. 1⅗–2⅖ oz. Found on several islands in Hudson Bay. Upperparts buffy gray with a *dark stripe* along middle of back and a tawny band across throat in summer. Ears and tail barely show through the long fur, which is *white in winter;* 3rd and 4th claws on front feet greatly enlarged, especially in winter. Skull (p. 245) has 16 teeth.

Similar species: (1) Northern Bog Lemming — uniform brownish gray; teeth grooved. (2) Voles (pp. 189 ff.) and (3) Phenacomys (p. 186) — tail more than 1 in. long.

Habitat: Tundra of Ungava and islands in Hudson Bay.

Habits: More active by day than at night during summer. Probably feeds on available vegetation. Nest (diam. about 8 in.) may be underground, among rocks, or, in winter, aboveground and beneath the snow. Digs numerous refuge burrows 1–2 ft. long; deposits feces in selected locations, may be 2–3 qts. of tiny fecal pellets in a pile. Populations may fluctuate widely. Has lived more than 2 years in captivity. Both parents care for young.

Young: Usually 3–4 (1–7); gestation period 19–21 days; 1–2 litters a year.   Map below

GREENLAND COLLARED LEMMING   p. 180
Dicrostonyx groenlandicus

Recognition: Head and body 4–5½ in.; tail ⅖–⅘ in.; wt. 1⅗–2⅖ oz. See Hudson Bay Collared Lemming (above) for description. This lemming occupies the *tundra* west and north of Hudson Bay and a strip in Greenland.

Those on St. Lawrence I., Alaska, considered as a distinct species (*D. exsul*) by most authors.

Similar species: (1) Brown Lemming — no dark streak down back; brown in winter. (2) Northern Bog Lemming — brownish gray; upper incisors grooved. (3) Voles (pp. 189 ff.) and (4) Phenacomys (p. 186) — tail longer than 1 in.   Map opposite

SOUTHERN BOG LEMMING *Synaptomys cooperi*   p. 180

Recognition: Head and body 3⅖–4⅖ in.; tail ⅗–⅞ in.; wt. ½–1⅖ oz. Upperparts brownish gray, belly grayish; ears *nearly concealed;* tail less than 1 in. long; *shallow groove* near outer edge of upper incisor. Skull (p. 245) has 16 teeth. There are 6–8 mammae.

Similar species: (1) Meadow Vole (p. 191) — tail more than 1 in. (2) Yellownose Vole (p. 198) — yellow nose. (3) Prairie Vole (p. 201) — front teeth not grooved. (4) Pine Vole (p. 201) — uniform-auburn color. (5) Boreal Redback Vole (p. 189) — tail longer than 1 in.; reddish on middle of back.

Habitat: Low damp bogs and meadows with heavy growth of vegetation.

Habits: Active day or night; feeds primarily on green vegeta-

Hudson Bay Collared Lemming
Dicrostonyx hudsonius, 183

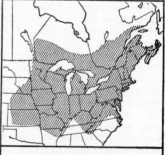

Southern Bog Lemming
Synaptomys cooperi, 184, **180**

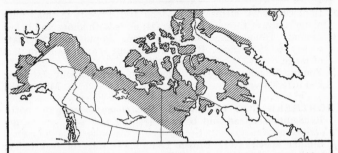

Greenland Collared Lemming, *Discrostonyx groenlandicus*, 184, **180**

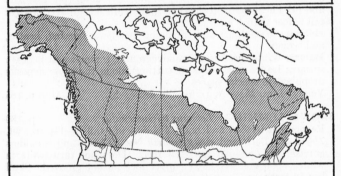

Northern Bog Lemming, *Synaptomys borealis*, 186

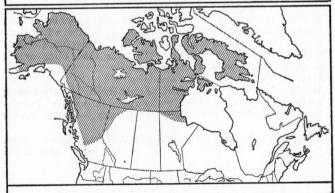

Brown Lemming, *Lemmus trimucronatus*, 186, **180**

tion; cuts grass stems 1–2 in. long and deposits in small piles along runways through heavy grass; nests both above and below ground. Home range about ⅓ acre. Populations fluctuate widely, to 35 per acre. Breeds throughout year in southern part of range.
Young: Usually 3–4 (2–6); gestation period about 23 days; 2–3 litters a year. Map p. 184

NORTHERN BOG LEMMING *Synaptomys borealis*
Recognition: Head and body 4–4⅗ in.; tail ⅘–1 in. As described above.
Similar species: (1) Brown Lemming — soles of feet hairy; teeth not grooved. (2) Collared Lemmings — tawny band across throat, summer; white, winter. (3) Voles (pp. 189–202) and (4) Phenacomys (below) — front teeth not grooved and/or tail longer than 1 in.
Habitat: Wet alpine and subalpine meadows, muskeg, heaths, and sedges.
Habits: Winter nest usually aboveground, summer nest beneath surface; leaves small piles of cuttings along runways; deposits droppings in special places.
Young: Born May–Aug.; usually 4–5 (2–8). Map p. 185

BROWN LEMMING *Lemmus trimucronatus* p. 180
Recognition: Head and body 4½–5½ in.; tail ⅘–1⅙ in.; wt. 2½–4 oz. Back and *rump reddish brown;* head and shoulders *grayish;* fur *long and soft; tail short.* Does not turn white in winter. Soles of feet hairy; upper incisors not grooved. Skull has 16 teeth.

Population on St. George I., Pribilofs, is considered a distinct species (*L. nigripes*).
Similar species: (1) Greenland Collared Lemming — dark median stripe down back, or all-white. (2) Northern Bog Lemming — brownish gray; incisors grooved. (3) Voles (pp. 189–202) and (4) Phenacomys (below) — tail more than 1 in., or not brightly colored; soles of feet not furred.
Habitat: Tundra and alpine meadows.
Habits: Active day and night. Feeds mostly on vegetation; nests aboveground in winter, underground in summer. Populations may fluctuate widely, with peaks every 3–4 years. Breeds June–Aug.
Young: Usually 2–6 (2–11); probably 2 or more litters a year. Map p. 185

Phenacomys

THESE vole-like rodents are inhabitants of grassy areas within the cold forested regions of Canada, the high mountaintops of w. U.S., and the humid nw. Pacific Coast. They occur where people seldom go, and therefore are not likely to be encountered. Most of them are ground-living, have relatively short tails, and rather long, soft, grayish-brown fur. The belly is pale grayish. The Tree Phenacomys is quite different from the others; it has a relatively long blackish tail, which contrasts with the bright rufous body; and it is arboreal.

Economic status: Neutral; occur mostly in wild areas.

MOUNTAIN PHENACOMYS *Phenacomys intermedius* p. 180
(Heather Phenacomys)
  Recognition: Head and body 3½–4⅜ in.; tail 1–1⅔ in.; wt. 1–1⅖ oz. Body *gray* washed with *brown to dark brown, white* feet and *silvery* belly sometimes tinged with buff; nose or face yellowish in some; tail bicolored. Skull (p. 245) has 16 teeth. There are 8 mammae.
  Similar species: (1) Mountain Vole (p. 192) — tail usually longer; difficult to distinguish. (2) Longtail Vole (p. 194) — tail longer than 2 in. (3) Yellow-cheeked and (4) Yellownose Voles (p. 198) — tail longer than 1⅔ in. (5) Tundra Vole (p. 193) — larger. (6) Redback Voles (below) — nose not yellowish; back reddish. (7) Others — not found near mountaintops, or measurements differ.
  Habitat: Open grassy areas near mountaintops; pine and spruce forests, rocky slopes, tundra, dry areas or near water; not restricted, but occupies several habitats.
  Habits: Most active at twilight and night. Feeds on bark of dwarf birch and willows, seeds, lichens, berries, green vegetation; caches food items. Nests aboveground in winter; below surface, under rocks, stumps, debris in summer.
  Young: Born June–Sept.; 2–8; gestation period about 21 days; 2 or more litters a season. Naked, blind. Females sexually mature at 4–6 weeks, breed 1st year. Map p. 188

PACIFIC PHENACOMYS *Phenacomys albipes*
  Recognition: Head and body 3⅘–4⅖ in.; tail 2½–2⅘ in. Body dark, *rich brown* above; gray washed with buff on belly; tail brown above, paler below. Skull has 16 teeth.
  Similar species: (1) Mountain Vole (p. 192) — high mt. meadows. (2) Townsend and (3) Longtail Voles (pp. 193, 194) — head and body over 4½ in. (4) Oregon Vole (p. 198) — tail under 2 in. (5) California Redback Vole (p. 190) — back chestnut. (6) Tree Phenacomys — reddish with blackish tail. (7) California Vole (p. 193) — larger, grayish brown.
  Habitat: Dense forests; near small streams. Map p. 190

TREE PHENACOMYS *Phenacomys longicaudus* p. 180
  Recognition: Head and body 4–4⅓ in.; tail 2⅖–3⅓ in.; wt. 1 oz.

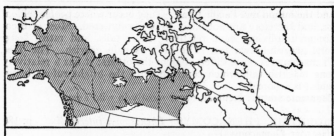

Tundra Redback Vole, *Clethrionomys rutilus*, 189

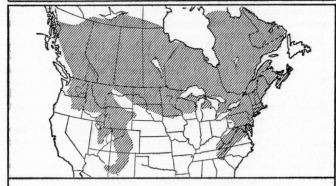

Boreal Redback Vole, *Clethrionomys gapperi*, 189, **180**

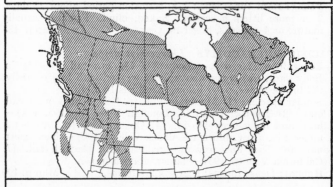

Mountain Phenacomys, *Phenacomys intermedius*, 187, **180**

A bright *reddish-brown* to *cinnamon* phenacomys with a blackish, *well-haired* tail. Color and size serve to distinguish this species from all others in area.

Authors have thought there are 2 species in Oregon; the other is *P. silvicola.* Externally it is difficult to distinguish them, so they are treated as one here. Further study is needed to resolve this problem. Skull has 16 teeth. There are 4 mammae.

Habitat: Spruce, hemlock, and fir forests.

Habits: Arboreal. Food consists almost entirely of leaves of tree in which they are living — spruce, hemlock, or fir. Bulky nest, up to the size of a half-bushel measure or larger, is built on branches, usually near the trunk, 15–100 ft. up in the trees; nest becomes larger with age, some probably occupied by many generations.

Young: Born any time of year; 1–3. Naked, blind.

Map p. 195

Redback Voles

THESE small forest rodents (5–6 in. overall length) usually have long, soft fur, *gray* or washed with *yellowish on sides* and *reddish down the back.* In southern part of the range they may be deep brown with little, if any, contrast between sides and back. Belly always *gray or silvery,* and tail bicolored. There are 8 mammae.

TUNDRA REDBACK VOLE *Clethrionomys rutilus*

Recognition: Head and body 4–4½ in.; tail 1⅕–1⅗ in.; wt. 1–1⅕ oz. Sides washed with yellowish; bright *reddish* (sometimes brown) *down middle of back;* belly silvery or washed with yellow; tail yellowish beneath, dark brown on top; winter pelage paler than that of summer. Skull has 16 teeth. There are 8 mammae.

Formerly known as *C. dawsoni.*

Similar species: (1) Lemmings (p. 183) — larger; no distinct reddish stripe down back. (2) Other voles — color of sides and back do not contrast.

Habitat: Tundra and damp forest floors, alpine conditions.

Young: Born May–Sept.; 4–9; probably 2 litters a year.

Map opposite

BOREAL REDBACK VOLE *Clethrionomys gapperi* p. 180

Recognition: Head and body 3⅔–4⅔ in.; tail 1⅕–2 in.; wt. ½–1⅖ oz. In North and East there are 2 color phases, red and gray (palest in Labrador). For most part, may be distinguished from all other voles of its area by *reddish back* and *gray sides,* but in North and East the gray phase may not have a reddish back and may be difficult to distinguish from other voles of the area without recourse to the skull. No grooves on upper incisors. Skull (p. 245) has 16 teeth. There are 8 mammae.

Similar species: (1) Lemmings (p. 183) — larger; shorter tails. (2) Phenacomys (p. 186) and (3) Other voles (below) — no contrast between color of sides and back.

Habitat: Coniferous, deciduous, or mixed forests; it prefers damp situations.

Habits: Active day or night; good climber for a vole. Feeds chiefly on green vegetation, but adds seeds, nuts, bark, fungi, and a few insects. Nest usually under roots or logs, simple platform. Home range about ¼ acre. Populations up to 10 per acre, usually fewer.

Young: Born March–Oct.; usually 4–6 (3–8); gestation period 17–19 days; probably 2 or more litters a year. Naked, blind.

Map p. 188

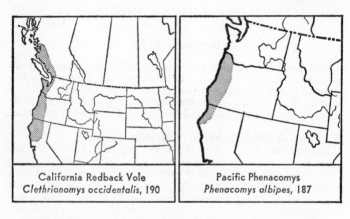

California Redback Vole
Clethrionomys occidentalis, 190

Pacific Phenacomys
Phenacomys albipes, 187

CALIFORNIA REDBACK VOLE *Clethrionomys occidentalis*

Recognition: Head and body 4⅛ in.; tail 2–2⅕ in. Body *dark sepia;* back *dark chestnut,* but does not contrast strikingly with sides; belly *buffy* or *soiled whitish;* feet *whitish* or *dusky.* Skull has 16 teeth. There are 8 mammae.

Formerly known as *C. californicus.*

Similar species: (1) Mountain Vole (p. 192) — grayish; high mt. meadows. (2) California Vole (p. 193) — grayish brown. (3) Townsend (p. 193), (4) Richardson (p. 198), and (5) Longtail (p. 194) Voles — head and body 4½ in. or more. (6) Oregon Vole (p. 198) — tail less than 2 in. (7) Mountain Phenacomys (p. 187) — tail less than 2 in.; high mts. (8) Pacific and (9) Tree Phenacomys (p. 187) — tail more than 2⅕ in.

Habitat: Forest floors, moist and strewn with logs.

Young: Embryos reported for July and Aug.; 2–4.

Map above

Other Voles

THROUGHOUT Canada and the U.S. where there is good *grass cover*, 1 or more species of voles are likely to be found. Their presence often may be detected by *narrow runways*, 1–2 in. wide, through the matted grasses. Small piles of brownish droppings and short pieces of grass stems along these runways are further evidence. In a few places, these voles are found among rocks or on forest floors where there is no grass. In areas of winter snow, their *round openings* to the surface of the snow also reveal their presence. They are active by day as well as by night. Mostly they are *brownish gray* with *long fur, small ears*, and relatively *short tails*, always less than length of head and body. They have small, black, beadlike eyes. Skull has 16 teeth.

Similar species: (1) Bog Lemmings (pp. 184, 186) — upper incisors have grooves down their front surfaces, tail never longer than 1 in. (2) Collared and (3) Brown Lemmings (pp. 183, 184, 186) — brightly colored. (4) Phenacomys (p. 186) — difficult to distinguish as a group; see special accounts. (5) Redback Voles (p. 189) — usually have reddish backs contrasting with gray sides.

Young: Hairless, blind.

Economic status: Voles can do severe damage to fruit trees by girdling the trunks or removing bark from roots, especially in winter under a protective covering of snow. Also, they may do damage to hay and grain crops, particularly if these are left in the shock during winter. On the credit side, they serve as a buffer species to predators and supply the food for many fur-bearing mammals as well as for hawks and owls.

MEADOW VOLE *Microtus pennsylvanicus*   p. 180
   Recognition: Head and body 3½–5 in.; tail 1⅖–2⅗ in.; wt. 1–2½ oz. The most widely distributed of the voles, this species varies from a gray, faintly washed with brown, in the West, to dark brown in the East. Belly *silvery to slightly buffy or dark gray*, and tail *bicolored*. Fur is *long* and soft. Upper incisors not grooved. Skull (p. 245) has 16 teeth. There are 8 mammae.
   The voles on Muskeget I., Massachusetts, *M. breweri*, and Gull I., off Long I., New York, *M. nesophilus*, probably extinct, may be distinct species.
Similar species: (1) Mountain Vole — characters not distinct; high mt. meadows. (2) Tundra Vole — larger where ranges meet. (3) Longtail Vole — tail more than 2 in.; may be difficult to distinguish. (4) Prairie Vole — tail usually less than 1⅖ in.; sometimes difficult to distinguish. (5) Alaska Vole — tail under 1⅖ in.; above timberline. (6) Yellow-cheeked and (7) Yellow-nose Voles — nose yellow. (8) Richardson Vole — head and body longer than 5½ in. (9) Redback Voles (p. 189) — back

reddish, sides gray or yellowish. (10) Mountain Phenacomys
(p. 187) — tail usually under 1⅖ in.; high mts. (11) Others —
tail never longer than 1 in.

Habitat: Low moist areas or high grasslands with rank growths
of vegetation; near streams, lakes, swamps, occasionally in
forests with little ground cover; orchards with grass undergrowth.

Habits: Active day or night. A good swimmer. Feeds on
grasses, sedges, seeds, grain, bark, and probably some insects.
Nests either above or below ground; makes burrows along
surface runways. Home range ⅒–1 acre. Populations fluctuate
markedly with highs at 3- to 4-year intervals. Lives 1–3 years
in wild. A good fighter; probably displays territorial behavior
during part of year. Breeds throughout year.

Young: Born any month of year; 1–9 (usually 3–5); gestation
period 21 days; several litters a year (in captivity, a female had
17 litters in 1 year).　　　　　　　　　　　　　　　　Map below

MOUNTAIN VOLE *Microtus montanus*

Recognition: Head and body 4–5½ in.; tail 1⅕–2⅗ in.; wt.
1–3 oz. Upperparts *grayish brown to blackish*, belly whitish;
feet usually *dusky;* found primarily in the *valleys* of the mountainous Great Basin area. There are 8 mammae.

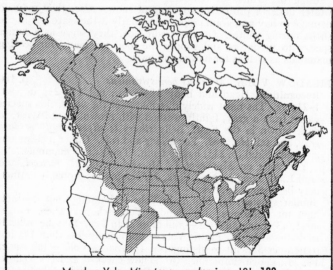

Meadow Vole, *Microtus pennsylvanicus*, 191, **180**

Similar species: (1) Longtail Vole — tail usually longer; may be difficult to distinguish. (2) Meadow Vole — usually not in mts.; difficult to distinguish. (3) California Vole — usually not in high mt. meadows; difficult to distinguish. (4) Mountain Phenacomys (p. 187) — near tops of mts.; difficult to distinguish. (5) Oregon Vole — dark brown, hair short. (6) Richardson Vole — head and body 5½ in. or more. (7) Prairie Vole — low prairies. (8) Mexican Vole — belly yellowish, not whitish. (9) Townsend Vole — tail blackish. (10) California Redback Vole (p. 190) — dark sepia and chestnut. (11) Pacific Phenacomys (p. 187) — not in high mts. Map p. 195

CALIFORNIA VOLE *Microtus californicus*

Recognition: Head and body 4¾–5⅔ in.; tail 1⅗–2⅘ in.; wt. 1½–3½ oz. This is a *grayish-brown* (blackish toward the coast, reddish in the desert) vole with *bicolored tail* and *pale feet* that contrast with the color of the back. There are 8 mammae.
Similar species: (1) Longtail Vole — tail usually longer; may be difficult to distinguish. (2) Mountain Vole — feet dusky; high mt. meadows. (3) Townsend Vole — tail blackish; feet dusky. (4) Oregon Vole — dark brown; fur short. (5) California Redback Vole (p. 190) — body sepia; back chestnut. (6) Mountain Phenacomys (p. 187) — tail usually under 1⅗ in.; high mts. (7) Pacific Phenacomys (p. 187) — smaller, rich brown. (8) Tree Phenacomys (p. 187) — reddish; tail blackish.
Habitat: Marshy ground, saltwater and fresh; wet meadows, dry, grassy hillsides. Seashore to mts.
Habits: Feeds on grasses, sedges, and other green vegetation. Breeds throughout year.
Young: 4–8; gestation period 21 days; more than 1 litter a year.
Map p. 195

TOWNSEND VOLE *Microtus townsendi* p. 180

Recognition: Head and body 4¾–6⅖ in.; tail 2–3 in. A large, *blackish-brown* vole with *gray belly*, *blackish tail*, and *dusky feet.* Ears project well above fur. Found also on San Juan and Shaw Is., Washington, and Bowen I., B.C. (not shown on map). May be distinguished from all others by size and color. There are 8 mammae.
Habitat: Moist fields; sedges, tules, meadows; from tidewater to alpine meadows. Usually near water.
Young: Born March–Sept.; usually 4–5 (1–9); gestation period 21 days. Map p. 195

TUNDRA VOLE *Microtus oeconomus*

Recognition: Head and body 5–6⅘ in.; tail 1⅖–2⅛ in.; wt. 1⅓–2⅘ oz. *Body dull brown* washed with buffy or fulvous. Belly *grayish,* tail *bicolored.* Its fairly uniform color above, and size, will distinguish it from most other small rodents in the area.

There are 8 mammae. Occurs on St. Lawrence, Big Punuk, Amak, Unalaska, Popof, Afognak, Kodiak, Chichagof, Montague, Baranof, and Barter Is., Alaska.

Similar species: (1) Yellow-cheeked Vole — large; nose yellowish. (2) Meadow Vole — smaller where ranges meet. (3) Alaska Vole — tail usually under 1⅗ in. (4) Longtail Vole — tail longer than 2 in. (5) Redback Voles (p. 189) — back reddish. (6) Mountain Phenacomys (p. 187) — smaller. (7) Lemmings (p. 183) — tail no longer than 1 in., or body brightly colored.

Habitat: Moist to wet tundra.

Habits: Makes runways through tundra vegetation; may store some food. Nests in shallow burrows or under debris.

Young: 3–11 embryos reported.   Map opposite

LONGTAIL VOLE *Microtus longicaudus*

Recognition: Head and body 4½–5⅓ in.; tail 2–3½ in.; wt. 1⅓–2 oz. A rather *large* vole with a *long tail*. Fur *dark gray washed with brown or blackish;* feet *soiled whitish;* tail *bicolored.* There are 8 mammae.

Similar species: (1) Meadow Vole — tail usually under 2 in.; may be difficult to distinguish. (2) California Vole — tail usually shorter; mostly in foothills and valleys; may be difficult to distinguish. (3) Mountain Vole — belly whitish; sometimes difficult to differentiate. (4) Mexican, (5) Prairie, (6) Oregon, (7) Alaska, and (8) Tundra Voles — tail usually under 2 in. (9) Townsend Vole — large; blackish tail. (10) Richardson Vole — head and body longer than 5½ in. (11) Phenacomys (p. 186) — either reddish or rich brown, or with tail under 2 in. (12) Redback Voles (p. 189) — back reddish, sides gray or yellowish. (13) Others — tail less than 2 in.

Habitat: Streambanks and mt. meadows, occasionally in dry situations; brushy areas in winter.

Habits: Feeds on grasses, bulbs, bark of small twigs. Nests aboveground in winter, in burrows in summer.

Young: Born May–Sept.; 4–8.   Map p. 199

CORONATION ISLAND VOLE *Microtus coronarius*

Recognition: Head and body 5–5⅜ in.; tail 2⅘–3⅜ in. Similar to Longtail Vole.

Range: Coronation, Forrester, and Warren Is., Alaska.

MEXICAN VOLE *Microtus mexicanus*

Recognition: Head and body 4–4⅜ in.; tail 1–1⅔ in.; wt. 1–1½ oz. A *small, brownish* vole. Feet *dusky;* tail *short.* There are 4 mammae.

Similar species: (1) Mountain Vole — belly whitish. (2) Longtail Vole — tail 2 in. or more. (3) Boreal Redback Vole (p. 189) — back red, sides gray.

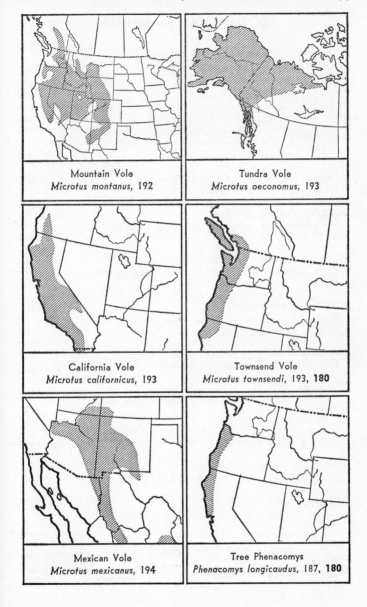

Mountain Vole
Microtus montanus, 192

Tundra Vole
Microtus oeconomus, 193

California Vole
Microtus californicus, 193

Townsend Vole
Microtus townsendi, 193, **180**

Mexican Vole
Microtus mexicanus, 194

Tree Phenacomys
Phenacomys longicaudus, 187, **180**

SOME ODD MAMMALS

Muskrat houses in marsh

Tree cut by Beaver

	Map	Text
FLORIDA WATER RAT, *Neofiber alleni*	200	202
Rich brown fur; round tail; water. SE.		
MUSKRAT, *Ondatra zibethica*	203	203
Rich brown fur; scaly tail flattened on sides; water. N, S, E, W.		
APLODONTIA, *Aplodontia rufa*	95	94
Dark brown; no apparent tail; moist situations. NW.		
NUTRIA, *Myocastor coypus*		210
Body grayish brown; tail long, round, scantily haired; water. S, NW.		
ARMADILLO, *Dasypus novemcinctus*	240	240
Covered with armor plate. S Central, SE.		
OPOSSUM, *Didelphis marsupialis*	2	1
White face, naked tail; size of House Cat. S, E, W.		
BEAVER, *Castor canadensis*	158	157
Tail scaly, paddle-shaped, flattened on top and bottom. N, S, E, W.		
PORCUPINE, *Erethizon dorsatum*	209	208
Long sharp spines on body and tail. N, W.		
PECCARY, *Pecari angulatus*	226	226
Piglike; 3 toes on hind foot. SW, S Central.		

Muskrat walking. Tail mark. R.F. R.H. 3 in.±

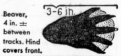

Beaver, 4 in. ± between tracks. Hind covers front. 3-6 in.

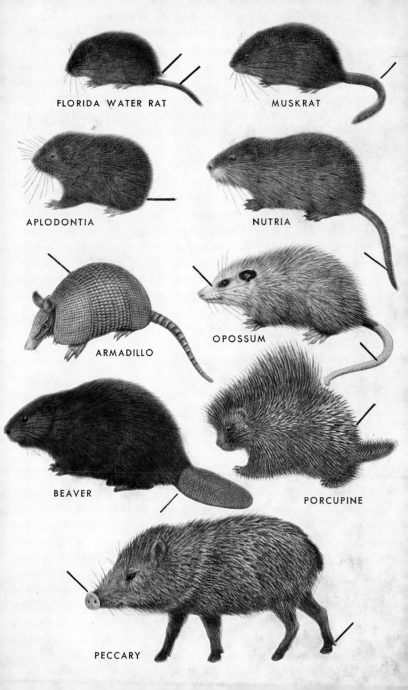

FLORIDA WATER RAT

MUSKRAT

APLODONTIA

NUTRIA

ARMADILLO

OPOSSUM

BEAVER

PORCUPINE

PECCARY

Winter

Summer

WHITETAIL JACKRABBIT

Winter

Summer

SNOWSHOE HARE

BLACKTAIL JACKRABBIT

ANTELOPE JACKRABBIT

EUROPEAN HARE

Winter

Summer

ARCTIC HARE

Plate 20   197

JACKRABBITS AND HARES

	Map	Text

WHITETAIL JACKRABBIT, *Lepus townsendi*   213 213
  Winter: White or pale gray; large; tail usually white.
  Summer: Brownish gray; tail usually white above
  and below.
  N Central, NW.

SNOWSHOE HARE, *Lepus americanus*   212 214
  Winter: White; hairs dark at bases; large hind feet.
  Summer: Dark brown; large hind feet.
  N, E, W.

BLACKTAIL JACKRABBIT, *Lepus californicus*   218 215
  Black on top of tail and rump; ears black-tipped.
  W, S Central.

ANTELOPE JACKRABBIT, *Lepus alleni*   218 215
  Whitish sides and hips; ears huge. SW.

EUROPEAN HARE, *Lepus europaeus*   218 214
  Black on top of tail; large size; open areas. NE.

ARCTIC HARE, *Lepus arcticus*   212 212
  Winter: Body hairs white to skin; tips of ears black.
  Summer: Gray, brown, or white; tail always white;
  tips of ears black.
  Arctic, Subarctic.

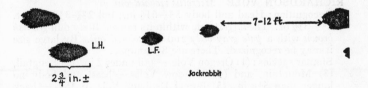

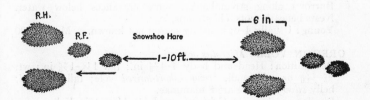

Habitat: Mt. meadows and parklike yellow pine forests; usually dry situations.
Habits: Active by day. May nest aboveground in winter, below in summer; makes runways and burrows through grass or herbaceous cover.
Young: Usually 3–4 (2–5). Map p. 195

YELLOW-CHEEKED VOLE *Microtus xanthognathus*
Recognition: Head and body 6–7 in.; tail 1⅘–2 in.; wt. 4–6 oz. A large, yellow-cheeked, dull brown vole. There are 8 mammae.
Similar species: (1) Lemmings (p. 183) — tail no longer than 1 in. (2) Other voles — smaller; cheeks not yellowish. (3) Mountain Phenacomys (p. 187) — tail under 1⅘ in.
Habitat: Spruce forests and bordering tundra.
Habits: Chiefly crepuscular, but may be active day or night. May construct dirt mounds 2–10 ft. in diam. and 1–2 ft. high; runways through sphagnum.
Young: 7–10 embryos reported. Map opposite

YELLOWNOSE VOLE *Microtus chrotorrhinus* p. 180
Recognition: Head and body 4–4⅘ in.; tail 1⅘–2 in.; wt. 1–2 oz. A medium-sized, *grayish-brown* vole with a rich *yellow nose.* There are 8 mammae.
Similar species: (1) Meadow Vole, (2) Pine Vole, (3) Boreal Redback Vole (p. 189), and (4) Bog Lemmings (pp. 184, 186) — none with grayish-brown body and rich yellow nose. (5) Mountain Phenacomys (p. 187) — tail under 1⅘ in.
Habitat: Cool, moist, rocky woodlands. Map opposite

RICHARDSON VOLE *Microtus richardsoni*
Recognition: Head and body 5⅗–6½ in.; tail 2⅖–3⅗ in.; wt. 2½–3½ oz. The *largest* vole within its range. Body dull *grayish brown* with a *pale gray belly* and a *bicolored tail.* By large size it may be recognized. There are 8 mammae.
Similar species: (1) Oregon Vole — tail under 2 in. (2) Longtail, (3) Mountain, and (4) Meadow Voles — head and body no longer than 5½ in. (5) Boreal Redback Vole (p. 189) — back reddish, sides gray. (6) Others — tail less than 2 in.
Habitat: Creekbanks and marshes; mts., to above timberline.
Habits: Semi-aquatic; swims well and takes to water readily. Burrows along streambanks; some entrances below water. Nests beneath roots, old stumps, logs.
Young: Usually 4–6; breeding season not known. Map p. 200

OREGON VOLE *Microtus oregoni*
Recognition: Head and body 4–4⅖ in.; tail 1⅕–1⅗ in.; wt. ⅗–7⁄10 oz. A small, *brown, short-haired* vole; tail *bicolored;* belly *silvery.* There are 8 mammae.
Similar species: (1) California and (2) Mountain Voles — fur

long. (3) Townsend, (4) Longtail, (5) Richardson Voles, (6) California Redback Vole (p. 190), and (7) Pacific and (8) Tree Phenacomys (p. 187) — tail longer than 2 in. (9) Mountain Phenacomys (p. 187) — near mountaintops.

Habitat: Forests, brush, grassy areas; usually on dry slopes.
Habits: Burrows through the duff on the forest floor or among the grass roots; seldom comes aboveground. Breeding season, May–Aug., possibly longer.
Young: Report of 3–5 per litter.   Map p. 200

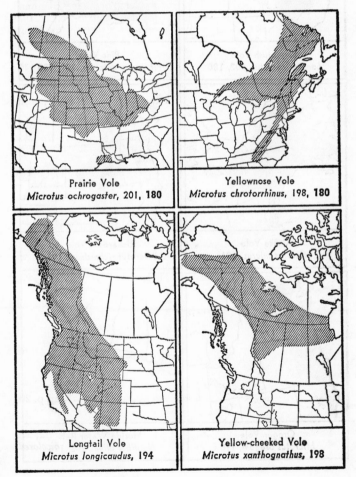

Prairie Vole
Microtus ochrogaster, 201, **180**

Yellownose Vole
Microtus chrotorrhinus, 198, **180**

Longtail Vole
Microtus longicaudus, 194

Yellow-cheeked Vole
Microtus xanthognathus, 198

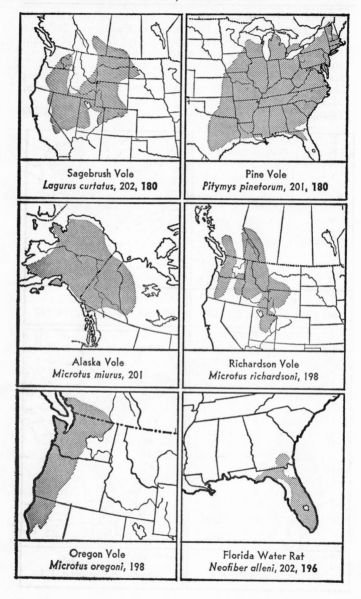

Sagebrush Vole
Lagurus curtatus, 202, **180**

Pine Vole
Pitymys pinetorum, 201, **180**

Alaska Vole
Microtus miurus, 201

Richardson Vole
Microtus richardsoni, 198

Oregon Vole
Microtus oregoni, 198

Florida Water Rat
Neofiber alleni, 202, **196**

ALASKA VOLE *Microtus miurus*

Recognition: Head and body $3\frac{1}{2}$–5 in.; tail 1–$1\frac{2}{5}$ in.; wt. 1–2 oz. Tail short; body *buffy*. May be distinguished by *small size* and *short tail*. There are 8 mammae.

Similar species: (1) Lemmings (p. 183) — larger; tail no longer than 1 in. or body brightly colored. (2) Mountain Phenacomys (p. 187) — body not buffy. (3) Other voles — either have reddish back or are larger; tail usually more than $1\frac{3}{5}$ in.

Habitat: High, well-drained slopes, tundra benches, scattered dwarf willows.

Habits: Active day or night. In autumn, constructs forage piles of 1 qt. to 8 gal. in volume. Digs own burrows, but may also occupy those of ground squirrels. Breeds June–Aug.

Young: 4–12 embryos reported. Map opposite

INSULAR VOLE *Microtus abbreviatus*

Recognition: Head and body $5\frac{2}{5}$–$5\frac{4}{5}$ in.; tail 1–$1\frac{1}{5}$ in.

Range: Hall and St. Matthew Is., Bering Sea, Alaska.

PRAIRIE VOLE *Microtus ochrogaster* p. 180

Recognition: Head and body $3\frac{1}{2}$–5 in.; tail $1\frac{1}{5}$–$1\frac{3}{5}$ in.; wt. 1–$1\frac{1}{2}$ oz. In the extensive *prairie* region, this is the typical vole. It is *grayish to dark brown*, with a good mixture of fulvous-tipped hairs — darkest in South and East, palest in Northwest. Tail *short* for a Vole; belly either *whitish or fulvous*. There are 6 mammae.

Some authors consider this a separate genus (*Pedomys*). The populations in Louisiana and Texas are considered distinct by some (*M. ludovicianus*).

Similar species: (1) Meadow Vole — tail usually more than $1\frac{3}{5}$ in.; sometimes difficult to distinguish. (2) Longtail Vole — tail 2 in. or more. (3) Mountain Vole and (4) Mountain Phenacomys (p. 187) — in mts. (5) Boreal Redback Vole (p. 189) — back red. (6) Sagebrush Vole — ash-gray. (7) Pine Vole — auburn; tail 1 in. or less. (8) Southern Bog Lemming (p. 184) — grooved upper incisors.

Habitat: Open prairies; fence rows, railway rights-of-way, and old cemeteries; usually fairly dry places.

Habits: Active day and night. Has extensive underground burrow system as well as runways on surface; nests more often underground.

Young: Born mostly March–Sept.; usually 3–4 (2–6); gestation period 21 days; 3–4 litters a season. Females breed at 30 days. Map p. 199

PINE VOLE *Pitymys pinetorum* p. 180

Recognition: Head and body $2\frac{4}{5}$–$4\frac{1}{5}$ in.; tail $\frac{2}{3}$–1 in.; wt. $\frac{3}{4}$–$1\frac{1}{3}$ oz. This handsome little vole is rarely found in the pines, as the name would imply, but is more characteristic of the eastern *deciduous forest. Auburn fur thick and soft,* does not have the scattered long guard hairs found in most other voles. Ears small; tail *short.* Upper incisors smooth. Skull (p. 245) has 16 teeth. There are 4 mammae.

Some authors place this in the genus *Microtus.* The Pine Vole in Florida is considered a distinct species (*P. parvulus*) by some.

Similar species: (1) Meadow and (2) Yellownose Voles — tail longer than 1 in. (3) Prairie Vole — not auburn. (4) Boreal Redback Vole (p. 189) — tail longer. (5) Southern Bog Lemming (p. 184) — upper incisors grooved.

Habitat: Usually a forest floor with a thick layer of duff, deciduous in North, pines in South; occasionally found in other situations, particularly in orchards.

Habits: Active day or night. Tunnels through leaf mold and loose soil, near surface; may burrow around orchard trees and eat bark from roots; also eats bulbs, tubers, seeds. Nests beneath stumps, logs, or other protection. Home range about ¼ acre. Populations fluctuate widely. Breeds Jan.–Oct. in North, probably all year in South.

Young: Usually 3–4 (2–7); gestation period about 21 days; 3–4 litters a year. Map p. 200

SAGEBRUSH VOLE *Lagurus curtatus* p. 180

Recognition: Head and body 3⅘–4½ in.; tail ⅗–1⅛ in.; wt. ⅘–1⅓ oz. An extremely pale, *ash-gray* vole with *whitish belly and feet;* tail usually *less than 1 in.* If found living in *sagebrush,* it is without doubt this species. Palest of the voles; also the one found in driest places. Skull (p. 245) has 16 teeth. There are 8 mammae.

Similar species: (1) Prairie Vole — tail longer than 1⅛ in. (2) Other voles — tail longer; not found in sagebrush.

Habitat: Scattered sagebrush, loose soil; arid conditions.

Habits: Active day or night. Makes shallow burrows, usually close to a sagebush. Feeds on green vegetation, particularly sagebrush. Breeds throughout year.

Young: Usually 4–6 (3–8); more than 1 litter a year.

Map p. 200

Water Rat and Muskrat

THESE are the largest and most nearly aquatic members of this family of rodents. Most of their lives are spent in or near water. There is but 1 species in each genus.

FLORIDA WATER RAT *Neofiber alleni* p. 196

Recognition: Head and body 7⅘–8⅗ in.; tail 4⅕–6⅘ in.; wt. 5½–11⅔ oz. A small *round-tailed* edition of the Muskrat;

rich brown fur, with *coarse guard hairs* over dense underfur, and size will distinguish it from any other water-living rodent in the area. Skull (p. 245) has 16 teeth. There are 6 mammae.

Habitat: Bogs, marshes, weedy borders of lakes; savannas bordering streams.

Habits: Builds bulky nest in stumps, mangroves, or open savannas. Constructs feeding platform in shallow water; feeds on water plants, crayfish. Probably breeds throughout year.

Young: 1–3 recorded.

Economic status: Of no importance; may do occasional damage to crops; an interesting part of our native fauna. Map p. 200

MUSKRAT *Ondatra zibethica* p. 196

Recognition: Head and body 10–14 in.; tail 8–11 in.; wt. 2–4 lb. *Fur dense, rich brown*, overlaid with coarse guard hairs; belly *silvery;* tail long, *naked*, scaly, and black; *flattened from side to side*. Character of tail alone is sufficient to distinguish the Muskrat from all other mammals. Their presence in marshes may be detected by the *conical houses*, 2–3 ft. above water, which are built of marsh vegetation. Skull (p. 245) has 16 teeth. There are 6 mammae.

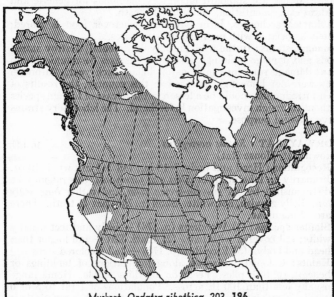

Muskrat, *Ondatra zibethica*, 203, **196**

The Muskrat on Newfoundland may be a distinct species (*O. obscura*).

Habitat: Marshes, edges of ponds, lakes, and streams; cattails, rushes, water lilies, open water.

Habits: Chiefly aquatic; moves overland, especially in autumn. Feeds on aquatic vegetation, also clams, frogs, and fish on occasion. Builds house in shallow water; also burrows in banks; entrances usually underwater; 1 family to each house. Breeds April–Aug. in North, in winter in South.

Young: Usually 5–6 (1–11); gestation period 22–30 days; 2–3 litters a year. Naked, blind.

Economic status: One of our most valuable fur animals; may cause some damage to dikes, by burrowing.   Map p. 203

Old World Rats and Mice: Muridae

THESE include the Norway Rat, Black Rat, and House Mouse, no one of which commonly occurs far from man-made structures. They are *dull grayish brown to black, with long naked tails* fairly uniform in color. Albino mutants of the Norway Rat and the House Mouse are standard laboratory mammals for genetic and medical experimentation. Skull has 16 teeth.

Habitat: Warehouses, farm buildings, wherever food is stored; closely associated with man and his structures.

Economic status: In the wild, entirely detrimental; destroy stored foods and damage buildings; also carry diseases communicable to man; damage runs into millions of dollars each year. Although they were not knowingly released in this country, the results of their introduction should be a lesson in the release of foreign species without thorough investigation beforehand. The laboratory strains serve a useful purpose.

NORWAY RAT   *Rattus norvegicus*   p. 181
(Brown Rat, House Rat)

Recognition: Head and body 7–10 in.; tail 5–8 in.; wt. 7–10 oz. Primarily an inhabitant of *cities and farmyards*, this rat may be distinguished by its *grayish-brown color* and rather *long scaly tail*. Belly grayish, not white. Skull (p. 245) has 16 teeth. There are 12 mammae.

Similar species: (1) Woodrats (p. 174) — belly and feet usually white; tail covered with hair. (2) Black Rat — tail longer than head and body. (3) Rice Rat (p. 178) — tail bicolored.

Habits: Colonial. Burrows along foundations of buildings or beneath rubbish piles. Feeds on anything edible. Home range usually less than 100 ft. across. Populations of 1 rat to 5 or 6 people is common in larger cities, probably higher populations in small communities.

Young: Usually 8–10 (6–22); gestation period 21–22 days; 12 litters a year possible. Females breed at 3 months.
Range: Throughout the continent where people are concentrated.

BLACK RAT (Roof Rat) *Rattus rattus*   p. 181
Recognition: Head and body 7–8 in.; tail 8⅔–10 in.; wt. 5–10 oz. There are 2 color phases (*brown* and *black*) in this species. Belly may be grayish but *never white*. *Naked* tail is *longer* than head and body. Found chiefly around *buildings;* rare in North, common in extreme South. Skull has 16 teeth. There are 10 mammae.
Similar species: (1) Norway Rat — tail shorter than head and body. (2) Woodrats (p. 174) and (3) Rice Rat (p. 178) — tail bicolored.
Habits: Lives mostly in tops of buildings; does not require soil to burrow into; occasionally found in fields some distance from buildings.
Range: Chiefly seaports; has been reported as far inland as Urbana, Illinois.

HOUSE MOUSE *Mus musculus*   p. 164
Recognition: Head and body 3⅕–3⅖ in.; tail 2⅘–3⅘ in.; wt. ⅖–⅘ oz. A small, *grayish-brown* mouse with *gray or buffy belly* and a *scaly tail* about the *same color above and below;* fur fairly short. Upper incisors not grooved. Skull (p. 245) has 16 teeth. There are 10 mammae.
Similar species: (1) White-footed and (2) Deer Mice (pp. 161–72) — white belly. (3) Pygmy Mouse (p. 172) — smaller; tail haired. (4) Harvest Mice (p. 159) — grooved upper incisors. (5) Jumping Mice (below) — white belly.
Habits: Occasionally found in fields, but usually in buildings. Eats anything edible. A prolific species; breeds year round.
Young: 3–11; gestation period 18–21 days; several litters a year. First breed at 6 weeks.
Range: Throughout the continent, wherever there are concentrations of people.

Jumping Mice: Zapodidae

MEMBERS of this family are rather small to *medium-sized* mice with extremely *long tails* and *large hind feet*. Body *yellowish to orange* along sides, darker on back, *belly white;* ears small, narrowly *edged with buff or white*. No external cheek pouches. Upper incisors have *grooves* down front surfaces. They prefer damp meadows and forests, and hibernate during the winter.
Similar species: (1) Pocket Mice (p. 137) and (2) Kangaroo Rats (pp. 151–57) — external cheek pouches.

Economic status: Neutral; rarely sufficiently numerous to do damage.

MEADOW JUMPING MOUSE *Zapus hudsonius* p. 148

Recognition: Head and body 3–3⅓ in.; tail 4–5⅘ in.; wt. ½–⅘ oz. If seen jumping through the grass, these *olive-yellow* mice might be mistaken for frogs. On close inspection, the *2-toned body* and the *long*, scantily haired tail, plus the *large hind feet*, will serve to distinguish this from most other small mammals. Skull (p. 245) has 18 teeth. There are 8 mammae.

Similar species: (1) Woodland Jumping Mouse — white tip on tail. (2) Western Jumping Mouse — head and body over 3⅓ in.; in mts.

Habitat: This mouse prefers low meadows for feeding, but appears in various land habitats; not restricted.

Habits: Primarily nocturnal. Feeds on seeds, insects, fruits. Winter nest 2–3 ft. beneath surface, in well-drained site; hibernates in Oct. or Nov., emerges April–May; summer nest on surface or beneath brush, logs, stumps. Home range ½–2 acres. Populations fluctuate, never very high. Lives 1–2 years in wild. Breeds June–Aug.

Young: Usually 4–5 (3–7); gestation period 18–21 days; 2–3 litters a season. Map opposite

WESTERN JUMPING MOUSE *Zapus princeps*

Recognition: Head and body 3½–4 in.; tail 5–6 in.; wt. ⅔–1⅓ oz. This is chiefly a *mt.* species. *Yellowish sides, darker back, white* (or buffy) *belly, long tail, large hind feet*, and no external cheek pouches set it apart from most other small rodents. Skull has 18 teeth. There are 8 mammae.

Similar species: (1) Meadow Jumping Mouse — head and body less than 3½ in.; usually not in mts. (2) Pacific Jumping Mouse — similar but more colorful; ranges known to overlap only at Allison Pass, B.C.

Habitat: Near streams, lush growths of grasses and herbs.

Habits: Chiefly nocturnal. Good swimmer. Feeds primarily on seeds. Hibernates Sept. or Oct. to April or May. Nests on surface under protection of grasses or herbs. Can jump 4–6 ft.

Young: Born June–July; 2–7; 1 litter a season. Map opposite

PACIFIC JUMPING MOUSE *Zapus trinotatus*

Recognition: Head and body 3⅗–3⅘ in.; tail 5⅕–6⅕ in. Similar to the Western Jumping Mouse but is more brightly colored. *Long tail, large hind feet*, and no external cheek pouches will serve to identify this species. Range separate, except at Allison Pass, B.C., from ranges of other jumping mice.

Habitat: Wet, marshy areas, open meadows, woods; to timberline. Map p. 208

WOODLAND JUMPING MOUSE
Napaeozapus insignis

p. 148

Recognition: Head and body 3⅗–4 in.; tail 5–6⅕ in.; wt.

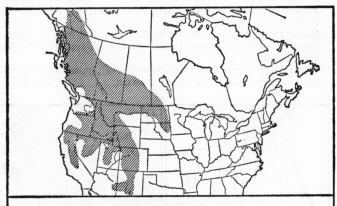

Western Jumping Mouse, *Zapus princeps*, 206

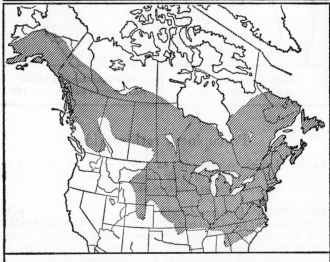

Meadow Jumping Mouse, *Zapus hudsonius*, 206, **148**

$\frac{7}{10}-1\frac{1}{10}$ oz. A handsome jumping mouse; *bright yellowish sides, brownish back, white belly, large hind feet,* and a *long white-tipped tail* should serve to identify it within its range. Skull (p. 245) has 16 teeth. There are 8 mammae.

Similar species: Meadow Jumping Mouse — no white tip on tail.

Habitat: Forested or brushy areas near water; wet bogs, stream borders.

Habits: Nocturnal. Feeds on seeds, fruits, and insects. Hibernates Nov.–April. Home range 1–2 acres. Populations of 3 per acre normal.

Young: Born June–Sept.; usually 3–5 (1–6); gestation period 29 days or more; possibly 2 litters a season.   Map below

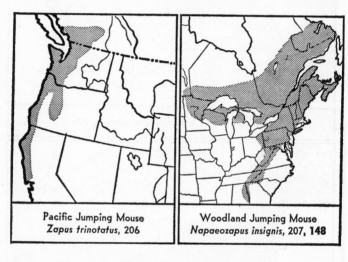

Pacific Jumping Mouse
Zapus trinotatus, 206

Woodland Jumping Mouse
Napaeozapus insignis, 207, **148**

Porcupine: Erethizontidae

LARGE, blackish rodents with an overlay of yellow-tipped hairs; size of small dog; most of body, especially rump and tail, *thickly set with long sharp spines.* Known as fossils from Oligocene.

PORCUPINE   *Erethizon dorsatum*   p. 196
    Recognition: Head and body 18–22 in.; tail 7–9 in.; wt. 10–28 lb. A *heavy-bodied, short-legged,* clumsy animal that may be seen lumbering through the forest or hunched into what appears to be a large black ball high in a tree. Often seen along shoulders of highways, especially where salt has been used, in evening or early morning. Many are killed by autos. Trees with tops

barked indicate presence of Porcupines nearby. Only N. American mammal with long sharp quills. Eyeshine deep red. Skull (p. 249) has 20 teeth. There are 4 mammae.

Habitat: Usually forested areas, but occasionally away from trees if brush is available.

Habits: Most active at night, but may be seen during day, especially in top of tree; climbs awkwardly, but is more at home in tree than on ground. Solitary in summer; may be colonial in winter. Feeds on buds, small twigs, and inner bark of trees; fond of salt. Dens in hollow trees or natural caves in rocks; does not hibernate. Grunts, groans, and high-pitched cries may be heard for ¼ mi., especially in fall rutting season. Breeds Sept.–Oct.

Young: Born April–May; 1; gestation period about 7 months; wt. about 1 lb. Furred, and eyes open; able to climb trees and eat solid foods a few hours after birth. Sexually mature at 3 years.

Economic status: May damage buildings, communication lines, and trees. Quills used for decorative purposes by Indians; meat edible, best if animal had not been feeding on pines. May be seen in many of the western parks and throughout Canada.

Map below

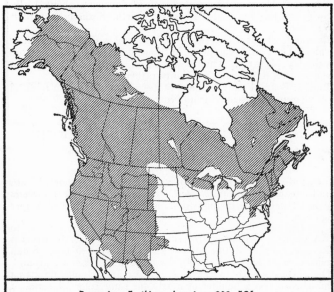

Porcupine, *Erethizon dorsatum*, 208, **196**

Nutria: Capromyidae

A LARGE S. American rodent that was introduced first into Louisiana as a possible fur-bearing mammal; now spread over much of U.S. Some raised in captivity for breeding stock and fur. Probably most numerous in marshes of Louisiana and Oregon.

NUTRIA (Coypu)   *Myocastor coypus*   p. 196
   Recognition: Head and body 22–25 in.; tail 12–17 in.; wt. 15–20 lb. A *large grayish-brown* rodent with *long, round, scantily haired* tail. Hind feet webbed. Skull has 20 teeth.
   Similar species: (1) Beaver (p. 157) and (2) Muskrat (p. 203) — flattened, naked tails. (3) Opossum (p. 1) — white face, pointed nose, no webs between toes.
   Habitat: Marshes, swamps, ponds, and lakes.
   Habits: Nocturnal. Feeds on nearly every kind of aquatic plant available; carries food to feeding station, log, brush, or vegetation that will support the animal. Burrows in banks with entrance above water; builds winter resting platforms 20–30 in. wide and 6–9 in. above water, in dense vegetation; builds simple nest in vegetation growing in shallow water. Lives 4 years in wild to 12 years in captivity. Breeds throughout year in South.
   Young: 2–11; gestation period 127–32 days; wt. about ½ lb. Swim and feed on solids 24 hrs. after birth. Sexually mature at 5 months.
   Economic status: The fur of wild-caught animals is of little value. The Nutria competes, in the wild, for food with the more valuable Muskrat. This is a case of an introduced foreign species that has become a liability rather than an asset.
   Range: Found locally in many states where it has been released or where it has escaped from Nutria ranches.

Pikas, Hares, and Rabbits: Lagomorpha

Pikas: Ochotonidae

SMALL, *rat-sized*, grayish to buffy or brownish, with short, broad, rounded ears and *no visible tail*. Found only in the *rockslides* and near timberline in high mts. Known as fossils from Upper Oligocene.

PIKA (Cony)   *Ochotona princeps*   p. 216
   Recognition: Head and body 6½–8½ in.; wt. 4–6⅓ oz. Small piles of *fresh hay* in the *rockslides* mean that Pikas are around. One of these *grayish* to *buffy* or *brownish* mammals may be sitting hunched up on a boulder of nearly the same color. A series of peculiar short squeaks is further evidence. *No visible tail*. Other

mammals seen in similar situations during daytime are marmots, Golden-mantled Squirrels, and chipmunks. All have
bushy tails. Skull (p. 249) has 26 teeth. There are 6 mammae.
Habitat: Talus slopes, rockslides; usually near timberline in
mts., down to sea level in North.
Habits: Active only by day. Colonial. Feeds on grasses and
herbs; stores food in small piles of "hay" beneath boulders;
does not hibernate. Each Pika has its territory within the
colony, at least in autumn. Breeds in spring and possibly in
summer.
Young: Born May–June and July–Aug.; 2–5; gestation period
30–31 days.
Economic status: Lives where few people ever go; does no harm;
an interesting part of our native fauna. May be seen at some of
the talus slopes along highway in Glacier Natl. Park; also in
Crater Lake, Kings Canyon, Mt. Rainier, Rocky Mt., Sequoia,
Yellowstone, and Yosemite Natl. Parks.   Map below

COLLARED PIKA *Ochotona collaris*
Recognition: Similar to *O. princeps* (above); may be same
species; geographic range separate.   Map below

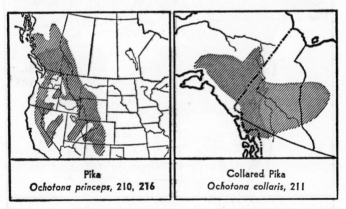

Pika
Ochotona princeps, 210, 216

Collared Pika
Ochotona collaris, 211

Hares and Rabbits: Leporidae

MEMBERS of this family usually have *long ears, long hind legs*, soft
fur, and a *short cottony tail*. Most species, particularly in warmer
climates, carry tularemia, or "rabbit disease." Sick rabbits should
be avoided. Meat should be well cooked; rubber gloves should
be worn when dressing-out rabbits, if in doubt. Skull has 28 teeth.
Known as fossils from Upper Eocene.

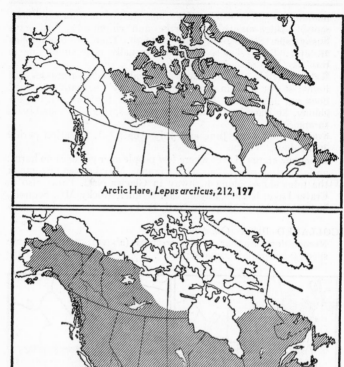

Arctic Hare, *Lepus arcticus*, 212, **197**

Snowshoe Hare, *Lepus americanus*, 214, **197**

ARCTIC HARE   *Lepus arcticus*   p. 197
   Recognition: Head and body 17–24 in.; ear 3–4 in.; wt. 6–12 lb.
A truly *arctic* mammal, this large hare occupies the barren
grounds. In Ellesmere and n. Baffin Is. and Greenland, these
hares remain *white throughout year;* elsewhere *gray or brown in*

summer, but tail remains *white*. In winter, fur *white to the base* (except tips of ears, which are black).
Similar species: Snowshoe Hare — smaller; tail brown in summer; fur not white to base in winter.
Habitat: Tundra of Far North.
Habits: Active throughout year; somewhat gregarious. Often stands up on hind feet, also hops kangaroo-fashion without touching forefeet to ground. Feeds on low-growing tundra plants. Populations fluctuate widely.
Young: Born June–July; 4–8. Fully furred, eyes open.
Economic status: Serves as food for foxes and dogs; also eaten by Eskimos, but meat not nourishing; skins used for clothing and robes. Map opposite

TUNDRA HARE *Lepus othus*
Recognition: Head and body 20–24 in.; ear 3–3½ in.; wt. 9–10 lb. This is the western representative of the Arctic Hare and probably should be in the same species. It turns *brown in summer*, but *tail remains white*. In winter, fur *white to the skin*.
Similar species: Snowshoe Hare — head and body less than 20 in.; tail brown in summer; fur not white to skin in winter.
Habits: Probably similar to those of Arctic Hare (above); young huddle together in a small depression; no nest.
Map below

WHITETAIL JACKRABBIT *Lepus townsendi* p. 197
Recognition: Head and body 18–22 in.; ear 5–6 in.; wt. 5–10 lb. On our northern *plains* and in the *western mts.* this is the largest hare. *Brownish gray* in summer, *white or pale gray* in winter. Tail nearly always *white above and below*. There are 8 mammae.
Similar species: (1) Snowshoe Hare — smaller; dark brown in

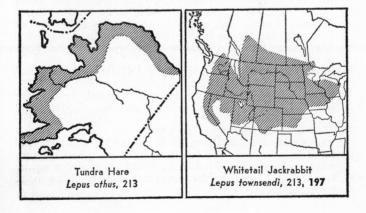

Tundra Hare
Lepus othus, 213

Whitetail Jackrabbit
Lepus townsendi, 213, **197**

summer; prefers forests and swamps. (2) Blacktail Jackrabbit —
top of tail black. (3) Cottontails — smaller; do not turn white
in winter.

Habitat: Open, grassy or sagebrush plains.

Habits: Nocturnal. Sits in form during day; does not burrow
in soil, but makes tunnels in deep snow. Feeds mostly on grasses
and other green vegetation in summer; may add buds, bark, and
small twigs in winter. When running, can clear 17 ft. at a jump;
has been clocked at 40 mph.

Young: 3–6. Furred, eyes open. Concealed in vegetation, not
in nest.

Economic status: Causes some damage to hay crops and small
trees; a good game mammal; meat edible.   Map p. 213

SNOWSHOE HARE *Lepus americanus*   p. 197
(Varying Hare, Jackrabbit)

Recognition: Head and body 13–18 in.; ear 3½–4 in.; wt. 2–4 lb.
A *large-footed* hare that turns *white* in winter; in summer, *dark
brown*. The white of winter is only on tips of hairs; beneath
these is a yellowish band. Ears relatively small for a hare. Eyeshine orange. There are 8–10 mammae.

Similar species: (1) Arctic and (2) Tundra Hares — tail always
white; fur white to skin in winter. (3) Whitetail Jackrabbit —
larger; tail nearly always white; long ears. (4) Cottontails —
brownish or grayish throughout year; feet usually whitish; nape
patch rusty. (5) Blacktail Jackrabbit — black stripe down
rump and on top of tail; open areas. (6) European Hare —
larger; top of tail black; open areas.

Habitat: Swamps, forests, thickets; mts. in West.

Habits: Nocturnal. Sits in form or beneath brush or trees during
day. Feeds on succulent vegetation in summer, twigs, buds,
bark in winter; fond of frozen meat. Does not build nest. Home
range about 10 acres, but may travel up to 1 mile. Populations
fluctuate tremendously, with highs about every 11 years. Few
live more than 3 years in the wild, up to 8 years in captivity.
May display territorial behavior during breeding season. Runs
in circle in front of dogs.

Young: Born April–Aug.; usually 2–4 (1–7); gestation period
36–37 days; 2–3 litters. Leverets furred, eyes open.

Economic status: An important game mammal; causes some
damage to new forest plantations and gardens.   Map p. 212

EUROPEAN HARE *Lepus europaeus*   p. 197

Recognition: Head and body 25–27 in.; ear 4½–5 in.; wt. 7–10
lb. This large introduced hare is *brownish gray;* does not turn
white in winter. Top of tail black. Within its present range, by
far the *largest* member of its group; may easily be distinguished
by size alone.

Habitat: Open fields and low, unforested hills.
Economic status: A good game mammal, but if sufficiently numerous could cause considerable damage to crops.

Map p. 218

ANTELOPE JACKRABBIT *Lepus alleni*   p. 197

Recognition: Head and body 19–21 in.; ear 7–8 in.; wt. 6–13 lb. A bounding white flash among the mesquite, giant cactus, and other desert vegetation — or a pair of *huge ears, without black* on them, erect and supported by a relatively small head — may be your introduction to this large, long-legged hare of the desert. Its pale *whitish sides and hips* will serve for identification. There are 6 mammae.

The population in extreme s. New Mexico may be of a distinct species (*L. gaillardi*).

Similar species: (1) Blacktail Jackrabbit — brown on sides and hips; ear tips bordered with blackish. (2) Cottontails — smaller; brownish or grayish; smaller ears.

Habitat: Grasses, mesquites, and catclaws; on slopes at moderate elevations; creosote desert.

Habits: Active from early evening to well after sunrise; sits in shade of a bush during day; may be seen in groups of 2–25 or more. May move some distance from daytime resting spot to feeding area. Feeds on various desert plants, including cacti. Home range usually no more than 1000 ft. across. Does not build nest. Populations fluctuate, occasionally seen in concentrations of 10 per acre. May run 30–40 mph. Many infected with tapeworm cysts (bladder worm). Breeding season, Dec.–Sept.

Young: Usually 1–3 (1–5). Furred, eyes open; scattered among bushes.

Economic status: An average of 8 rabbits will eat as much as 1 sheep, 41 as much as 1 cow; on desert grazing range these large jackrabbits compete with livestock. A fair game mammal.

Map p. 218

BLACKTAIL JACKRABBIT *Lepus californicus*   p. 197

Recognition: Head and body 17–21 in.; ear 6–7 in.; wt. 3–7 lb. Throughout the *grasslands* and *open areas* of the West this is the common jackrabbit. Its grayish-brown body, *large black-tipped ears*, and *black streak* on top of the tail will serve to distinguish it from all near-relatives. Eyeshine reddish. Skull (p. 249) has 28 teeth. There are 6 mammae.

Similar species: (1) Antelope Jackrabbit — white sides, no black on ears. (2) Whitetail Jackrabbit — usually no black on top of tail; whitish in winter. (3) Snowshoe Hare — tail not black; white in winter; forests. (4) Cottontails — much smaller; ears not black-tipped. (5) Swamp Rabbit — smaller; no black on ears or tail. (6) Brush Rabbit — smaller.

COTTONTAILS AND PIKAS

Pika and haystack
in rockslide

	Map	*Text*
PYGMY RABBIT, *Sylvilagus idahoensis*	222	223

PYGMY RABBIT, *Sylvilagus idahoensis*   222   223
Body slate-gray with pinkish tinge; ears short; small
size; desert brush. NW.

BRUSH RABBIT, *Sylvilagus bachmani*   222   221
Body brown; ears relatively short; small, inconspicuous tail; brush. W.

PIKA, *Ochotona princeps*   211   210
No visible tail; rounded ears; small size; rockslides.
W.

DESERT COTTONTAIL, *Sylvilagus auduboni*   222   220
Pale gray washed with yellow; large ears. W.

MOUNTAIN COTTONTAIL, *Sylvilagus nuttalli*   219   220
Grayish; mts. W.

EASTERN COTTONTAIL, *Sylvilagus floridanus*   219   219
Feet whitish; nape patch rusty and distinct. E,
Central, SW.

MARSH RABBIT, *Sylvilagus palustris*   222   221
Body dark brown; fur coarse; marshes. SE.

SWAMP RABBIT, *Sylvilagus aquaticus*   222   223
Body brownish gray; feet rusty above; fur coarse.
SE.

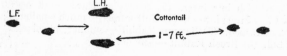

L.F.   L.H.   Cottontail   1-7 ft.

4 in.±

PYGMY RABBIT

BRUSH RABBIT

PIKA

DESERT COTTONTAIL

MOUNTAIN COTTONTAIL

EASTERN
COTTONTAIL

MARSH RABBIT

SWAMP RABBIT

BARREN GROUND CARIBOU

WOODLAND CARIBOU

MUSKOX

ELK

MOOSE

Plate 22   217

NORTHERN BIG GAME MAMMALS

	Map	Text
BARREN GROUND CARIBOU, *Rangifer arcticus*	233	234

BARREN GROUND CARIBOU, *Rangifer arcticus*   233   234
Whitish; small antlers. Arctic.

WOODLAND CARIBOU, *Rangifer caribou*   233   232
Body dark chocolate color; neck whitish; white on
rump and above hoofs. Arctic, Subarctic.

MUSKOX, *Ovibos moschatus*   237   238
Long, silky, brown hair reaches nearly to ground.
Arctic.

ELK, *Cervus canadensis*   226   227
Neck chestnut-brown; rump patch pale yellowish.
W, Central.

MOOSE, *Alces alces*   231   231
Body dark brown; antlers (on male) palmate; overhanging snout; "bell" on throat; no white; large
size. N.

Caribou

20-40 in. to next track

4 in. ±

Elk

4½ in. ±

2-3 ft. to next track

7 in. ±

Moose

2-5 ft. to next track

Habitat: Open prairies and sparsely vegetated deserts.

Habits: Most active early evenings through early mornings; sits in form at base of bush or clump of grass during day. Often feeds on green vegetation along edges of highways. Populations may fluctuate. Can run 30–35 mph. Breeds Dec.–Sept. in South.

Young: Usually 2–4 (1–6). Fully furred, eyes open. Probably no nest prepared.

Economic status: Average of 12 rabbits will eat as much as 1 sheep, 59 as much as 1 cow. Consumes considerable vegetation that could be utilized by stock. A fair game animal. Commonly seen along highways in early morning and evenings.

Map below

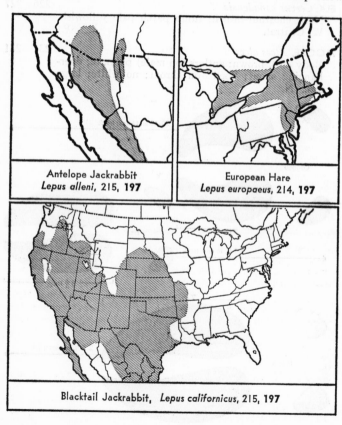

Antelope Jackrabbit
Lepus alleni, 215, **197**

European Hare
Lepus europaeus, 214, **197**

Blacktail Jackrabbit, *Lepus californicus,* 215, **197**

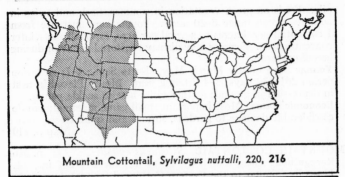

Mountain Cottontail, *Sylvilagus nuttalli*, 220, **216**

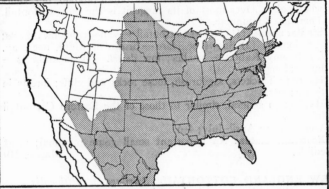

Eastern Cottontail, *Sylvilagus floridanus*, 219, **216**

EASTERN COTTONTAIL *Sylvilagus floridanus*   p. 216
  Recognition: Head and body 14–17 in.; ear 2½–3 in.; wt. 2–4 lb.
  Body brownish or grayish; *cottony tail white;* nape patch rusty,
  feet whitish. Skull (p. 249) has 28 teeth. There are 8 mammae.
  Similar species: (1) Desert Cottontail — smaller; ears longer;
  not in forests. (2) New England Cottontail — rusty nape patch
  pale or absent; reddish in summer; mts. (3) Swamp and (4)
  Marsh Rabbits — no distinct rusty nape patch; feet not pale
  whitish. (5) Snowshoe Hare — larger; dark brown in summer,
  white in winter. (6) European Hare and (7) Jackrabbits —
  larger; ears longer; open areas.
  Habitat: Heavy brush, strips of forest with open areas nearby,
  edges of swamps, weed patches.
  Habits: Active from early evening to late morning; spends day
  in partially concealed form, burrow in ground, or beneath brush-

pile. Feeds on green vegetation in summer, bark and twigs in winter. Home range 3–20 acres. Populations fluctuate from 1 cottontail per 4 acres to several per acre, especially in winter concentrations. Females may display territorial behavior during breeding season.

Young: Born mostly March–May, also to Sept.; 4–7; gestation period 26½–30 days; 3–4 litters a year. Blind. Placed in nest in depression in ground; mother visits nest to suckle young.

Economic status: Most important small game mammal; can do considerable damage to gardens, shrubs, and small trees.

Map p. 219

MOUNTAIN COTTONTAIL *Sylvilagus nuttalli*   p. 216

Recognition: Head and body 12–14 in.; ear 2⅕–2⅖ in.; wt. 1½–3 lb. Similar to the Eastern Cottontail (above), but somewhat paler. Over most of its range it is the only cottontail. There are 8 mammae.

Similar species: (1) Desert Cottontail — valleys and low deserts; ears longer. (2) Snowshoe Hare — brown or white, not gray. (3) Pygmy Rabbit — smaller; low *desert.* (4) Jackrabbits — larger; long ears.

Habitat: Thickets, sagebrush, loose rocks and cliffs; forests in South; mts.

Habits: In general, similar to those of the Eastern Cottontail (above).

Young: Born April–July; 4–6.

Economic status: An important small game mammal; meat edible.   Map p. 219

NEW ENGLAND COTTONTAIL *Sylvilagus transitionalis*

Recognition: Head and body 17 in.; ear 2½ in.; wt. 2¼–3 lb. This mt. cottontail is *reddish* in summer and sprinkled with white to give it a *reddish-gray* appearance in winter; nape patch behind ears *pale, small, or absent;* a *dark patch* between ears.

Similar species: (1) Eastern Cottontail — distinct rusty nape patch; lower areas. (2) Snowshoe Hare — feet brown in summer; white in winter. (3) European Hare — larger; top of tail black.

Habitat: Brushy areas, open forests, rough mt. terrain.

Map p. 222

DESERT COTTONTAIL *Sylvilagus auduboni*   p. 216

Recognition: Head and body 12–15 in.; ear 3–4 in.; wt. 1⅖–2¾ lb. This is the common cottontail of the *valleys* in the arid Southwest. Body *pale gray washed with yellow.* Ears large. There are 8 mammae.

Similar species: (1) Mountain Cottontail — ears shorter; mts. (2) Eastern Cottontail — larger; ears shorter. (3) Brush Rab-

bit — smaller; dark brown; shorter ears; heavy brush. (4) Snowshoe Hare — dark brown or white; high in mts. (5) Pygmy
Rabbit — smaller; heavy brush. (6) Jackrabbits — larger; open
areas.
Habitat: Open plains, foothills, and low valleys; grass, sagebrush, scattered piñons and junipers.
Habits: Most active from late afternoon throughout the night,
but may be seen at any time of day. Seeks safety in thickets or
burrows. Home range from 1 (females) to 15 (males) acres.
May live 2 years or more in wild.
Young: Born throughout year in some part of range; 2–6. Blind.
Deposited in grass-lined nest in depression in ground; female
returns to nest to suckle young.
Economic status: An important small game mammal; does little
damage to gardens and green crops.   Map p. 222

BRUSH RABBIT *Sylvilagus bachmani*   p. 216
Recognition: Head and body 11–13 in.; ear 2–2⅗ in.; wt. 1¼–
1⅘ lb. A *small brown* rabbit; ears and tail relatively *small*.
There are 8 mammae.
Similar species: (1) Desert Cottontail — larger; grayish; ears
longer. (2) Blacktail Jackrabbit — larger; open areas.
Habitat: Chaparral or thick brush.
Habits: Least active in middle of day, but may be seen feeding
on green vegetation at any time. Never ventures far from thick
cover. Rarely uses burrows; makes runways through thick
vegetation. Home range ¼–1 acre. Populations 1–3 per acre.
Breeding season, Jan.–June.
Young: 2–5. Covered with fine, short hair; blind.
Economic status: Meat excellent, but small size discourages
hunters; does little damage; in cities, feeds mostly on lawns near
dense cover.   Map p. 222

MARSH RABBIT *Sylvilagus palustris*   p. 216
Recognition: Head and body 14–16 in.; ear 2½–3 in.; wt. 2½–
3½ lb. A *dark brown*, coarse-haired, *small-footed* rabbit; feet
reddish brown above, darker below; tail small and inconspicuous,
dingy white below.
Similar species: Eastern Cottontail — hind feet whitish; large
rusty nape patch; conspicuous white tail.
Habitat: Wet bottomlands, swamps, hammocks.
Habits: Chiefly nocturnal. Feeds on various marsh vegetation,
including rhizomes and bulbs. Breeding season, Feb.–Sept.
Young: Usually 2–4 (2–5). Placed in nest in depression in
ground.
Economic status: A good game mammal; does little damage.
                                                      Map p. 222

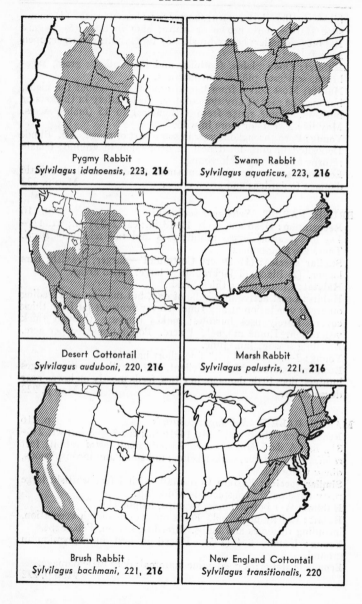

Pygmy Rabbit
Sylvilagus idahoensis, 223, **216**

Swamp Rabbit
Sylvilagus aquaticus, 223, **216**

Desert Cottontail
Sylvilagus auduboni, 220, **216**

Marsh Rabbit
Sylvilagus palustris, 221, **216**

Brush Rabbit
Sylvilagus bachmani, 221, **216**

New England Cottontail
Sylvilagus transitionalis, 220

SWAMP RABBIT *Sylvilagus aquaticus* p. 216
(Cane-cutter)
Recognition: Head and body 14–17 in.; ear 3½–4 in.; wt.
3½–6 lb. This is a rich *brownish-gray* rabbit with coarse hair;
feet *rusty;* nape patch *small* and indistinct.
Similar species: (1) Eastern Cottontail — rusty nape patch
distinct; hind feet whitish. (2) Blacktail Jackrabbit — larger;
black on ears and tail.
Habitat: Swamps, marshes, wet bottomlands.
Habits: Takes to water readily, a good swimmer; rarely uses
burrows; nests beneath logs, at bases of stumps, or in depression
in ground. Runs in circles in front of dogs. Home range 11–27
acres. Lives 1–4 years. Breeds Jan.–Sept.
Young: Usually 2–3 (1–5); gestation period 36–40 days. Furred,
eyes open in 2–3 days.
Economic status: Does some damage to crops near swamps; a
good game mammal. Map opposite

PYGMY RABBIT *Sylvilagus idahoensis* p. 216
Recognition: Head and body 8½–11 in.; ear 2¼–2½ in.; wt.
½–1 lb. Small, *slate-gray* rabbit with a *pinkish tinge;* difficult
to see in dense cover; *smallest* of the rabbits; may be distinguished from all others by size alone. Skull (p. 249) has 28
teeth. There are 10 mammae.
Considered by some to belong in a distinct genus (*Brachylagus*).
Similar species: Cottontails — larger; conspicuous white tails.
Habitat: Tall sagebrush growing in clumps.
Habits: Appears throughout the day, but is chiefly nocturnal
and crepuscular. Digs simple burrows, generally 2 or more
entrances. Feeds primarily on sagebrush. Home range usually
within 30 yds. of burrow or other home site. May issue a barking
sound while sitting at burrow mouth.
Young: Born June–July; 5–8. Map opposite

Even-toed Hoofed Mammals:
Artiodactyla

WEIGHT distributed equally on digits 3 and 4; 2 or 4 toes on each
foot (except peccaries); medium-sized to large mammals; young
able to walk a few minutes after birth.

Peccaries: Tayassuidae

PECCARIES are truly wild pigs of the New World. Primarily
tropical and subtropical, they occur south into S. America.

PRONGHORN AND DEER

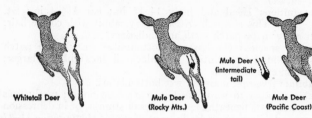

Whitetail Deer   Mule Deer   Mule Deer
                      (Rocky Mts.)   (Pacific Coast)

Mule Deer
(intermediate
tail)

	Map	Text

PRONGHORN, *Antilocapra americana*   235   235
Body pale tan; bands on throat, rump patch, and
lower sides white. W.

MULE DEER, *Odocoileus hemionus*   229   228
Northwest Pacific Coast: Winter, black on tip of tail.
Rocky Mts.: Winter, whitish rump, large ears, black-
tipped tail.
Antlers in velvet, summer.
W.

WHITETAIL DEER, *Odocoileus virginianus*   229   230
Winter, male: Body blue-gray; large tail white
beneath; antlers branch from main beam.
Summer, female: Body reddish; large tail white
beneath.
Fawn: Spotted; tail white beneath.
N, S, E, W.

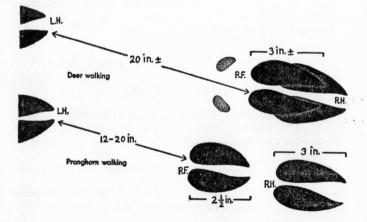

L.H.

20 in. ±

Deer walking

R.F.

3 in. ±

R.H.

L.H.

12-20 in.

Pronghorn walking

R.F.

2½ in.

3 in.

R.H.

PRONGHORN

MULE DEER

Northwest Pacific Coast: Winter

Rocky Mountains: Winter

Head in velvet: Summer

Summer, female

Fawn

Winter, male

WHITETAIL DEER

MOUNTAIN GOAT

Gray phase

WHITE SHEEP

Black phase

BIGHORN SHEEP

WHITE SHEEP
White phase

BISON

Plate 24   225

GOAT, SHEEP, AND BISON

	Map	Text

MOUNTAIN GOAT, *Oreamnos americanus* — 235 · 237
White; horns and hoofs black; beard. NW.

WHITE SHEEP, *Ovis dalli* — 239 · 239
Horns massive, yellowish, coiled. NW.
Gray phase: Grayish.
Black phase: Blackish.
White phase: White.

BIGHORN SHEEP, *Ovis canadensis* — 239 · 238
Creamy-white rump; massive coiled horns. W.

BISON, *Bison bison* — 237 · 236
Body dark brown all over; hump over shoulders;
massive head; horns in both sexes. W.

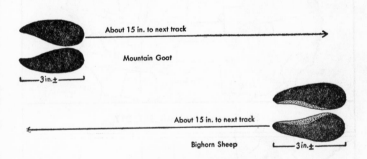

About 15 in. to next track

Mountain Goat

3 in. ±

About 15 in. to next track

Bighorn Sheep   3 in. ±

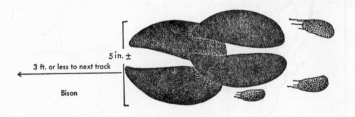

5 in. ±

3 ft. or less to next track

Bison

PECCARY (Javelina)   *Pecari angulatus*   p. 196
  Recognition: Head and body 34–36 in.; height 20–24 in.; wt.
40–50 lb. *Piglike* mammal. Hair coarse, mixed black and gray,
lighter over front of shoulder; *3 toes* on each hind foot. Upper
tusks point downward. Young, reddish with black stripe down
back. Skull (p. 260) has 38 teeth. There are 2 mammae.
  Similar species: Wild Boar (below) — upper tusks curve upward; 4 toes on each hind foot.
  Habitat: Brushy, semidesert; cacti, oaks, chaparral, mesquite;
along cliffs; near waterholes.
  Habits: Most active mornings and late afternoons; usually seen

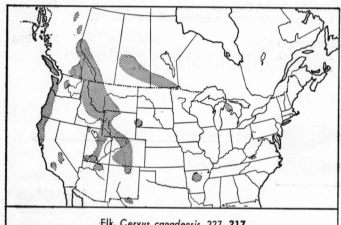

Elk, *Cervus canadensis*, 227, **217**

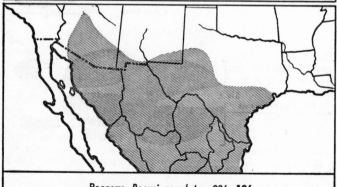

Peccary, *Pecari angulatus*, 226, **196**

in bands of 2–25. Omnivorous; feeds on nuts, mesquite beans, berries, fruits, cacti, grubs, bird eggs. Apparently breeds throughout year.

Young: Usually 2 (1–5); gestation period 142–48 days. Able to follow mother 1 day after birth.

Economic status: Beneficial; does not compete with grazing animals for food; destroys much prickly pear cactus; a good game mammal. Musk gland on rump should be removed, or meat will be tainted; hides make fine leather. May be seen in Organ Pipe Cactus and Saguaro Natl. Monuments, Arizona.

Map opposite

Old World Swine: Suidae

MEMBERS of this family have been introduced mostly as domesticated farm aminals. Some of these have become feral. Also, wild stock (same species) from Europe has been released in several places as big game.

WILD BOAR (Swine)   *Sus scrofa*
   Recognition: Head and body 3½–5 ft.; height to 3 ft.; wt. to 400 lb. Hair coarse and thin; *upper tusks curve upward;* 4 toes on each foot. Skull has 44 teeth. Normally 12 mammae.
   Similar species: Peccary (above) — upper tusks point downward; 3 toes on each hind foot.
   Young: 4–12; gestation period 16–17 weeks.
   Range: Feral domestic swine and/or the introduced Wild Boar from Europe may be found in the following states: Arkansas, California (Santa Cruz I. and Monterey and San Luis Obispo Cos.), Georgia, Missouri, New Hampshire, North Carolina, Oregon, Tennessee, and Texas.

Deer: Cervidae

THIS family includes *hoofed* mammals that have *antlers* which are shed *each year*. They all chew their cud. There are no upper incisors. It includes our deer, Elk, Moose, and caribou. Known as fossils from Lower Oligocene.

ELK (Wapiti)   *Cervus canadensis*   p. 217
   Recognition: Height 4–5 ft. Wt.: males, 700–1000 lb.; females, 500–600 lb. Beam length of antlers to 64¾ in.; record spread 74 in. A large deer with pale yellowish rump patch, small *white* tail, general *reddish-brown* body (chestnut-brown neck with a mane in males), and *huge spreading antlers* on males in late summer and autumn. Skull (p. 261) has 34 teeth. There are 4 mammae.

The Dwarf, or Tule Elk, now confined to a reserve in Kern Co., California, is considered a distinct species (*C. nannodes*) by some authors.

Similar species: (1) Moose — large overhanging snout, brown rump. (2) Mule Deer — smaller; black on tail. (3) Whitetail Deer — smaller; no rump patch. (4) Woodland Caribou — whitish neck.

Habitat: Semi-open forest, mt. meadows (in summer), foothills, plains, and valleys.

Habits: Most active mornings and evenings. Usually seen in groups of 25 or more; both sexes together in winter, old bulls in separate groups during summer. Feeds on grasses, herbs, twigs, bark. Migrates up mts. in spring, down in fall; males shed antlers Feb.–March; velvet shed in Aug. Attains adult dentition at $2\frac{1}{2}$–3 years. Calf has high-pitched squeal when in danger; cow has similar squeal, also sharp bark when traveling with herd; males have high-pitched bugling call that starts with a low note and ends with a few low-toned grunts, heard during rutting season, especially at night. Lives 14 years (25 in captivity). Females breed at $2\frac{1}{2}$ years. Rut starts in Sept.; old males round up harems.

Young: Born May–June; normally 1, rarely 2; gestation period about $8\frac{1}{2}$ months. Spotted. Able to walk a few minutes after birth.

Economic status: Can do considerable damage to vegetables, pastures, grainfields, and haystacks; a prize game mammal for meat and trophies; formerly ranged over much of continent, now restricted. There have been numerous attempts to re-establish them, some successful, others not. May be seen commonly in following national parks: Grand Teton, Yellowstone, Olympic, Glacier, Rocky Mt., Banff, and Jasper; also other places where they have been introduced. Apparently established on Afognak I., Alaska (not on map).   Map p. 226

MULE DEER (Blacktail Deer)   *Odocoileus hemionus*   p. 224
Recognition: Height 3–$3\frac{1}{2}$ ft. Wt.: males, 125–400 lb.; females, 100–150 lb. Largest in Rocky Mts. Record antler spread $47\frac{1}{2}$ in. *Reddish* in summer, *blue-gray* in winter; some have whitish rump patch. Tail either *black-tipped or black on top*. Ears *large*. Antlers, on males, branch *equally*, are not prongs from a main beam. Skull has 32 teeth. There are 4 mammae.

The deer of the nw. Pacific Coast (Blacktail Deer), formerly regarded as a distinct species (*O. columbianus*), is now considered a subspecies of the Mule Deer.

Similar species: (1) Whitetail Deer — tail broad and white below; antlers with main beam and prongs from it. (2) Elk — larger; no black on tail. (3) Woodland and (4) Barren Ground Caribou — no black on tail; neck whitish. (5) Moose — larger;

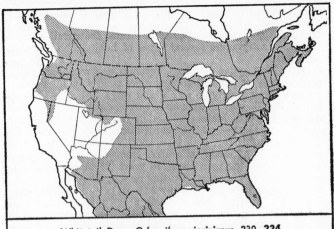

Whitetail Deer, *Odocoileus virginianus*, 230, **224**

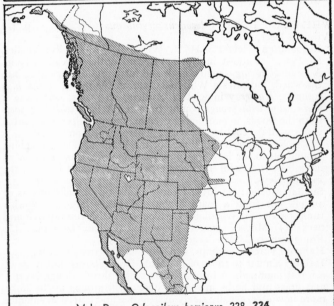

Mule Deer, *Odocoileus hemionus*, 228, **224**

dark brown; overhanging snout. (6) Pronghorn (p. 235) — no black on tail, white on sides.

Habitat: Coniferous forests, desert shrubs, chaparral, grassland with shrubs; occupies several types of habitat; browse plants necessary.

Habits: Most active mornings, evenings, and moonlight nights; occurs singly or in small groups; more gregarious in winter. A browser, feeds mostly on shrubs and twigs, but adds grass and herbs. In mts. may migrate up in spring, down in fall; on plains does not migrate. Males shed antlers Jan.–Feb. Voice of fawns and does, a bleat — seldom heard; bucks have guttural grunt, especially during rut; both sexes snort when alarmed. Follows definite trails, noticeably in winter. Home range 90–600 acres or more. Normal life span about 16 years (25 in captivity). Females breed at 1½ years. Rutting season, Oct.–Dec.

Young: Born June–July; usually 2 (1–3); gestation period about 7 months. Spotted. Able to walk a few minutes after birth.

Economic status: The most important big game mammal of the West; can do considerable damage to crops, range, and forest land if allowed to become too numerous. May be seen in most western parks.   Map p. 229

WHITETAIL DEER *Odocoileus virginianus*   p. 224
(Virginia Deer, Whitetail)

Recognition: Height 3–3½ ft. Wt.: males, 75–400 lb.; females, 50–250 lb. Largest in North. Record antler spread 33½ in. A large *white flag* wagging back and forth and disappearing into the woods indicates a Whitetail Deer on the move. *Reddish* in summer, *blue-gray* in winter. Antlers, on males, consist of a *main beam with prongs* issuing from it. A loud *whistling snort* from the woods, in morning or evening, means a deer has scented you. Skull (p. 261) has 32 teeth. There are 4 mammae.

The Key Deer, a "toy" race of the Whitetail Deer, weighing around 50 lb. or less, was once endangered. Conservationists have been successful in having a preserve set aside for it in the Florida Keys.

Similar species: (1) Mule Deer — black tip on tail; prongs of antlers not from a main beam. (2) Elk — larger; yellowish rump patch. (3) Woodland Caribou — whitish rump patch and neck. (4) Moose — larger; no white; overhanging snout. (5) Pronghorn (p. 235) — large white rump.

Habitat: Forests, swamps, and open brushy areas nearby.

Habits: Similar to those of the Mule Deer (above), but more of a forest mammal. A browser; eats twigs, shrubs, fungi, acorns, and grass and herbs in season. Occurs in groups up to 25 or more in winter, usually singly or 2–3 (doe and fawns) in summer and fall; some in North migrate to swamps in winter. Home range rarely more than 1 mi. across. Voice rarely heard, low bleat by fawns, guttural grunts by old bucks in rut; both sexes snort when alarmed. Full dentition at 13 months; males occasionally have upper canine teeth. Can run 35–40 mph and jump 30 ft. horizontally, 8½ ft. vertically. Lives to 16½ years in wild. Females breed at 1½ years (rarely at ½); breeding season, Nov.–Feb.

Young: Usually 2 (1–3) to adult does; gestation period about 6½ months. Weaned at 4 months. May run with mother for nearly 1 year.

Economic status: The most important big game mammal of the East; can do considerable damage to young orchards and vegetable crops if populations are not controlled. Tame deer are common along the road through Algonquin Provincial Park, Ontario. May be seen along back roads mornings and evenings.

Map p. 229

MOOSE *Alces alces*   p. 217
Recognition: Height 5–6½ ft. Wt.: males, 850–1180 lb.; females, 600–800 lb. Record antler spread 77⅝ in. A large, dark brown animal with gray legs. By its *large size, overhanging snout,* and pendent *"bell"* on throat, as well as its ungainly appearance, it may be distinguished from all other mammals. Males have massive, *palmate, flat antlers* with small prongs projecting from the borders. Often seen *in or near water.* Skull (p. 261) has 32 teeth. There are 4 mammae.

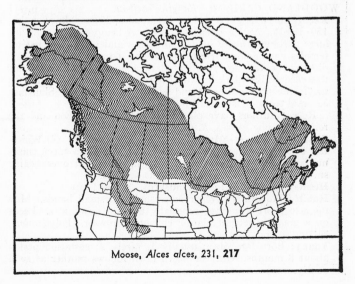

Moose, *Alces alces,* 231, **217**

Similar species: (1) Elk — pale yellow rump patch, snout not enlarged. (2) Deer — smaller; white on some part of body. (3) Caribou — whitish on rump and neck, no overhanging snout.

Habitat: Forests with lakes and swamps.

Habits: Maximum activity at night, but may be seen at any time. Occurs singly or by twos (cow and calf) or threes (bull, cow, calf), rarely in small groups. Browses on many woody plants in winter, twigs, bark, saplings; feeds primarily on aquatic vegetation in summer. Males shed antlers mostly Dec.–Feb.; velvet shed Aug.–Sept. Voice, seldom heard, low *moo* with upward inflection at end, also low grunts. Attains full dentition at about 16 months. Can swim as fast as 2 men can paddle a canoe; speeds up to 35 mph on land. Populations of 4 per sq. mi. are high. Lives 20 years or more in wild. Females first breed at 2–3 years. Rutting season, Sept.–Oct.

Young: Born May–June; usually 1, rarely 2; gestation period about 8 months. Light reddish brown, with dark stripe down back; follows mother after 3 days.

Economic status: A magnificent game mammal, for meat and trophies, where hunting is allowed; chiefly of scenic and scientific value in U.S. May be seen either at edge of forest or feeding in shallow lake in following parks: Grand Teton, Yellowstone, Glacier, Banff, Jasper, Isle Royale, Algonquin Provincial.

Map p. 231

WOODLAND CARIBOU   *Rangifer caribou*   p. 217

Recognition: Height 3½–4 ft. Wt.: males, 250–600 lb.; females, 150–350 lb. Antler spread to 60 in. A heavy-set "deer" with *large feet* and *rounded* hoofs. All males and more than half of females have *antlers*, *semipalmated* with 1 prominent brow tine down over the nose; antlers dark mahogany-brown, beams flattened; velvet dark brown. Body dark chocolate-brown with *whitish on neck* and *rump* and *white above each hoof*. Skull has 32 or 34 teeth. There are 4 mammae.

Recent authors have placed all species of caribou and the reindeer in one species, *R. tarandus*.

Similar species: (1) Mule Deer — black-tipped tail. (2) Whitetail Deer — neck and rump not whitish. (3) Elk — neck chestnut-brown. (4) Moose — dark brown, no white; overhanging snout; wholly palmate antlers; hoofs pointed.

Habitat: Coniferous forests, muskegs.

Habits: Moderately gregarious; usually in small bands. May migrate short distances, especially up and down mts. Feeds on a great variety of plants; chiefly a browser. Polygamous; rutting season, late Sept.

Young: Born late May; usually 1, rarely 2; gestation period about 8 months. Grayish-brown fawn follows mother as soon as dry.

Greenland Caribou, *Rangifer tarandus*, 234

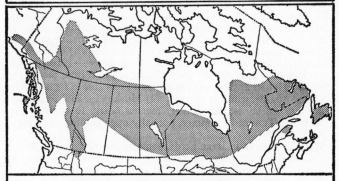

Woodland Caribou, *Rangifer caribou*, 232, **217**

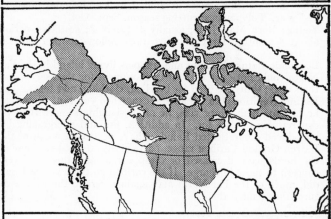

Barren Ground Caribou, *Rangifer arcticus*, 234, **217**

Economic status: Occurs in wildest areas; an excellent game mammal; supplies food for Indians and white trappers; skins used for tents, clothing, and bedding.   Map p. 233

BARREN GROUND CARIBOU *Rangifer arcticus*   p. 217
Recognition: Height 3¼–4 ft. Wt.: males, 250–400 lb.; females, 150–250 lb. Record antler spread 44 in. Similar, in general, to Woodland Caribou, but paler (in Far North *nearly white*). Antlers on both sexes; pale brown or ivory, beams cylindrical, velvet light brown to gray. After the southward migration in autumn this and the Woodland Caribou may occur together, in winter, in n. Manitoba and n. Saskatchewan, but in summer, after the northward migration, their ranges are usually separate. Skull (p. 261) has 32 or 34 teeth. There are 4 mammae.
Similar species: (1) Moose — larger; dark brown; overhanging snout; antlers wholly palmate. (2) Mule Deer — black on tail. (3) Reindeer (introduced, domesticated animals from Siberia) — smaller; larger antlers, with prominent brow tine in female; color often variable, white or spotted. (4) Muskox (p. 238) — massive unbranched horns; hair of body reaches nearly to ground.
Habitat: Tundra in summer, partially open coniferous forest in winter.
Habits: Always in large herds, some numbering in the tens of thousands; migratory; never stays in one place for long; an excellent swimmer, will often cross a lake rather than go around. Feeds mostly on lichens (reindeer moss), but also takes herbs, mosses, willows, and grasses. Voice, a coughlike grunt. Foot joints make clicking noise as animal walks. Females breed in 2nd year. Polygamous; rutting season, Sept.–Oct.
Young: Born May–June; usually 1, rarely 2; gestation period about 8 months. Grayish-brown fawn follows mother as soon as dry.
Economic status: Eskimos and trappers living inland in the Far North could not exist without caribou meat for themselves and their dogs; skins are used for bedding, clothing, and tents. The Eskimo tradition is to kill all you can, when you can. Now that he has the high-power rifle, he often slaughters more than he can retrieve or care for. In addition, fire and overgrazing by introduced domesticated Reindeer have destroyed much of the Barren Ground Caribou range, particularly in Alaska. Some of the herds have decreased or disappeared, and this is of real concern to those in charge. If the caribou go the way the Bison did, much of the Far North may again revert to the wild creatures that remain there.   Map p. 233

GREENLAND CARIBOU (Reindeer)   *Rangifer tarandus*
Recognition: Height 3½ ft.; wt. 150–300 lb. Found chiefly along coast of *Greenland*. The domesticated Reindeer (*R. tarandus*) from Siberia has been introduced in parts of Alaska

and Canada without too much success. It is considered to be the same species as the Greenland Caribou.

Similar species: (1) Muskox (p. 238) — massive unbranched horns; hair of body reaches nearly to ground.   Map p. 233

Pronghorn: Antilocapridae

THERE is but one species in this family. It is a strictly N. American mammal. The Pronghorn has true horns — bone cores covered with horny sheaths made up of agglutinated hair — but peculiar in that the sheaths are shed each year. *Both sexes have horns.* Known as fossils from Middle Miocene.

PRONGHORN (Antelope) *Antilocapra americana*   p. 224
  Recognition: Height 3 ft.; wt. 75–130 lb.; record spread of horns $22\frac{5}{16}$ in. A pale tan, medium-sized mammal; distinguished by its *large white rump patch*, white lower sides, 2 broad *white bands across throat,* and slightly curved horns, each with a single *prong projecting forward;* 2 toes on each foot. Skull (p. 261) has 32 teeth. There are 4 mammae.
  Similar species: (1) Bighorn Sheep (p. 238) — massive coiled horns; no white bands across throat. (2) Mule Deer (p. 228) — black on tail; no white along sides. (3) Whitetail Deer (p. 230) — no large white rump patch; no white along sides.
  Habitat: Open prairies and sagebrush plains.
  Habits: Chiefly diurnal, most active mornings and evenings, but may be seen at any time. Usually occurs in small bands.

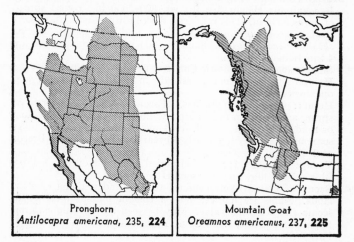

Pronghorn
Antilocapra americana, 235, **224**

Mountain Goat
Oreamnos americanus, 237, **225**

Mainly a browser; eats many weeds, some grass, but fond of sagebrush. In some areas migrates between summer and winter ranges. Home range for a band usually 2–4 mi. across. May attain speed of 40 mph. Erects hair on large white rump patch and makes animal more conspicuous; usually done only when fleeing from danger. Full dentition acquired at 3½ years. Lives to 14 years in wild. Breeds at 1½ years, Aug.–Oct.; some males collect small harems. Horn coverings shed after breeding season.

Young: Born April–May in South, May–June in North; usually 2 (1–3); gestation period 230–40 days. Grayish-brown kids are left alone for a few days, except at nursing time, then follow mother.

Economic status: Slight competition for food with cattle and sheep, but feeds mostly on vegetation not eaten by domestic stock. A big game mammal, but more important as an interesting element in our fauna. Commonly seen on western plains and in Yellowstone and Wind Cave Natl. Parks; also Petrified Forest Natl. Monument. Map p. 235

Bison, Goats, Muskox, and Sheep: Bovidae

THIS is the family to which our domestic cattle, sheep, and goats belong. Members have *true horns*, which are *never shed* and are *not branched*. Horns are present in *both sexes*. Known as fossils from Lower Miocene.

BISON (Buffalo) *Bison bison* p. 225
Recognition: Height 5–6 ft.; wt. 800–2000 lb.; record spread of horns 35⅜ in. This is a large, dark brown beast with *massive head*, a *high hump on its shoulders*, and *long shaggy hair on shoulders and front legs*. Skull (p. 261) has 32 teeth. There are 4 functional mammae.
Similar species: Domestic Cattle — not dark brown.
Habitat: Open plains; grasslands in South, woodlands and openings in North.
Habits: Diurnal; gregarious. Formerly migrated north in spring and south in fall. Forms wallows, where it rolls in dust or mud. A grazing animal, feeds mostly on grasses, but takes some browse. May live nearly 30 years, normally 15–20. Breeds at 2–3 years, July–Oct.
Young: Normally 1; gestation period about 9 months. Yellowish-red calf follows mother soon after birth.
Economic status: Now confined to zoos and national or state lands. Some are harvested as a control measure; chiefly of scenic and scientific value. May be seen at the following national parks: Platt, Wind Cave, Yellowstone, and Wood Buffalo Park, Alberta. Map opposite

MOUNTAIN GOAT *Oreamnos americanus* p. 225
Recognition: Height 3–3½ ft.; wt. 100–300 lb.; record spread
of horns 11⅜ in. On the *rocky crags near snowline*, this *white*
goat with long fur, a definite beard, and short, *smooth, black
horns* that curve slightly backward may be seen at a distance by
the adventurer. The hoofs are black. Skull has 32 teeth. There
are 4 mammae.

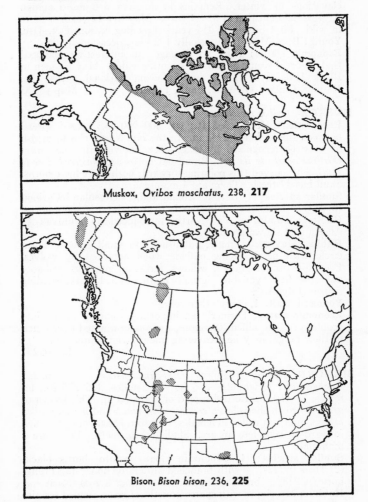

Muskox, *Ovibos moschatus*, 238, **217**

Bison, *Bison bison*, 236, **225**

Similar species: (1) Bighorn and (2) White Sheep — horns massive, yellowish, and spiral-shaped.

Habitat: Steep slopes and benches along cliffs; usually at or above timberline.

Habits: Primarily diurnal. Usually seen in groups of less than 10. Part grazer and part browser, feeds on various high-mt. vegetation; usually above timberline in summer, moves to lower elevations in winter. Remains in an area 3–6 miles across. Attains full dentition at 3½–4 years. May live 12 years or more in wild. First breeds at 2½ years; breeding season, Oct.–Dec.

Young: Born May–June; usually 1–2 kids, occasionally 3.

Economic status: Does no damage; an interesting mammal that has real scenic as well as scientific value. May be seen in Black Hills, S. Dakota, and following national parks: Mt. Rainier, Glacier, Olympic, Banff, Jasper.   Map p. 235

MUSKOX *Ovibos moschatus*   p. 217

Recognition: Height 3–5 ft.; wt. 500–900 lb.; record spread between tips of horns 29¾ in. In the *Far North*, this brownish ox may be recognized by long, silky, brown hair that *hangs skirtlike nearly to its feet.* Broad flat horns are *plastered close to skull*, with curved tips pointing forward; both sexes have horns. Skull has 32 teeth. There are 4 mammae.

Similar species: (1) Barren Ground and (2) Greenland Caribou (p. 234) — hair not reaching nearly to ground; antlers, not horns.

Habitat: Tundra of Far North; introduced on Nunivak I., Alaska (not shown on map).

Habits: May occur singly, but usually in small groups. Form circle with heads facing outside when attacked by wolves. Feeds on tundra grasses, willows, forbs, sedges, and probably any other food available. Sexually mature at 3–4 years; breeding season, July–Aug.

Young: Usually 1, every other year.

Economic status: Formerly an important item in the Eskimo economy; easily killed, therefore, were exterminated over much of their range; may be recovering under strict protection.

Map p. 237

BIGHORN SHEEP (Bighorn) *Ovis canadensis*   p. 225

Recognition: Height 2½–3½ ft. Wt.: males, 125–275 lb.; females, 75–150 lb. Record spread of horns 33 in. This brown to grayish-brown sheep has a *creamy white rump* and *massive coiled horns* (small, not coiled in females) that spiral back, out, and then forward to complete an arc. Skull has 32 teeth. There are 2 mammae.

Similar species: (1) Mountain Goat — white; horns black. (2) Deer (p. 227) — with branched antlers or none. (3) Pronghorn (p. 235) — branched horns; white bands across throat.

Habitat: Mt. slopes with sparse growths of trees, rugged terrain.

Habits: Gregarious. Sexes usually separate in summer; rams join ewes and lambs in fall. May move to lower elevations in winter. Both a browser and grazer, feeds on great variety of plants. Full dentition attained at 4 years. Probably lives to 15 years in wild. Females breed at 2½ years. Rutting season, Nov.–Dec.

Young: Born May–June; 1, occasionally 2; gestation period about 180 days. Lambs follow mother soon after birth.

Economic status: Little competition with domestic stock for food; has been exterminated in much of former range. Most likely to be seen in Yellowstone and Glacier Natl. Parks and in Death Valley Natl. Monument. Map below

WHITE SHEEP (Dall Sheep) *Ovis dalli* p. 225

Recognition: Height 3–3⅓ ft.; wt. 125–200 lb.; record spread of horns 35 in. This stocky *white or whitish* to nearly black (in the south of its range) sheep is found in the *inaccessible mt. areas* of the Northwest. Horns are yellowish, massive in males, smaller in females. Usually seen in bands of 6 or more. Included here is the "Stone Sheep," a blackish color phase, and the "Fannin Sheep," an intermediate phase. Skull (p. 261) has 32 teeth. There are 2 mammae

Similar species: Mountain Goat — long fur, a beard; small, slender, black horns that curve slightly backward.

Habitat: Rough terrain, mt. slopes.

Habits: Similar to those of the Bighorn Sheep (above). Map below

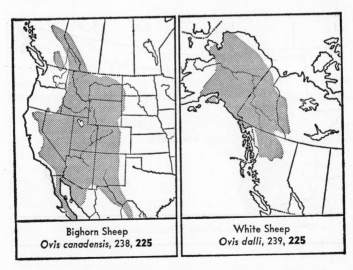

Bighorn Sheep
Ovis canadensis, 238, **225**

White Sheep
Ovis dalli, 239, **225**

Sloths and Armadillos: Xenarthra

Armadillos: Dasypodidae

THIS is chiefly a tropical family. They have *degenerate teeth* (simple pegs), and the body is covered with a *protective "armor" of horny material*. Small, scattered hairs grow from between the plates. Known as fossils from Paleocene.

ARMADILLO *Dasypus novemcinctus* p. 196
Recognition: Head and body 15–17 in.; tail 14–16 in.; wt. 8–17 lb. This peculiar *"armored"* mammal is about the size of a House Cat. Body, tail, and top of head *covered with horny material*. The only mammal here included that has a protective cover of armor plate; commonly seen along highways at night; many killed by autos. Skull (p. 260) usually has 32 (28–32) peglike teeth. There are 4 mammae.
Habitat: Woodlands, brushy areas, rock outcrops and cliffs.
Habits: Occasionally out by day, especially in winter, but mostly mornings, evenings, and at night in summer. Seeks safety by dashing to a burrow or dense thicket; rarely rolls into a ball for protection; frequents waterholes and streams for mud baths as well as drinking water. Feeds almost entirely on insects and other small invertebrates; eats a few berries, fruits, and bird eggs; roots in leaf mold for much of its food. Dens in open-

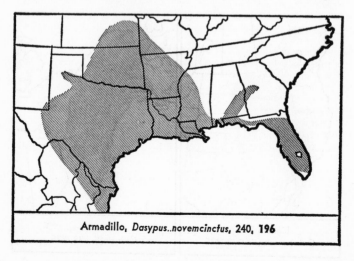

Armadillo, *Dasypus..novemcinctus,* 240, **196**

ings in rock outcroppings or in burrows 10–15 ft. long that it digs. One armadillo to 3–10 acres is normal population.

Young: Born March–April; always 4 of same sex; gestation period reported at about 150 days.

Economic status: Almost entirely beneficial; destroys many insects; burrows serve as home sites for other mammals; meat edible; shells made into baskets for tourist trade. Map opposite

Dugong and Manatee: Sirenia

WHOLLY aquatic mammals, *not* related to whales. Two living species, each in a separate family.

Manatee: Trichechidae

THE 1 species in this family is confined to warm coastal waters. For characters see below. Known as fossils from Pleistocene.

MANATEE (Sea Cow) *Trichechus manatus* p. 259

Recognition: Length 7–13 ft.; wt. up to 1300 lb. A large sluggish aquatic mammal with *broad head*, *thick, cleft upper lips,* front flippers, and a broad, horizontally flattened and rounded tail; no hind legs (flippers). Muzzle adorned with stiff bristles. Skull usually has 24 teeth (all alike) in use at one time; teeth move forward and are replaced from behind. There are 2 mammae.

Similar species: (1) Whales and (2) Porpoises (below) — usually in deep water some distance from shore; tails not rounded.

Habitat: Brackish water, lagoons, mouths of rivers; usually shallow.

Habits: A sluggish animal, usually seen in small groups; cannot tolerate water temperatures below 46° F.; can remain underwater for 30 min. Feeds on aquatic vegetation.

Young: No definite season known; 1 calf; gestation period about 11 months.

Economic status: Does no harm; a most interesting part of our fauna; meat edible; protected in U.S.

Range: From Beaufort, N. Carolina, south to the Florida Keys, and along coast of Gulf of Mexico.

Whales, Dolphins, and Porpoises: Cetacea

THESE are strictly *marine* mammals as far as N. America is concerned. They are *fishlike* in general appearance except that the *tail fluke is horizontal*, not vertical. Also, they breathe air and must come to the surface periodically. Just before or as they break water, they expel warm, moisture-laden air from the lungs, and the vapor one sees as they "blow" is mostly condensation of moisture in the expelled air. The large whales usually are not seen at close range, unless washed up on a beach, and are difficult for the novice to identify. Porpoises and dolphins play off bows of boats and may be seen at close range, thus making identification easier. Whales normally give birth to 1 young (calf) on alternate years; some migrate thousands of miles each year. There are 2 mammae. Known as fossils from Upper Eocene.

Economic status: Whaling was a big and profitable industry in the past. With no restrictions on numbers or kinds taken, some of the large whales were threatened with extinction. Now there is international control over kinds, sizes, and numbers of whales taken. In addition to their commercial value, there is a definite scenic or aesthetic value. Who at sea has not been thrilled at seeing one of the large whales surface nearby — or at seeing a school of dolphins or porpoises coming toward the boat to play across the bow?

Toothed Whales: Odontoceti

THIS suborder contains the beaked and sperm whales and the large group of dolphins and porpoises. All have simple, peglike teeth (variable in number).

Beaked Whales: Ziphiidae

MEMBERS of this family have *vestigial teeth* in the upper jaw; functional teeth (2–4) in the lower jaw (some females and young have no teeth showing); 2 grooves on throat converge anteriorly to form a V; snout elongated into a beak; small dorsal fin between tail and middle of back; food probably consists of fish and squids for most part. Known as fossils from Lower Miocene.

BAIRD BEAKED WHALE *Berardius bairdi*   p. 247
Recognition: Length to 42 ft. This is a rare and little-known whale. It is black with a *whitish area on lower belly*. Snout is formed into a definite beak; dorsal fin small and set far back on body. There are 4 functional teeth, 2–3 in. long and flattened laterally, in the lower jaw.
Range: Pacific Coast, south to California.

SOWERBY BEAKED WHALE *Mesoplodon bidens*
Recognition: Length to 16 ft. A rare and little-known species; dorsal fin well back on the body. *Dark gray* above, paler on sides and belly. There are 2, *small*, laterally flattened teeth near tip of lower jaw.

It has recently been suggested that *Nodus* is the proper generic name, and should replace *Mesoplodon*.
Range: North Atlantic Coast, south to Massachusetts.

ATLANTIC BEAKED WHALE   *Mesoplodon densirostris*
Recognition: Length to 15 ft.; wt. to 1800 lb. Nearly completely black; pale patches beneath flippers and on belly; 2 *large* teeth about 6 in. long near front of lower jaw.
Range: North Atlantic Coast.

GERVAIS BEAKED WHALE   *Mesoplodon gervaisi*
Recognition: Length to 15½ ft. Black above, paler on sides and belly; 2 small teeth near front of lower jaw.
Range: South Atlantic Coast, north to New York.

TRUE BEAKED WHALE   *Mesoplodon mirus*   p. 247
Recognition: Length to 17 ft. Slaty black on top, paler on belly; 2 *small* laterally compressed teeth at *tip* of lower jaw.
Range: North Atlantic Coast, occasionally south to Florida.

PACIFIC BEAKED WHALE   *Mesoplodon stejnegeri*
Recognition: Length to 17 ft. Blackish with anterior of body, especially head, grayish to whitish; 2 *large* laterally compressed teeth about 8 in. long near tip of lower jaw.
Range: Pacific Coast, south to California.

GOOSEBEAK WHALE   *Ziphius cavirostris*   p. 247
Recognition: Length to 28 ft. Variable in color; gray to black on back, with occasional white on head and middle of back; sides black to brownish or spotted; belly usually whitish; body thick; a distinct *keel from dorsal fin to tail;* 2 teeth 2½ in. long in lower jaw of male.
Range: Atlantic Coast, north to Rhode Island; Pacific Coast, south to California.

BOTTLENOSE WHALE   *Hyperoodon ampullatus*   p. 247
Recognition: Length to 30 ft.; at birth, 10 ft. Grayish black to light brown or yellowish, with *whitish about head* and a whitish belly; forehead of male *rises abruptly* from short beak; old males may be recognized by *whitish patch on forehead* and *white dorsal fin.* There are 2 *small* teeth about 1½ in. long at *tip* of lower jaw.
Range: Arctic and North Atlantic Coasts.

Sperm Whale: Physeteridae

THIS family contains but 1 species. Occurs in all oceans. For characters, see below. Known as fossils from Lower Miocene.

BATS, SHREWS, AND MOLES
(Skulls natural size)

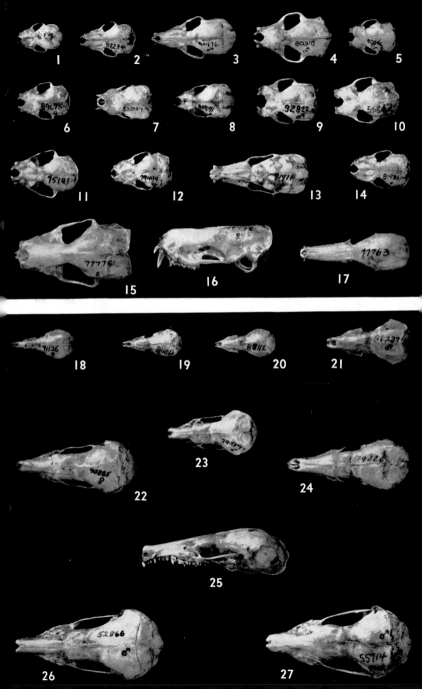

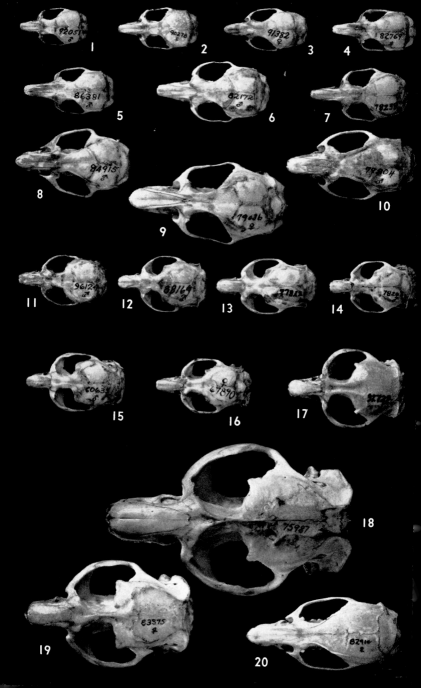

Plate 26   245

MICE, VOLES, AND RATS
(Skulls natural size)

SPERM WHALE (Cachalot)   *Physeter catodon*   p. 253
  Recognition: Length: males to 60 ft.; females to 30 ft.; at birth 12–14 ft. Wt. to 53 tons. *Snout square;* head large, about ⅓ of length of animal; *lower jaw small, narrow; no dorsal fin;* row of bumps on posterior half of back; bluish gray above, paler below; 20–25 teeth in each lower jaw; teeth up to 8 in. long. The spout is prolonged and *directed forward* at a distinct angle.
  Habits: Females and young tend to remain in warmer waters, males in colder waters in summer. Can remain submerged 75 min. Feeds mostly on squids and octopuses.
  Economic status: This is one of the large whales that has been hunted for centuries, and still is. It is the whale that produces ambergris. Spermaceti oil is located in the head.
  Range: Atlantic and Pacific Coasts.

Pygmy Sperm Whale: Kogiidae

THIS family contains but 1 species. Occurs in Atlantic, Pacific, and Indian Oceans. For characters, see below. Known as fossils from Lower Pliocene.

PYGMY SPERM WHALE   *Kogia breviceps*   p. 253
  Recognition: Length to 13 ft. One of the *smallest* whales; *snout broad, protruding; lower jaw narrow;* body black above, grayish white below; a pale bracket-shaped mark behind eye. A distinct dorsal fin. There are 18–30 needlelike teeth in lower jaw.
  Range: Warm waters of both coasts; north to Nova Scotia and Washington.

White Whale and Narwhal: Monodontidae

No dorsal fin; snout blunt; no grooves on throat. Inhabit cold arctic waters. Feed mostly on fish and cuttlefish. Teeth present. Known as fossils from Pleistocene.

WHITE WHALE (Beluga)   *Delphinapterus leucas*   p. 247
  Recognition: Length to 14 ft. This small *white* whale may be recognized by size and color. No other cetaceans have these characters. Young are bluish gray. Skull has 32–40 small, pointed teeth; both jaws have teeth.
  Range: Arctic and North Atlantic Coasts; Hudson Bay; chiefly in cold waters; rarely south as far as Cape Cod and Alaska.

NARWHAL   *Monodon monoceros*   p. 247
  Recognition: Length to 12 ft. Peculiar in that the male has a *long, spirally twisted "unicorn" tusk projecting forward* from the blunt snout. This tusk may reach a length of 9 ft. Back is mottled gray and the belly is white; young are bluish gray.
  Range: Arctic Coast.

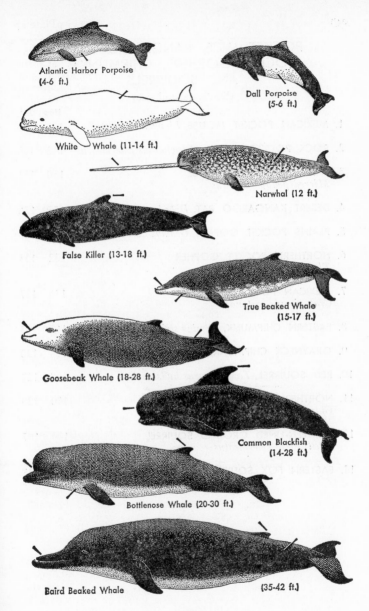

Atlantic Harbor Porpoise
(4-6 ft.)

Dall Porpoise
(5-6 ft.)

White Whale (11-14 ft.)

Narwhal (12 ft.)

False Killer (13-18 ft.)

True Beaked Whale
(15-17 ft.)

Goosebeak Whale (18-28 ft.)

Common Blackfish
(14-28 ft.)

Bottlenose Whale (20-30 ft.)

Baird Beaked Whale   (35-42 ft.)

POCKET MICE, KANGAROO RATS, POCKET GOPHERS, CHIPMUNKS, AND SQUIRRELS

(Skulls natural size)

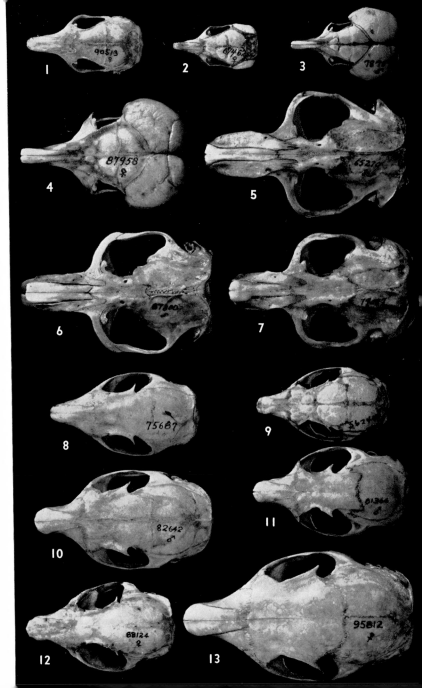

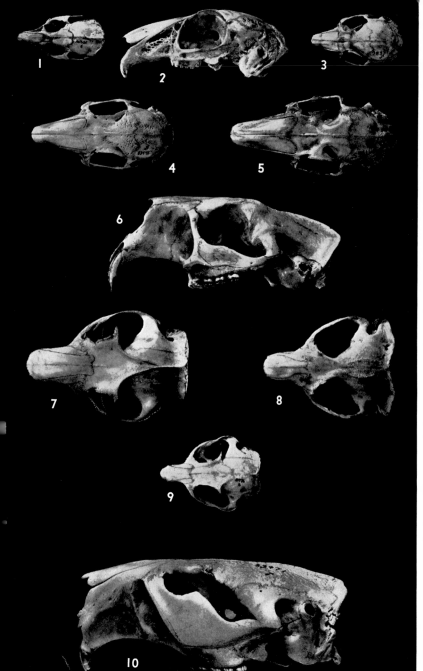

Plate 28   249

RABBITS, HARES, AND MISCELLANEOUS RODENTS

(Skulls one-half natural size)

Dolphins and Porpoises: Delphinidae

SMALL representatives of the order, length to 30 ft.; tail fluke notched in middle; dorsal fin usually well developed. Feed principally on fish and squids. Commonly travel in groups of up to 50 or more. Teeth in both jaws. Known as fossils from Lower Miocene.

CUVIER DOLPHIN *Stenella frontalis*
 Recognition: Length to 6 ft. Back blackish, sides mottled grayish, belly whitish; dorsal fin present; 35–44 small teeth on each side of upper and lower jaws.
 Range: South Atlantic Coast, north to N. Carolina.

SPOTTED DOLPHIN *Stenella plagiodon*   p. 253
 Recognition: Length to 7 ft. Grayish black, with numerous small *white spots* on back; belly pale gray; *long snout* separated from forehead by distinct *transverse groove;* dorsal fin present; 34–37 teeth on each side of upper and lower jaws.
 Range: Atlantic Coast, N. Carolina to Texas.

LONGSNOUT DOLPHIN *Stenella styx*
 Recognition: Length to 8 ft. Black above, white below; narrow black streak from eye along lower side, another from eye to front flipper; 44–50 teeth on each side of upper and lower jaws.
 Range: Atlantic Coast, north to Greenland; Pacific Coast, from Bering Sea to Oregon.

LONGBEAK DOLPHIN *Steno bredanensis*
 Recognition: Length to 8 ft. Black above, white (including beak) below; sides spotted; *no transverse groove* between beak and forehead; slender beak *compressed* from side to side; 20–27 teeth on each side of upper and lower jaws.
   Formerly known as *S. rostratus.*
 Range: Atlantic and Pacific Coasts, north to Virginia and California.

COMMON DOLPHIN *Delphinus delphis*   p. 253
 Recognition: Length to 8½ ft. Back and flippers black; flanks yellowish; belly white; 2 white lines across groove that separates beak from forehead; beak about 6 in. long; dorsal fin present. Likely to be seen playing in front of a ship; leaps high out of water when traveling. This is one of the dolphins that has been displayed at the Marinelands of Florida and California. There are 30–40 small teeth on each side of upper and lower jaws.
   The Pacific Dolphin is considered a distinct species by most authors (*D. bairdi*).
 Range: Atlantic and Pacific Coasts; warm and temperate waters, usually some distance from shore.

ATLANTIC BOTTLENOSE DOLPHIN *Tursiops truncatus*
   Recognition: Length to 12 ft. This is the *commonest* dolphin along the Atlantic Coast. May be recognized by *large* size and general *grayish* coloration, slightly paler beneath than on back. The relatively *short beak* (about 3 in. long) is separated from the forehead by a *transverse groove*. Lower jaw is slightly *longer* than the upper; 20–26 teeth on each side of upper and lower jaws.
   It has been proposed that the proper specific name is *nesarnack*.
   Habits: This species has been successfully maintained in captivity at the Marinelands of Florida and California; the dolphin that does most of the performing. Females are sexually mature at 4 years.
   Young: 1 calf; gestation period 10–12 months.
   Range: Atlantic Coast, north to Cape Cod.

PACIFIC BOTTLENOSE DOLPHIN *Tursiops gilli*   p. 253
   Recognition: Length to 12 ft. Similar to Atlantic Bottlenose Dolphin (above). Grayish black above, white beneath, except for dark area from vent to fluke; *white on upper lip*. May be seen off West Coast.
   Range: Pacific Coast, north to California.

RIGHT WHALE DOLPHIN *Lissodelphis borealis*   p. 253
   Recognition: Length to 8 ft. A small black dolphin with a narrow *white belly stripe* from breast to tail and *no dorsal fin* will most certainly be of this species. There are 43–45 teeth on each side of upper and lower jaws.
   Range: Pacific Coast, north to Bering Sea.

ATLANTIC WHITE-SIDED DOLPHIN
Lagenorhynchus acutus
   Recognition: Length to 9 ft. This dolphin may be recognized by its blackish back, white belly, and a *pale area* along either side below the *prominent dorsal fin*. *Yellowish streaks* along the sides. *Short, blunt nose.* There are 30–37 teeth on each side of upper and lower jaws.
   Range: Atlantic Coast, south to Cape Cod.

PACIFIC WHITE-SIDED DOLPHIN
Lagenorhynchus obliquidens   p. 253
   Recognition: Length to 9 ft.; wt., 1 female 6 ft. long, 190 lb. This dolphin has a greenish-black back, a *pale stripe along each side*, and a white belly. Dorsal fin is definitely hooked. Nose is blunt. There are 29–31 teeth on each side of upper and lower jaws.
   Habits: Frequents near-shore waters in winter, moves offshore in summer; travels in groups of up to 1000. Feeds mostly on anchovies and sauries, also squids and other sea animals. Performs well in captivity, but is not as versatile as Bottlenose

Dolphin; may be seen at Marineland of the Pacific, California.
Range: Pacific Coast.

WHITEBEAK DOLPHIN   *Lagenorhynchus albirostris*   p. 253
Recognition: Length to 10 ft. In the North Atlantic one is
likely to encounter this medium-sized blackish dolphin with a
pale stripe along each side, a whitish belly, and a *white beak*
about 2 in. long. There are 26–27 teeth on each side of upper
and lower jaws.
Range: North Atlantic Coast, south to Labrador.

ATLANTIC KILLER WHALE   *Orcinus orca*   p. 253
(Sea Wolf)
Recognition: Length to 30 ft. If seen at sea, the first indication
of a killer whale would probably be the *large, exposed dorsal fin*
cutting the surface of the water. If it exposes a jet-black body
with *white extending up on the side* posteriorly, it is this species.
It also has a clear white spot behind each eye and white underparts. Nose is blunt. There are 10–15 teeth on each side of
upper and lower jaws.
    Formerly known as *Grampus.*
Habits: Travels in packs of 5–40. Feeds on other whales (some
much larger), seals, sea lions, birds, and fish. This is the "wolf
of the sea."
Range: Atlantic Coast, south to New Jersey.

PACIFIC KILLER WHALE (Sea Wolf)   *Orcinus rectipinna*
Recognition: Length to 30 ft. Characters as given for Atlantic
Killer Whale.
    Formerly known as *Grampus.*
Range: Pacific Coast.

GRAMPUS   *Grampus griseus*   p. 253
Recognition: Length to 13 ft.; at birth 5 ft. Rather *blunt-nosed*,
with a dark gray or blackish body marked with numerous
irregular streaks. Head tinged with *yellow*, belly grayish white;
slender flippers are mottled grayish. Dorsal fin prominent.
There are 2–7 teeth in each lower jaw, usually none in the uppers.
    Formerly known as *Grampidelphis.*
Range: Atlantic and Pacific Coasts.

FALSE KILLER   *Pseudorca crassidens*   p. 247
Recognition: Length to 18 ft. This small, black, *slender* whale
has a relatively small, *recurved dorsal fin* just in front of the
middle of the body. Snout blunt and rounded; head flattened;
8–10 teeth on each side of upper and lower jaws.
Range: Atlantic and Pacific Coasts; north to N. Carolina and
Washington.

Spotted Dolphin
(5–7 ft.)

Common Dolphin
(6½–8½ ft.)

Right Whale Dolphin
(5–8 ft.)

Pacific White-sided Dolphin
(7–9 ft.)

Pacific Bottlenose Dolphin
(10–12 ft.)

Whitebeak Dolphin
(7–10 ft.)

Pygmy Sperm Whale
(9–13 ft.)

Grampus
(9–13 ft.)

Atlantic
Killer Whale
(15–30 ft.)

Sperm Whale
(40–60 ft.)

COMMON BLACKFISH *Globicephala melaena*   p. 247
(Pilot Whale)
  Recognition: Length to 28 ft. *Uniformly black;* large recurved
  dorsal fin well forward of middle of body; flippers about ⅕
  length of body; forehead *high, bulges forward;* 7–12 teeth on each
  side of upper and lower jaws.
     Formerly known as *G. ventricosa.*
  Habits: Normally travels in large schools; occasionally stranded
  on the beach.
  Range: Atlantic Coast, south to Virginia.

SHORT-FINNED BLACKFISH *Globicephala macrorhyncha*
  Recognition: Length to 20 ft.; flipper 2½–3 ft. This species is
  difficult to distinguish from the Common Blackfish. Flipper is
  about ⅙ as long as body.
     Formerly known as *G. brachyptera.*
  Range: Atlantic Coast, north to New Jersey.

PACIFIC BLACKFISH (Pilot Whale) *Globicephala scammoni*
  Recognition: Length to 16 ft. Similar to Common Blackfish
  (above); 8–12 teeth on each side of upper and lower jaws. A
  captive at Marineland of the Pacific, in California, performed
  nearly as well as the Bottlenose Dolphin.
  Range: Pacific Coast.

ATLANTIC HARBOR PORPOISE *Phocoena phocoena* p. 247
  Recognition: Length to 6 ft.; wt. 100–120 lb. A *small,* thick-
  bodied animal with a blunt snout, *black* back, triangular fin,
  pinkish sides, and *white* belly. A *dark line* runs from corner of
  mouth to flipper; 16–27 spade-shaped teeth on each side of
  upper and lower jaws. Common near shore and in harbors.
  Range: Atlantic Coast south to Delaware River.

PACIFIC HARBOR PORPOISE *Phocoena vomerina*
  Recognition: Length to 6 ft. Similar to Atlantic Harbor Porpoise. There are 23–27 teeth on each side of upper and lower
  jaws.
     Some authors consider this as a race of *P. phocoena.*
  Range: Pacific Coast.

DALL PORPOISE *Phocoenoides dalli*   p. 247
  Recognition: Length to 6 ft. Strikingly marked; *black* except
  for a *large white area* across the vent region and extending
  slightly over halfway up the sides, the front edge about even
  with front of dorsal fin; 23–27 teeth on each side of upper and
  lower jaws.
  Range: Pacific Coast, south rarely to Long Beach. California.

Baleen Whales: Mysticeti

WHALES *without teeth*, but with *strips of whalebone*, baleen, hanging from roof of mouth. These strips are frayed along the edges and serve to strain from the water the small organisms on which these largest of the whales feed.

Gray Whale: Eschrichtiidae

THIS family contains but 1 species. Occurs in North Pacific Ocean. For characters, see below. Not known as fossils.

GRAY WHALE *Eschrichtius glaucus*   p. 259
   Recognition: Length to 45 ft.; wt., 1 female (44 ft. long), 34⅜ tons. Medium-sized, *blotched, grayish-black* whale, rather slender; spouts are *quick and low* (about 10 ft. high). Has *2–4 longitudinal folds* on throat; a slight hump, but *no fin*, on back. Baleen plates may be more than 1 ft. long.
   Formerly known as *Rhachianectes*.
   Habits: Migrates southward, from latter part of Dec. to early Feb.; returns in March and April after about 3 months in breeding waters in Baja California, Mexico. May be seen in great numbers off coast of San Diego, California, during migrations.
   Range: Pacific Coast.

Finback Whales: Balaenopteridae

THIS family includes the largest whales. Each has many longitudinal grooves on its throat, and a small dorsal fin far back on the body. Gestation period is about 12 months. Known as fossils from Upper Miocene.

FINBACK WHALE *Balaenoptera physalus*   p. 259
   Recognition: Length to 70 ft.; length at birth 22 ft. This large, *flat-headed* whale is *gray* with a *white* belly and white inner sides of flippers and underside of fluke. The columnar spout (15–20 ft. high) is accompanied by a loud *whistling sound;* it rises as a narrow column, then expands into an ellipse. Baleen is streaked *purple and white.* Sometimes these whales come close to ships
   Range: Atlantic and Pacific Coasts.

RORQUAL (Sei Whale) *Balaenoptera borealis*   p. 259
   Recognition: Length to 50 ft. or more. Similar to the Finback Whale, but smaller and darker, and with a relatively larger dorsal fin; undersurface of fluke never white. Baleen is *black* except for the white frayed edges.
   Range: Atlantic and Pacific Coasts.

PIKED WHALE *Balaenoptera acutorostrata*   p. 259
   Recognition: Length to 30 ft.; length at birth 9 ft. This small

WEASEL AND RACCOON FAMILIES

(Skulls one-half natural size)

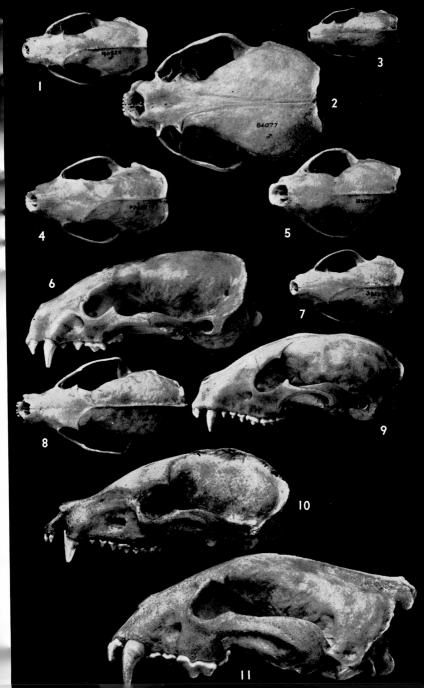

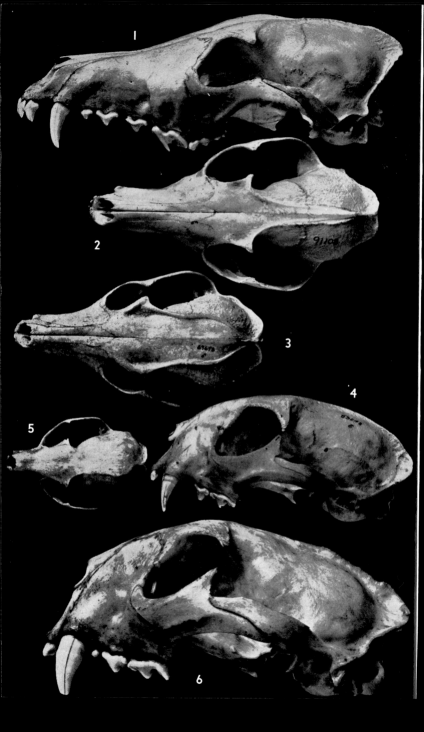

Plate 30   257

DOGS AND CATS
(Skulls one-half natural size)

	Map	*Text*
1. **COYOTE,** *Canis latrans*	74	73
2. **RED FOX,** *Vulpes fulva*	78	77
3. **GRAY FOX,** *Urocyon cinereoargenteus*	80	81
4. **BOBCAT,** *Lynx rufus*	85	86
5. **RINGTAIL,** *Bassariscus astutus*	56	56
6. **MOUNTAIN LION,** *Felis concolor*	82	82

finback prefers coastal waters. It is bluish-gray above, white below. Dorsal fin has a *curved tip*. A broad *white band* crosses the upperside of flipper. *Baleen whitish*.
Range: Atlantic and Pacific Coasts.

BLUE WHALE (Sulphurbottom) *Sibbaldus musculus* p. 259
Recognition: Length to 100 ft.; wt. to 150 tons; length at birth 23–25 ft. This is the *largest animal* known to man, past or present. It is slaty to *bluish gray* above, *yellowish or whitish* on belly; undersurface of flippers white. Spout is *almost vertical* and may be 20 ft. high. Baleen *black*.
Range: Atlantic and Pacific Coasts; commonest near pack ice.

HUMPBACK WHALE *Megaptera novaeangliae* p. 259
Recognition: Length to 50 ft.; length at birth about 16 ft. This is a thick-bodied whale with *long pectoral fins* (nearly ⅓ total length of animal) and a small dorsal fin well back on the body. Black except for the *white throat, breast*, and lower sides of fluke and flippers. Flippers have *fleshy knobs* along front borders and fluke is *irregular* in outline on posterior border. Spout is an *expanding column* about 20 ft. high. Baleen is nearly black.
Range: Pacific and Atlantic Coasts.

Right and Bowhead Whales: Balaenidae

HEAD relatively large, about ⅓ length of body; no dorsal fin; *no grooves* on throat. Known as fossils from Lower Miocene.

ATLANTIC RIGHT WHALE *Eubalaena glacialis*
Recognition: Length to 55 ft. A large, *blackish* whale, sometimes pale on the belly. Spout, 10–15 ft. high, comes out *in 2 columns*, which diverge to form a V. Baleen plates about 8 ft. long, black.
Range: Chiefly North Atlantic Coast; south in winter to S. Carolina.

PACIFIC RIGHT WHALE *Eubalaena sieboldi* p. 259
Recognition: Length to 70 ft. This large whalebone whale is similar to the Atlantic Right Whale, but larger; spout *in 2 divergent columns*, V-shaped, 15 ft. high.
Range: Pacific Coast.

BOWHEAD WHALE *Balaena mysticetus* p. 259
Recognition: Length to 65 ft. The Bowhead is found only in *polar* and *subpolar* seas, usually near *edge of the ice*. Has an extremely large head, *more than ½ the animal's length;* body dark, grayish brown. When resting, it may have a part of its back projecting above water.
Range: Circumpolar; polar and subpolar seas.

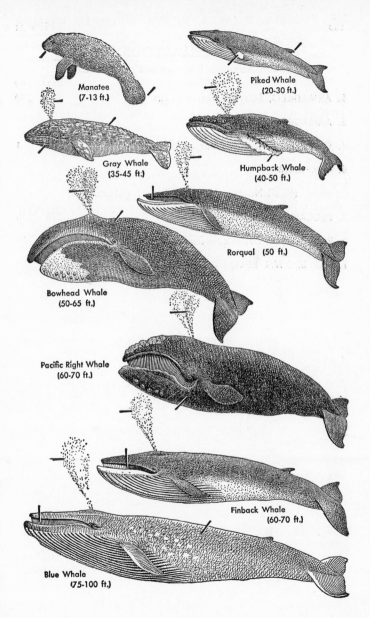

Manatee
(7-13 ft.)

Piked Whale
(20-30 ft.)

Gray Whale
(35-45 ft.)

Humpback Whale
(40-50 ft.)

Bowhead Whale
(50-65 ft.)

Rorqual (50 ft.)

Pacific Right Whale
(60-70 ft.)

Finback Whale
(60-70 ft.)

Blue Whale
(75-100 ft.)

MISCELLANEOUS
(Skull Numbers 1–4, one-half natural size)

		Map	Text
1. **ARMADILLO,** *Dasypus novemcinctus*		240	240
2. **ARMADILLO**			
3. **OPOSSUM,** *Didelphis marsupialis*		2	1
4. **OPOSSUM**			

(Skull Numbers 5–7, one-fourth natural size)

		Map	Text
5. **PECCARY,** *Pecari angulatus*		226	226
6. **BLACK BEAR,** *Ursus americanus*		51	48
7. **BIG BROWN BEAR,** *Ursus middendorffi*		49	50

THE following list of dental formulae for the land mammals may aid in identifying skulls picked up in the field. The symbols I, C, P, and M refer to incisors, canines, premolars, and molars, respectively. The formula

$$I\frac{5\text{-}5}{4\text{-}4}, \quad C\frac{1\text{-}1}{1\text{-}1}, \quad P\frac{3\text{-}3}{3\text{-}3}, \quad M\frac{4\text{-}4}{4\text{-}4} = \frac{26}{24} = 50$$

means that there are 5 incisors on each side in the upper jaw and 4 on each side in the lower jaw; and similarly for the canines, premolars, and molars. Further, that there are 26 teeth in all in the upper and 24 in the lower jaw, or a total of 50 teeth. There is only one North American land mammal with this formula, the Opossum (*Didelphis*). Identification from the Opossum skull can therefore be positive by counting the teeth. Suppose that you have a skull with 38 teeth. It could be either a myotis bat (*Myotis*), Peccary (*Pecari*), Marten (*Martes*), or Wolverine (*Gulo*). You examine the small front (incisor) teeth and find that there are 6 above and 6 below (total, 12). This eliminates *Myotis* and the Peccary, each of which has 4 above and 6 below (total, 10). The Marten and Wolverine have the same arrangement of teeth, so you turn to the pictures of the skulls (p. 256) and find that the Marten skull is slightly more than ½ the size of that of the Wolverine. You should be able to determine which it is on size of your specimen. For many of the rodents with 16, 20, or 22 teeth, one cannot come so close to the species as in the above examples. The pictures, again, might help some, but for positive identification they should be sent to a specialist. Scientific names of the genera are given after the dental formulae. Reference to the text location may be gained through the Index (p. 273).

262

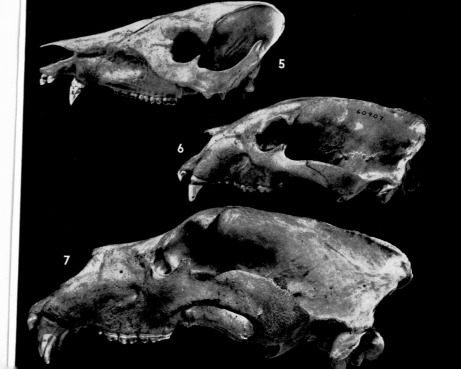

Plate 32

HOOFED MAMMA

(Skulls one-sixth natural s

1. **MOOSE,** *Alces alces* (antlers shed)

2. **BARREN GROUND CARIBOU,** *Rangifer a* (antlers removed)

3. **WHITETAIL DEER,** *Odocoileus virginianus* shed)

4. **ELK,** *Cervus canadensis* (female, no antle

5. **PRONGHORN,** *Antilocapra americana* (h sheaths removed)

6. **WHITE SHEEP,** *Ovis dalli* (horn sheaths

7. **BISON,** *Bison bison* (horn sheaths remo

Dental Formulae

DENTAL FORMULAE

	Incisors	Canines	Premolars	Molars	U and L	Total	Identifies Land Mammals Below
U	5-5	1-1	3-3	4-4	26	= 50	*Didelphis*
L	4-4	1-1	3-3	4-4	24		
U	3-3	1-1	4-4	3-3	22	= 44	*Condylura, Parascalops, Scapanus, Sus*
L	3-3	1-1	4-4	3-3	22		
U	3-3	1-1	4-4	2-2	20	= 42	*Alopex, Canis, Thalarctos, Urocyon, Ursus, Vulpes*
L	3-3	1-1	4-4	3-3	22		
U	3-3	1-1	4-4	2-2	20	= 40	*Bassariscus, Nasua, Procyon*
L	3-3	1-1	4-4	2-2	20		
U	2-2	1-1	3-3	3-3	18	= 38	*Myotis, Pecari*
L	3-3	1-1	3-3	3-3	20		
U	3-3	1-1	4-4	1-1	18	= 38	*Gulo, Martes*
L	3-3	1-1	4-4	2-2	20		
U	3-3	1-1	3-3	3-3	20	= 36	*Scalopus*
L	2-2	0-0	3-3	3-3	16		
U	2-2	1-1	3-3	3-3	18	= 36	*Neurotrichus*
L	1-1	1-1	4-4	3-3	18		
U	2-2	1-1	2-2	3-3	16	= 36	*Lasionycteris, Plecotus*
L	3-3	1-1	3-3	3-3	20		
U	3-3	1-1	4-4	1-1	18	= 36	*Lutra*
L	3-3	1-1	3-3	2-2	18		

DENTAL FORMULAE (continued)

	Incisors	Canines	Premolars	Molars	U and L	Total	Identifies Land Mammals Below
U	2-2	1-1	2-2	3-3	16		Macrotus, Mormoops
L	2-2	1-1	3-3	3-3	18	= 34	
U	2-2	1-1	2-2	3-3	16		Enderma, Pipistrellus
L	3-3	1-1	2-2	3-3	18	= 34	
U	3-3	1-1	3-3	1-1	16		Mephitis, Mustela, Spilogale, Taxidea
L	3-3	1-1	3-3	2-2	18	= 34	
U	0-0	1-1	3-3	3-3	14		Cervus, Rangifer
L	3-3	1-1	3-3	3-3	20	= 34	
U	3-3	1-1	3-3	3-3	20		Blarina, Microsorex, Sorex
L	1-1	1-1	1-1	3-3	12	= 32	
U	2-2	1-1	1-1	3-3	14		Eptesicus
L	3-3	1-1	2-2	3-3	18	= 32	
U	1-1	1-1	2-2	3-3	14		Lasiurus borealis, L. cinereus, L. seminolus, Tadarida brasiliensis
L	3-3	1-1	2-2	3-3	18	= 32	
U	3-3	1-1	3-3	1-1	16		Enhydra
L	2-2	1-1	3-3	2-2	16	= 32	
U	3-3	1-1	2-2	1-1	14		Conepatus
L	3-3	1-1	3-3	2-2	18	= 32	
U	0-0	0-0	3-3	3-3	12		Alces, Antilocapra, Bison, Odocoileus, Oreamnos, Ovibos, Ovis, Rangifer
L	3-3	1-1	3-3	3-3	20	= 32	

DENTAL FORMULAE (continued)

	Incisors	Canines	Premolars	Molars	U and L	Total	Identifies Land Mammals Below
U	0-0	0-0	{8-8		16}	= 32	Dasypus
L	0-0	0-0	8-8}		16}		
U	3-3	1-1	2-2	3-3	18}	= 30	Cryptotis
L	1-1	1-1	1-1	3-3	12}		
U	2-2	1-1	2-2	3-3	16}	= 30	Choeronycteris
L	0-0	1-1	3-3	3-3	14}		
U	2-2	1-1	2-2	2-2	14}	= 30	Leptonycteris
L	2-2	1-1	3-3	2-2	16}		
U	1-1	1-1	1-1	3-3	12}	= 30	Lasiurus ega, L. intermedius, Nycticeius
L	3-3	1-1	2-2	3-3	18}		
U	1-1	1-1	2-2	3-3	14}	= 30	Eumops, Tadarida femorosacca, T. molossa
L	2-2	1-1	2-2	3-3	16}		
U	3-3	1-1	3-3	1-1	16}	= 30	Felis
L	3-3	1-1	2-2	1-1	14}		
U	3-3	1-1	1-1	3-3	16}	= 28	Notiosorex
L	1-1	1-1	1-1	3-3	12}		
U	1-1	1-1	1-1	3-3	12}	= 28	Antrozous
L	2-2	1-1	2-2	3-3	16}		
U	3-3	1-1	2-2	1-1	14}	= 28	Lynx
L	3-3	1-1	2-2	1-1	14}		

DENTAL FORMULAE (continued)

	Incisors	Canines	Premolars	Molars	U and L	Total	Identifies Land Mammals Below
U	2-2	0-0	3-3	3-3	16		
L	1-1	0-0	2-2	3-3	12	= 28	Lepus, Sylvilagus
U	0-0	0-0	{7-7		14		
L	0-0	0-0	7-7}		14	= 28	Dasypus
U	2-2	0-0	3-3	2-2	14		
L	1-1	0-0	2-2	3-3	12	= 26	Ochotona
U	1-1	0-0	2-2	3-3	12		Ammospermophilus, Aplodontia, Citellus, Cynomys, Eutamias, Glaucomys, Marmota, Sciurus aberti, S. carolinensis, S. griseus, Tamiasciurus
L	1-1	0-0	1-1	3-3	10	= 22	
U	1-1	0-0	1-1	3-3	10		Castor, Cratogeomys, Dipodomys, Erethizon, Geomys, Liomys, Microdipodops, Myocastor, Perognathus, Sciurus apache, S. arizonensis, S. niger, Tamias, Tamiasciurus, Thomomys
L	1-1	0-0	1-1	3-3	10	= 20	
U	1-1	0-0	1-1	3-3	10		
L	1-1	0-0	0-0	3-3	8	= 18	Zapus
U	1-1	0-0	0-0	3-3	8		Baiomys, Clethrionomys, Dicrostonyx, Lagurus, Lemmus, Microtus, Mus, Napaeozapus, Neofiber, Neotoma, Ondatra, Onychomys, Oryzomys, Peromyscus, Phenacomys, Pitymys, Rattus, Reithrodontomys, Sigmodon, Synaptomys
L	1-1	0-0	0-0	3-3	8	= 16	

References

FOR the student whose interest carries him beyond the limits of this book, there is given below a short list of general references and the most recent accounts for the states and provinces. These lists are far from complete, but the bibliography within each publication listed will guide the reader to additional literature. Older publications which often are not available except in the larger universities and colleges have been omitted purposely.

General

Hall, E. R., and K. R. Kelson. The mammals of North America. New York: Ronald Press, 1959. 2 vols. A general reference with short descriptions, technical keys for identification, and distribution maps.

Hamilton, W. J. American mammals. New York: McGraw-Hill, 1939. Contains information on habits of many mammals.

Journal of Mammalogy. 1919 to present. A quarterly published by The American Society of Mammalogists; devoted to articles on mammals, chiefly of N. America.

Journal of Wildlife Management. 1937 to present. A quarterly published by The Wildlife Society; devoted to articles on management practices; contains many articles on mammals.

Miller, Gerrit S., and Remington Kellogg. List of North American Recent mammals. U.S. Natl. Mus. Bull. 205. 1955. A checklist; no aid to identification beyond giving names of species and subspecies, and approximate ranges.

North American Fauna. 1889 to present. No regular time of publication; a series published by U.S. Dept. of the Interior (formerly the Dept. of Agriculture); revisions of groups and state lists.

States and Provinces

Alabama
Howell, A. H. A biological survey of Alabama. North Amer. Fauna, 45:1–88. 1921.

Alaska
Bee, J. W., and E. R. Hall. Mammals of northern Alaska. Univ. Kans. Mus. Nat. Hist., Misc. Publ. no. 8.

Cahalane, V. H. A biological survey of Katmai National Monument. Smithsonian Misc. Publ., vol. 138, no. 5. 1959.

Dufresne, Frank. Alaska's animals and fishes. New York: Barnes, 1946.

Murie, O. J. Fauna of the Aleutian Islands and Alaska Peninsula. North Amer. Fauna, 61. 1959.

Alberta

Banfield, A. W. F. Mammals of Banff National Park, Alberta. Natl. Mus. of Canada, Bull. 159. 1958.

Rand, A. L. Mammals of the eastern Rockies and western plains of Canada. Natl. Mus. of Canada, Bull. 108. 1948.

Soper, J. D. Mammals of Wood Buffalo Park, northern Alberta and District of Mackenzie. Jour. Mamm., 23:119–45. 1942.

——. Mammal notes from the Grande Prairie–Peace River region, Alberta. Jour. Mamm., 29:49–64. 1948.

Arizona

Cockrum, E. L. The Recent mammals of Arizona. Tucson, Ariz.: Univ. Ariz. Press, 1960.

Arkansas

Sealander, J. A., Jr. A provisional check-list and key to the mammals of Arkansas (with annotations). Amer. Mid. Nat., 56:257–96. 1956.

British Columbia

Cowan, I. McT., and C. J. Guiguet. The mammals of British Columbia. B.C. Prov. Mus., Handbook no. 11. 1956.

California

Grinnell, J., J. S. Dixon, and J. M. Linsdale. Fur-bearing mammals of California, their natural history, systematic status, and relations to man. Berkeley, Calif.: Univ. Calif. Press, 1937. 2 vols.

Ingles, L. G. Mammals of California and its coastal waters. Stanford, Calif.: Stanford Univ. Press, 1954. 2nd ed.

Colorado

Rodeck, H. G. Guide to the mammals of Colorado. Univ. Colo. Mus., Leaflet no. 10. 1952.

Warren, E. R. The mammals of Colorado, their habits and distribution. Norman, Okla.: Univ. Okla. Press, 1943.

Connecticut

Goodwin, G. G. The mammals of Connecticut. State of Conn., Geol. and Nat. Hist. Survey Bull., 53:1–221. 1935.

Delaware (see *New York*)

Florida (see also *New York*)

Sherman, H. B. A list of the Recent land mammals of Florida. Proc. Fla. Acad. Sci., 1:102–28. 1936.

Georgia

Golley, F. B. Mammals of Georgia. Athens, Ga.: Univ. Ga. Press, 1962.

Harper, Francis. The mammals of the Okefenokee Swamp region of Georgia. Proc. Boston Soc. Nat. Hist., 38 (7):191–396. 1927.

——. Mammal notes from Randolph County, Georgia. Jour. Mamm., 10:84–85. 1929.

Idaho

Davis, W. B. The Recent mammals of Idaho. Caldwell, Idaho: Caxton Printers, 1939.

Illinois

Hoffmeister, D. F., and Carl O. Mohr. Fieldbook of Illinois mammals. Ill. Nat. Hist. Survey Div., Manual 4. 1957.

Indiana

Lyon, M. W., Jr. Mammals of Indiana. Amer. Mid. Nat., 17:1–384. 1936.

Iowa

Scott, T. G. Mammals of Iowa. Iowa State College, Jour. Sci., 12 (1):43–97. 1937.

Kansas

Cockrum, E. L. Mammals of Kansas. Univ. Kans. Publ., Mus. Nat. Hist., 7:1–303. 1952.

Hall, E. R. Handbook of mammals of Kansas. Univ. Kans. Mus. Nat. Hist., Misc. Publ. no. 7. 1955.

Keewatin District

Harper, Francis. The mammals of Keewatin. Univ. Kans. Mus. Nat. Hist., Misc. Publ. no. 12. 1956.

Sutton, G. M., and W. J. Hamilton, Jr. The mammals of Southampton Island. Mem. Carnegie Mus., vol. 12, pt. 2, sec. 1, pp. 9–111. 1932.

Kentucky (see also *New York*)

Bailey, Vernon. Cave life in Kentucky. Mainly in the Mammoth Cave region. Amer. Mid. Nat., 14 (5):385–635. 1933.

Hamilton, W. J., Jr. Notes on the mammals of Breathitt County, Kentucky. Jour. Mamm., 11:306–11. 1930.

Welter, W. A., and D. E. Sollberger. Notes on the mammals of Rowan and adjacent counties in eastern Kentucky. Jour. Mamm., 20:77–81. 1939.

Labrador

Hantzsch, B. Contributions to the knowledge of extreme northeastern Labrador [translated by M. B. A. Anderson]. Canad. Field-Nat., 46 (1):7–12; 46 (2):34–36. 1932.

Jackson, C. F. Notes on the mammals of southern Labrador. Jour. Mamm., 19:429–34. 1938.

Strong, W. D. Notes on mammals of the Labrador interior. Jour. Mamm., 11:1–10. 1930.

Weaver, R. L. Notes on a collection of mammals from the southern coast of the Labrador Peninsula. Jour. Mamm., 21:417–22. 1940.

Louisiana

Lowery, G. H., Jr. Checklist of the mammals of Louisiana and adjacent waters. La. State Univ. Mus. Zool., Occ. Paper no. 13, pp. 213–57. 1943.

Mackenzie District

Harper, Francis. Mammals of the Athabaska and Great Slave Lakes region. Jour. Mamm., 13:19–36. 1932.

Maine (see also *New York*)

Manville, R. H. Notes on the mammals of Mount Desert Island, Maine. Jour. Mamm., 23:391–98. 1942.

Norton, A. H. Mammals of Portland, Maine, and vicinity. Proc. Portland Soc. Nat. Hist., 4:1–151. 1930.

Manitoba

Breckenridge, W. J. Mammals collected in northern Manitoba. Jour. Mamm., 17:61–62. 1936.

Green, H. U. Mammals of the Riding Mountain National Park, Manitoba. Canad. Field-Nat., 46 (7):149–52. 1932.

Maryland (see also *New York*)

Gardner, M. C. A list of Maryland mammals. Pt. I, Marsupials and Insectivores, pt. II, Bats. Proc. Biol. Soc. Washington, 63:65–68, 111–14. 1950.

Goldman, E. A., and H. H. T. Jackson. Natural history of Plummers

Island, Maryland. IX, Mammals. Proc. Biol. Soc. Washington, 52:131–34. 1939.

Massachusetts (see also *New York*)

Parker, H. C. A preliminary list of the mammals of Worcester County, Massachusetts. Proc. Boston Soc. Nat. Hist., 41:403–15. 1939.

Warfel, H. E. Notes on some mammals of western Massachusetts. Jour. Mamm., 18:82–85. 1937.

Michigan

Burt, William H. Mammals of the Great Lakes Region. Ann Arbor, Mich.: Univ. Mich. Press, 1957.

Minnesota

Gunderson, H. L., and J. R. Beer. The mammals of Minnesota. Minn. Mus. Nat. Hist., Occ. Paper no. 6. 1953.

Mississippi (see also *New York*)

Cook, F. A. Game animals of Mississippi. Survey Bull. Miss. State Game and Fish Comm. 1943. Mimeo.

Missouri

Schwartz, C. W., and E. R. Schwartz. The wild mammals of Missouri. Columbia, Mo.: Univ. Mo. Press and Mo. Conserv. Comm., 1959.

Montana

Lechleitner, R. R. Mammals of Glacier National Park. Glacier Nat. Hist. Assoc., Bull. no. 6. 1955.

Nebraska

Jones, J. K. Checklist of mammals of Nebraska. Trans. Kans. Acad. Sci., 60:273–82. 1957.

Nevada

Hall, E. Raymond. Mammals of Nevada. Berkeley, Calif.: Univ. Calif. Press, 1946.

New Brunswick

Morris, R. F. The land mammals of New Brunswick. Jour. Mamm., 29:165–76. 1948.

Newfoundland

Bangs, Outram. The land mammals of Newfoundland. Bull. Mus. Comp. Zool., Harvard College, 54:507–16. 1913.

New Hampshire (see also *New York*)

Jackson, C. F. Notes on New Hampshire mammals. Jour. Mamm., 3:13–15. 1922.

New Jersey (see also *New York*)

Connor, P. F. Notes on the mammals of a New Jersey pine barrens area. Jour. Mamm., 34:227–35. 1953.

New Mexico

Bailey, Vernon. Mammals of New Mexico. North Amer. Fauna, 53:1–412. 1931.

New York

Hamilton, W. J., Jr. The mammals of Eastern United States. Ithaca, N. Y.: Comstock, 1943.

North Carolina (see also *New York*)

Conaway, C. H., and J. C. Howell. Observations on the mammals of Johnson and Carter Counties, Tennessee, and Avery County, North Carolina. Jour. Tenn. Acad. Sci., 28:53–61. 1953.

Komarek, E. V., and Roy Komarek. Mammals of the Great Smoky Mountains. Bull. Chicago Acad. Sci., 5:137–62. 1938.

Odum, E. P. Small mammals of the Highlands (North Carolina) Plateau. Jour. Mamm., 30:179–92. 1949.

North Dakota
  Bailey, Vernon. A biological survey of North Dakota. I, Physiography and life zones. II, The mammals. North Amer. Fauna, 49:1–226. 1927.

Nova Scotia
  Smith, R. W. The land mammals of Nova Scotia. Amer. Mid. Nat., 24:213–41. 1940.

Ohio (see also *Michigan*)
  Bole, B. P., Jr., and P. N. Moulthrop. The Ohio Recent mammal collection in the Cleveland Museum of Natural History. Cleveland Mus. Nat. Hist., Sci. Publs., 5 (6):83–181. 1942.

Oklahoma
  Blair, W. F. Faunal relationships and geographic distribution of mammals in Oklahoma. Amer. Mid. Nat., 22:85–133. 1939.

Ontario (see also *Michigan*)
  Cross, E. C., and J. R. Dymond. The mammals of Ontario. Royal Ont. Mus. Zool. Handbook no. 1. 1929.
  Downing, S. C. A provisional check-list of the mammals of Ontario. Royal Ont. Mus. Zool., Misc. Publ. no. 2, pp. 1–11. 1948.

Oregon
  Bailey, Vernon. The mammals and life zones of Oregon. North Amer. Fauna, 55:1–416. 1936.

Pennsylvania (see also *Michigan*)
  Gifford, C. L., and Ralph Whitebread. Mammal survey of south central Pennsylvania. Penna. Game Comm. 1951.
  Grimm, W. C., and H. A. Roberts. Mammal survey of southwestern Pennsylvania. Penna. Game Comm. 1950.
  Grimm, W. C., and Ralph Whitebread. Mammal survey of northeastern Pennsylvania. Penna. Game Comm. 1952.
  Richmond, N. D., and H. R. Rosland. Mammal survey of northwestern Pennsylvania. Penna. Game Comm. and U.S. Fish and Wildlife Service. 1949.

Quebec
  Cameron, A. W. The mammals of southeastern Quebec. Prov. Soc. Nat. Hist. Canada, Report for 1950–51, pp. 20–86. 1953.
  Doutt, J. K. Observations on mammals along the east coast of Hudson Bay and the interior of Ungava. Annals Carnegie Mus., 33:235–49. 1954.

Rhode Island (see *New York*)

Saskatchewan
  Beck, W. H. A guide to Saskatchewan mammals. Sask. Nat. Hist. Soc., Spec. Publ. no. 1. 1958.

South Carolina (see also *New York*)
  Penney, J. T. Distribution and bibliography of the mammals of South Carolina. Jour. Mamm., 31:81–89. 1950.

South Dakota
  Over, William H., and Edward P. Churchill. Mammals of South Dakota. Univ. South Dakota Mus. and Dept. Zool. 1941. Mimeo.

Tennessee (see also *New York*)
  Kellogg, Remington. Annotated list of Tennessee mammals. Proc. U.S. Natl. Mus., 86 (3051):245–303. 1939.

Texas
  Davis, W. B. The mammals of Texas. Texas Game and Fish Comm. Bull., 41:1–252. 1960.

Utah

    Durrant, S. D. Mammals of Utah. Univ. Kans. Publ., Mus. Nat. Hist., 6:1–549. 1952.

Vermont (see also *New York*)

    Osgood, F. L., Jr. The mammals of Vermont. Jour. Mamm., 19:435–41. 1938.

Virginia

    Handley, C. O., Jr., and C. P. Patton. Wild mammals of Virginia. Richmond, Va.: Comm. Game and Inland Fisheries, 1947.

Washington

    Dalquest, W. W. Mammals of Washington. Univ. Kans. Publ., Mus. Nat. Hist., 2:1–444. 1948.

West Virginia (see also *New York*)

    Kellogg, Remington. Annotated list of West Virginia mammals. Proc. U.S. Natl. Mus., 84 (3022):443–79. 1937.

    Wilson, L. W., and J. E. Friedel. A list of mammals collected in West Virginia. Proc. West Va. Acad. Sci. for 1941, vol. 15 (West Va. Univ. Bull. ser. 42, nos. 8–11), pp. 85–92. 1942.

Wisconsin

    Jackson, H. H. T. Mammals of Wisconsin. Madison, Wisc.: Univ. Wisc. Press, 1961.

Wyoming

    Bailey, Vernon. Animal life of Yellowstone Park. Sierra Club Bull., 12 (4):333–45. 1927.

    Negus, N. C., and J. S. Findley. Mammals of Jackson Hole, Wyoming. Jour. Mamm., 40:371–81. 1959.

Index

PAGE numbers in boldface type refer to illustrations other than those of skulls. They are placed only after the common English names of species and are not used after the scientific names. Page references to the illustrations of skulls are given under the subentry *Recognition* in the text for the ones illustrated. References to the maps are given at the end of each species account.

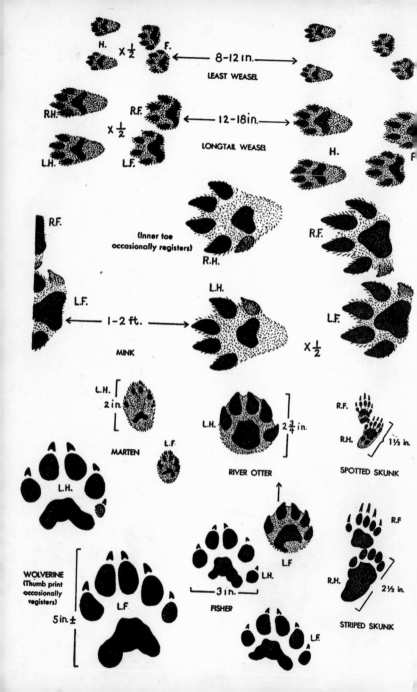